SCHOLASTIC

100 SCIENCE LESSONS

NEW EDITION

TERMS AND CONDITIONS

IMPORTANT - PERMITTED USE AND WARNINGS - READ CAREFULLY BEFORE USING

Licence

SCOTTISH PRIMARY 3

YEAR 2

Minimum specification:
- PC with a CD-ROM drive and 512 Mb RAM (recommended)
- Windows 98SE or above/Mac OSX.1 or above
- Recommended minimum processor speed: 1 GHz

O
507
ONE

S.2008

Gay Wilson
and Carole Creary

Authors
Gay Wilson
Carole Creary

Series Editor
Peter Riley

Editors
Nicola Morgan
Tracy Kewley
Kate Pedlar

Project Editor
Fabia Lewis

Illustrator
Ann Kronheimer

Series Designers
Catherine Perera and Joy Monkhouse

Designer
Catherine Perera

CD-ROM developed in association with
Vivid Interactive

Published by Scholastic Ltd
Villiers House
Clarendon Avenue
Leamington Spa
Warwickshire CV32 5PR

www.scholastic.co.uk

Designed using Adobe InDesign.

Printed by Bell and Bain Ltd, Glasgow

1 2 3 4 5 6 7 8 9   7 8 9 0 1 2 3 4 5

Text © 2007 Gay Wilson and Carole Creary

© 2007 Scholastic Ltd

British Library Cataloguing-in-Publication Data
A catalogue record for this book is available from the British Library.

ISBN 978-0439-94504-2

ACKNOWLEDGEMENTS

All Flash activities developed by Vivid Interactive

Material from the National Curriculum © Crown copyright. Reproduced under the terms of the Click Use Licence.

Extracts from the QCA Scheme of Work © Qualifications and Curriculum Authority.

Extracts from the Primary School Curriculum for Ireland, www.ncca.ie, National Council for Curriculum and Assessment.

Every effort has been made to trace copyright holders for the works reproduced in this book, and the publishers apologise for any inadvertent omissions.

Post-It is a registered trademark of 3M.

UNIVERSITY OF CHICHESTER

507
ONE

This new edition of *100 Science Lessons* follows the QCA Science Scheme of Work and also meets many of the demands of the curricula for England, Wales, Scotland, Northern Ireland and Eire. The book is divided into seven units – one unit to match each unit of the QCA scheme for Year 2, and one enrichment unit.

The planning grid at the start of each unit shows the objectives and outcomes of each lesson, and gives a quick overview of the lesson content (starter, main activity, group activities and plenary). The QCA objectives for Year 2 provide the basis for the lesson objectives used throughout the book.

After the planning grid is a short section on Scientific Enquiry. It is based on a QCA activity and provides a context for children to develop certain enquiry skills and for you to assess them. The section ends by showing where the activity can be embedded within one of the lessons.

Each unit is divided into a number of key lessons, which closely support the QCA scheme and all units end with an assessment lesson which is based on those key lessons. In addition to the key lessons, a unit may also contain one or more enrichment lessons to provide greater depth or a broader perspective. They may follow on from a key lesson or form a whole section, near the end of the unit, before the assessment lesson. The lesson objectives are based on the statements of the national curricula for England, Wales, Scotland, Northern Ireland and Eire, which are provided, in grid format, on the CD-ROM.

Lesson plans

There are detailed and short lesson plans for the key and enrichment lessons. About 60 per cent of the lesson plans in this book are detailed lesson plans. The short lesson plans are closely related to them and cover similar topics and concepts. They contain the essential features of the detailed lesson plans, allowing you to plan for progression and assessment. The detailed lesson plans have the following structure:

OBJECTIVES

The objectives are stated in a way that helps to focus on each lesson plan. At least one objective is related to content knowledge and there may be one or more relating to Scientific Enquiry. When you have read through the lesson you may wish to add your own objectives. You can find out how these objectives relate to those of the various national curricula by looking at the relevant grids on the CD-ROM. You can also edit the planning grids to fit with your own objectives (for more information see 'How to use the CD-ROM' on page 6).

RESOURCES AND PREPARATION

The Resources section provides a list of everything you will need to deliver the lesson, including any photocopiables presented in this book. The Preparation section describes anything that needs to be done in advance of the lesson, such as collecting environmental data.

As part of the preparation of all practical work, you should consult your school's policies on practical work and select activities for which you are confident to take responsibility. The ASE publication *Be Safe!* gives very useful guidance on health and safety issues in primary science.

BACKGROUND

This section may briefly refer to the science concepts which underpin the teaching of individual lessons. It may also highlight specific concepts which children tend to find difficult and gives some ideas on how to address these during the lesson. Suggestions may be given for classroom displays as well as useful tips for obtaining resources. Safety points and sensitive issues may also be addressed in this sections, where appropriate.

VOCABULARY

There is a vocabulary list of science words associated with the lesson which children should use in discussing and presenting their work. Time should be spent defining each word at an appropriate point in the lesson.

STARTER

This introductory section contains ideas to build up interest at the beginning of the lesson and set the scene.

MAIN TEACHING ACTIVITY

This section presents a direct, whole-class (or occasionally group) teaching session that will help you deliver the content knowledge outlined in the lesson objectives before group activities begin. It may include guidance on discussion, or on performing one or more demonstrations or class investigations to help the children understand the work ahead.

The relative proportions of the lesson given to the starter, main teaching activity and group activities vary. If you are reminding the children of their previous work and getting them onto their own investigations, the group work may dominate the lesson time; if you are introducing a new topic or concept, you might wish to spend all or most of the lesson engaged in whole-class teaching.

GROUP ACTIVITIES

The group activities are very flexible. Some may be best suited to individual work, while others may be suitable for work in pairs or larger groupings. There are usually two group activities provided for each lesson. You may wish to use one after the other; use both together (to reduce demand on resources and your attention); or, where one is a practical activity, use the other for children who successfully complete their practical work early. You may even wish to use activities as follow-up homework tasks.

Some of the group activities are supported by a photocopiable sheet. These sheets can be found in the book as well as on the CD-ROM. For some activities, there are also accompanying differentiated ideas, interactive activities and diagrams - all available on the CD-ROM (for more information, see 'How to use the CD-ROM' on page 6).

The group activities may include some writing. These activities are also aimed at strengthening the children's science literacy and supporting their English literacy skills. They may involve writing labels and captions, developing scientific vocabulary, writing about or recording investigations, presenting data, explaining what they have observed, or using appropriate secondary sources. The children's mathematical skills are also developed through number and data handling work in the context of science investigations.

ICT LINKS
Many lessons have this section in which suggestions for incorporating ICT are given. ICT links might include: using the internet and CD-ROMs for research; preparing graphs and tables using a computer; using the graphing tool, interactive activities and worksheets from the CD-ROM.

DIFFERENTIATION
Where appropriate, there are suggestions for differentiated work to support less able learners or extend more able learners in your class. Some of the photocopiable sheets are also differentiated into less able support, core ability, and more able extension to support you in this work. The book contains the worksheets for the core ability while the differentiated worksheets are found on the accompanying CD-ROM.

ASSESSMENT
This section includes advice on how to assess the children's learning against the lesson objectives. This may include suggestions for questioning or observation opportunities, to help you build up a picture of the children's developing ideas and guide your future planning. A separate summative assessment lesson is provided at the end of each unit of work. One may also be provided for a group of enrichment lessons if they form a section towards the end of a unit.

PLENARY
Suggestions are given for drawing together the various strands of the lesson in this section. The lesson objectives and outcomes may be reviewed and key learning points may be highlighted. The scene may also be set for another lesson.

HOMEWORK
On occasions, tasks may be suggested for the children to do at home. These may involve using photocopiables or the setting of a research project, perhaps involving the use the books on display (as suggested in the background section) to broaden the knowledge of the topic being studied.

OUTCOMES
These are statements related to the objectives; they describe what the children should have achieved by the end of the lesson.

LINKS
These are included where appropriate. They may refer to subjects closely related to science, such as technology or maths, or to content and skills from subjects such as art, history or geography.

ASSESSMENT LESSONS
The last lesson in every unit focuses on summative assessment. This assessment samples the content of the unit, focusing on its key theme(s); its results should be used in conjunction with other assessments you have made during the teaching of the unit. The lesson usually comprises of two assessment activities, which may take the form of photocopiable sheets to complete or practical activities with suggested assessment questions for you to use while you are observing the children. These activities may include a mark scheme, but this will not be related directly to curriculum attainment targets and level descriptors. These tasks are intended to provide you with a guide to assessing the children's performance.

PHOTOCOPIABLE SHEETS
These are an integral part of many of the lessons. They may provide resources such as quizzes, instructions for practical work, worksheets to complete whilst undertaking a task, information, guidance for written assignments and so on.

Photocopiable sheets printed in the book are suitable for most children. The CD-ROM includes differentiated versions of many photocopiables to support less confident learners and stretch more confident learners.

How to use the CD-ROM

SYSTEM REQUIREMENTS
Minimum specifications:
● PC or Mac with CD-ROM drive and at least 512 MB RAM (recommended)
● Microsoft Windows 98SE or above/Mac OSX.1 or above
● Recommended minimum processor speed: 1GHz

GETTING STARTED
The accompanying CD-ROM includes a range of lesson and planning resources. The first screen requires the user to select the relevant country (England, Scotland, Wales, Northern Ireland, Eire). There are then several menus enabling the user to search the material according to various criteria, including lesson name, QCA unit, National Curriculum topic and resource type.

Searching by lesson name enables the user to see all resources associated with that particular lesson. The coloured tabs on the left-hand side of this screen indicate the differentiated worksheets; the tabs at the top of the page lead to different *types* of resource (diagram, interactive or photocopiable).

PHOTOCOPIABLES
The photocopiables that are printed in the book are also provided on the CD-ROM, as PDF files. In addition, differentiated versions of the photocopiables are provided where relevant:
● green indicates a support worksheet for less confident children;
● red indicates the core photocopiable, as printed in the book;
● blue indicates an extension worksheet for more confident children.

There are no differentiated photocopiables for assessment activities.

The PDF files can be annotated on screen using the panel tool provided (see below). The tools allow the user to add notes, highlight items and draw lines and boxes.

PDF files of photocopiables can be printed from the CD-ROM and there is also an option to print the full screen, including any drawings and annotations that have been added using the tools. (NB where PDF files are landscape, printer settings may need to be adjusted.)

INTERACTIVE ACTIVITIES
The CD-ROM includes twelve activities for children to complete using an interactive whiteboard or individual computers. Each activity is based on one of the photocopiables taken from across the units. Activities include: dragging and dropping the body parts into the correct place; clicking on objects in the home to see if they light up; putting the baby animals next to their parents; sorting objects according to whether they are living or not living. *Note that the 'check' button should only be pressed, once the interactive task has been fully completed!*

GRAPHING TOOL
The graphing tool supports lessons where the children are asked to gather and record data. The tool enables children to enter data into a table, which can then be used to create a block graph, pie chart or line graph.

When inserting data into the table, the left-hand column should be used for labels for charts; the right-hand column is for numeric data only (see example below). The pop-up keypad can be used to enter numbers into the table.

DIAGRAMS
Where appropriate, diagrams printed in the book have been included as separate files on the CD-ROM. These include examples of tables and diagrams for children to refer to when undertaking experiments or building objects, such as the marble run in 'Pushes and pulls'. These can be displayed on an interactive whiteboard.

GENERAL RESOURCES
In addition to lesson resources, the CD-ROM also includes the planning grids for each unit, as printed in the book, and the relevant curriculum grid for England, Scotland, Wales, Northern Ireland and Eire. The curriculum grids indicate how elements of each country's National Curriculum are addressed by lessons in the book. The planning grids are supplied as editable Word files; the curriculum grids are supplied as Word and PDF files. Selection of a planning grid leads to a link, which opens the document in a separate window; this then needs to be saved to the computer or network before editing.

CHAPTER 1   Health and growth

Lesson	Objectives	Main activity	Group activities	Plenary	Outcomes
Lesson 1 Giant face	• To know that food can be put into different groups. • To understand that a knowledge of food groups can help us to build healthy diets.	Allocate foods to different groups. Assess a healthy diet. Know that humans also need water. (Revision from Y1/P2.)	Make giant faces and list some foods found in each of the main food groups on the tongues. Devise a healthy, balanced main course that includes all the food groups.	Discuss how humans need different foods and water to stay alive and healthy.	• Can arrange food into groups. • Can show how knowledge of food groups can help to build a healthy diet. • Can state that food and water are needed to stay alive.
Lesson 2 Healthy menu	• To know how to arrange a meal into food groups.	Look at a meal brought into school and sort into food groups.	Devise healthy menus for a week.	Discuss the menus and healthy eating.	• Can arrange the food in a meal into food groups. • Can assess how healthy a meal is.
Lesson 3 Everything in moderation	• To know that an occasional meal that is not well balanced does no harm. • To produce a simple block graph.	Discuss 'party food' for birthdays or other special occasions. Make a block graph.		Interpret the data on the graph.	• Know that an occasional meal that is not well balanced does no harm. • Know that some foods should be eaten in moderation. • Can produce and interpret a simple block graph.
Enrichment Lesson 4 Sleep diary	• To know that enough and regular sleep is needed for good health.	Keep a diary of bedtimes to help understand the need for rest and sleep.		Consider the importance of sleep.	• Know that a certain amount of sleep is needed every night for good health.
Enrichment Lesson 5 Tooth care	• To know that the mouth needs care and attention to keep it healthy.	Discuss oral hygiene, with a talk from an expert, if possible.	Write and decorate a letter to the Tooth Fairy. Write an oral hygiene poem.	Discuss how to keep teeth and mouths healthy.	• Can describe the care needed to keep teeth and gums healthy.
Enrichment Lesson 6 Skin care	• To know that the skin needs to be kept clean for good health.	Discuss the importance of keeping clean and the dangers of dirty skin. Learn how to wash hands properly.	Investigate who needs really clean hands. Write hygiene rules.	Review and prioritise the hygiene rules.	• Can describe how to care for the skin and keep it clean.
Enrichment Lesson 7 Wash those hands!	• To know that the skin needs to be kept clean for good health.	Observe how dirty hands can be.		Groups report back on their discussion on dirty hands.	• Understand how dirty the skin gets and why it needs to be kept clean.
Lesson 8 Safety with medicines	• To know that people who are ill take medicines to help them.	Talk about medicines and safety. Learn about the appropriate use of syringes.	Compare the packaging of sweets and drugs. Design packaging for a medicine with warnings.	Discuss safety issues of medicines.	• Know that medicines are drugs that can be dangerous if they are not taken as instructed. • Know that children should only take medicines under adult supervision. • Can explain that people take medicines to keep them well or make them better.
Lesson 9 Hazard symbols	• To know that some household substances are dangerous.	Talk about substances that must not be touched or played with. Discuss hazard symbols and safe storage.	Sort labels with hazard symbols. Write about safe storage for dangerous household substances.	Talk about dangerous substances and how they can be kept safe.	• Can identify dangerous household substances. • Can suggest ways in which dangerous household substances might be kept away from children.

Lesson	Objectives	Main activity	Group activities	Plenary	Outcomes
Lesson 10 Exercise diary	• To know that regular exercise is needed to maintain good health. • To know the difference between exercise and inactivity.	Discuss how regular exercise is needed for health. Observe changes in the body during exercise.	Complete a personal exercise timetable. Choose a favourite form of inactivity and write about it.	Discuss the need for exercise and a balance between activity and inactivity.	• Can explain why exercise is needed. • Can describe the changes in the body caused by exercise. • Can describe the difference between exercise and inactivity.
Lesson 11 Adults and babies	• To know that animals (including humans) produce young which grow into adults. • To know that different animals mature at different rates.	Comparing human and animal growth more closely. If possible, keeping butterfly or moth pupae in the classroom.	Match and name more unusual animals and their young. Sort out animals that need care or are independent from birth.	Talk about the names of animals and their babies. Discuss the ways that different animals grow and develop.	• Can compare the growth of some animals with that of humans. • Can match parent to offspring. (Revision from Y1/P2.)
Lesson 12 Caring for children	• To know that young humans need care while they are growing up.	Interview a parent about how to care for children of different ages.		Make a list of ways that parents care for children.	• Can describe some of the ways in which young humans need care as they grow up.

Assessment	Objectives	Activity 1	Activity 2
Lesson 13	• To assess whether the children can sort foods into different groups. • To assess whether the children can identify dangerous household substances	Sort food into groups. Explain the need for a balanced diet.	Identify household substances that are dangerous and need to be stored safely.

SC1 SCIENTIFIC ENQUIRY

Parts of the body and movement

LEARNING OBJECTIVES AND OUTCOMES
● To explore, using the senses; make and record observations about changes in the body
● To communicate what happened in a variety of ways (exercise diary)

ACTIVITY
After a vigorous warm-up, before a PE lesson, the children describe the changes that have taken place in their bodies as they exercise. For example, being warmer, out of breath, thirsty and more energetic. They then collect data in the form of a diary.

LESSON LINKS
This Sc1 activity forms an integral part of Lesson 10, Exercise diary.

Lesson 1 ▪ Giant face

Objective
● To know that food can be put into different groups.
● To understand that a knowledge of food groups can help us to build healthy diets.

Vocabulary
fruit, vegetables, cereals, starch, processed, balanced, healthy, energy, high-energy

RESOURCES 💿
Main activity: A story such as 'The Giant Jam Sandwich' by John Vernon (Picture Piper) or possibly versions of traditional stories such as: 'The Magic Porridge Pot', 'The Gingerbread Boy', 'The Enormous Pancake' or 'The Enormous Turnip'; a flipchart or board with columns headed: 'Fruit and vegetables'; 'Meat, fish, eggs and dairy products'; 'Cereals'; 'High energy foods'; a collection of foods including a small range from each food group such as: meat, eggs, milk, cereals (including bread) and fruit and vegetables. include some processed foods such as crisps (which can be high in salt and fat) and sweets (which are high in sugar).
Group activities: 1 A3 copies of photocopiable page 27 (also 'Giant face' (red), available on the CD-ROM); drawing and colouring materials; collage materials such as wool, wood shavings and hole-punched circles to create features such as hair, spots and freckles; scissors, adhesive. **2** One A4 sheet of stiff paper or light card for each child, writing and drawing materials.

PREPARATION
On the flipchart draw four columns and head these with the names of the main food groups: 'Fruit and vegetables'; 'Meat, fish, eggs and dairy products'; 'Cereals'; 'High energy foods'.

BACKGROUND
It is difficult to divide food into exact categories since many foods contain significant amounts of more than one type of ingredient. At this stage the foods are being divided into four main groups: fruit and vegetables (containing mostly sugars, carbohydrates, minerals and other trace elements); meat, fish, eggs and dairy products (containing mainly proteins and fats); cereals (containing mainly carbohydrates, minerals and trace elements); high energy foods such as sweets, crisps and chocolate (containing mainly sugars, salts and fats).

Children should be encouraged not to view some foods as 'bad'. Instead they need to appreciate that it is important to eat a balanced diet that contains items from all the food groups. Ideally, they should be eating large amounts of fruit and vegetables and cereals and medium amounts of proteins and fats. Sweets, sugars and salt should be eaten in moderation.

Differentiation
Group activity 1
To support children, use 'Giant face' (green), from the CD-ROM, which allows them to draw rather than write the different foods.
Group activity 2
Some children will need help writing their words. Some may draw pictures. Others may be able to label each food, in their meal, with the name of the food group to which it belongs.

Vegetarians and vegans also need protein in their diets but will obtain this from dairy products, nuts or pulses.

STARTER
There is a wealth of food-related stories or songs that could be used as initial stimulation for this lesson. Read the story, 'The Giant Jam Sandwich' or sing 'Food Glorious Food', from the musical 'Oliver'. Remind the whole class that they talked about food and their favourite meals in Year 1/Primary 2 and that food and water are needed to stay alive.

MAIN ACTIVITY
Gather the whole class around you. Ask a few children to tell you some of the things that they ate for breakfast, lunch and their evening meal yesterday. Make a list of these foods on the flipchart under the main food group headings (Fruit and vegetables; Meat, fish, eggs and dairy products; Cereals; High energy foods). Add to the lists what you had for your own meals yesterday. (This is a good opportunity to extend the lists, for example, if the children were short on ideas for fruit and vegetables.) Look at the lists with the children and talk about the fact that all foods can be grouped in this way. Ask the children: *Can anyone think of another food that could go in the fruit and vegetable list?* Add their suggestions to the lists.

Then ask: *Does anyone think that any of these foods are bad for you? Can a food be bad for you?* Tell the children that no food is bad unless you eat too much of it and talk about the need for a balanced diet. Explain to them that in order to balance our diet and keep healthy we need to eat a large amount of fruit and vegetables, a medium amount of things like meat, fish and dairy products and a large amount of cereals. Sweets, chocolate and salt are all right if they are eaten in small amounts. Remind them that we also need to drink, and that water is an important part of our diet too.

Look at the collection of foods together and ask the children to name them. *Can we sort them into the correct groups? Where do we put the processed foods, such as the crisps?* Although they are made from a vegetable, they are not a fresh vegetable and have been made into something else. Explain that crisps sometimes contain a lot of salt and fat, so we should not eat too many of them.

GROUP ACTIVITIES
1 Give each child a copy of the 'Giant face' sheet on photocopiable page 27. Ask them to draw the face of a greedy giant (male or female). Tell them that they should draw a big mouth, slightly open so that they can cut out the tongue and stick it in the right place. They should then list some foods found in each of the main food groups on the tongue. They can now finish off their faces by using the collage materials to make the giant's face as horrid as possible! These could form the basis of a class display.
2 Ask each child to devise a healthy, balanced main course, including all the food groups. Give each child an A4 sheet of stiff paper or light card. Ask them to decorate their sheet with pictures of any foods they have included.

ASSESSMENT
Check the children's work to assess whether they have listed foods correctly under the various groups. Does the main course that they have devised contain at least one food from each main group?

PLENARY
Read out the names of some of the foods the children have listed in their work and ask the class which group each food belongs to. Add these to the list made on the flipchart in the Main activity. Ask the children to tell you why it is important to know about foods and which group they belong to. Ask them to tell you again what else humans need to stay alive and healthy (water).

OUTCOMES
- Can arrange food into groups.
- Can show how knowledge of food groups can help to build a healthy diet.
- Can state that food and water are needed to stay alive.

Lesson 2 ▪ Healthy menu

Objective
- To know how to arrange a meal into food groups.

Vocabulary
healthy, balanced, food groups, excretion

RESOURCES
Main activity: A packed lunch, including something from all the food groups but making sure that the meal is not well-balanced, for example: jam sandwich, cold sausages, chocolate bar, crisps, yoghurt, apple, cake, sweets; large sheets of paper on which to write the names of the food groups, cards on which to write the children's suggestions.
Group activity: Writing materials; painting, drawing or collage materials for decorating the menu sheets.

BACKGROUND
For this activity, it is best not to use the children's packed lunches, but to provide one of your own. The contents of children's lunch boxes can be a sensitive issue; children of this age are not responsible for what is sent to school for them to eating. Children do need to know, however, that a balanced diet is necessary to maintain good health and growth and that there are no bad foods, just some that we should eat or drink in moderation.

They should also be aware of the need to drink in order to replace fluids lost through excretion (sweating and urinating) and that they should drink lots of water and not just sweet or fizzy drinks. Any discussions on food and nutrition should be handled sensitively - some children may come to school without breakfast, others may only have one meal a day. Some children have little choice and may have to eat whatever they can find in the house that day. Others may be given too many crisps, sweets and fizzy drinks. Young children need to learn about healthy eating, but should not be made to feel guilty when they have no say in what is given to them.

STARTER
Remind the whole class about what they learned in the last lesson. Ask: *Can anyone remember the food groups that we were talking about?* Write the names of the groups on individual sheets of paper and lay them down where the children can see them.

MAIN ACTIVITY
Ask the whole class if they can remember which food groups we should eat freely (fruit and vegetables and cereals) and which we should eat in moderation (meat, fish, eggs, dairy produce). Ask: *What types of food should we eat only small amounts of?* (Crisps, sweets, chocolate, and anything with large amounts of fat, sugar or salt.) With the children, look at the packed lunch you have brought in. Ask them to sort the various foods into the appropriate groups and place them on the relevant sheets of paper. When this is done say: *We have some things in each of the food groups but is this a healthy meal?* (No.) Explain that this is because there are too many sweet and fatty things and not enough fruit and vegetables. Talk to the children about how the meal could be changed or improved to make it more balanced. Ask for their ideas on what could be added or removed to turn the meal into a healthy one. Add these items by drawing them or writing their names on cards and placing these on the correct sheet. Take away the foods that the children suggest should be removed. Look at the result with the children and ask if the meal is now a healthy one.

Differentiation
All the children should be able to take part in this activity.

GROUP ACTIVITY

Sort the children into seven groups with one child who is able to scribe in each group. Provide writing and drawing materials to create menu sheets, then ask each group to think of a healthy menu for one day. Remind them, before they begin, that they should have at least one thing from every food group for lunch and tea, but that breakfast may be slightly different. It should still be healthy, and may be a good opportunity to have some of the milk they need for strong teeth and bones. Remind the children that they should include plenty of fruit and vegetables. Be sensitive to any children who have a food allergy. Each child in the group could then select one of the foods or courses to illustrate and add it to the menu sheet that the group has devised. The menus could then be put together to make a class 'Healthy Menu Book', with the addition of decorated covers.

ASSESSMENT

Use the children's work to assess whether they have understood the difference between a balanced and an unbalanced meal. Ask them what is meant by a healthy meal.

PLENARY

Ask the groups to tell the rest of the class what they have put into their day's menu. Discuss each day with the children. If they ate like that for a week would their diet be really healthy? Is anything missing? Should anything be added?

OUTCOMES
- Can arrange the food in a meal into food groups.
- Can assess how healthy a meal is.

Lesson 3 ◗ Everything in moderation

Objective
- To know that an occasional meal that is not well balanced does no harm.
- To produce a simple block graph

RESOURCES

Flipchart or board, large squared paper for making block graphs, pencils.

MAIN ACTIVITY

Ask the children to tell you about some of their favourite party foods. List them on the flipchart. Ask: *Are they healthy or not?* Remind the children that less healthy foods are not bad for them, they should just eat them in moderation. Discuss the fact that an occasional meal that is not well balanced does no harm if their overall diet is a healthy one. The occasional special treat is also allowed. Make a block graph of favourite party foods.

ASSESSMENT

Note which children are able to make a block graph and interpret the data. Question the children to find out if they understand that the occasional unbalanced meal does no harm if their overall diet is healthy.

ICT LINK ⊙

Children could use the graphing tool on the CD-ROM to make block graphs.

PLENARY

Look at the graph of favourite party foods, with all of the children and ask them to interpret the data. Ask questions such as: *Which is the favourite party food? Which is the least favourite?*

OUTCOMES
- Know that an occasional meal that is not well balanced does no harm.
- Know that some foods should be eaten in moderation.
- Can produce and interpret a simple block graph.

Differentiation
All the children should be able to take part in this activity.

ENRICHMENT
Lesson 4 ▪ Sleep diary

Objective
- To know that enough and regular sleep is needed for good health.

RESOURCES
Paper, card for diary covers, writing and drawing materials.

MAIN ACTIVITY
Ask the children why we need to sleep. Do they understand that we all need a certain amount of sleep every night to keep us healthy, and that our bodies and our brains need proper rest in order to help them grow and develop? Talk about the effects of too little sleep. (Tiredness, lack of concentration, grumpiness!) Ask the children to keep a bedtime diary (for whatever time period suits the unit of work you are doing). They could decorate the cover with appropriate pictures and illustrate each page.

ASSESSMENT
During the Plenary session ask the children why they need to sleep.

PLENARY
Talk to the children about the earlier discussion and the importance of sleep. What happens if they don't get enough, regular sleep? (They feel tired during the day and find it more difficult to concentrate.) When the children have completed their bedtime diaries, use these as the basis for a further Plenary session to reinforce what has been learned.

Differentiation
To challenge children, ask them to add the time they get up every morning to their diaries and calculate the number of hours they spend sleeping each day or each week.

OUTCOME
- Know that a certain amount of sleep is needed for good health.

ENRICHMENT
Lesson 5 ▪ Tooth care

Objective
- To know that the mouth needs care and attention to keep it healthy.

Vocabulary
teeth, gums, hygiene, dental, decay, filling, healthy, clean, fluoride

RESOURCES
Main activity: A copy of the poem 'Oh I wish I'd looked after my teeth' by Pam Ayres, from 'Pam Ayres – The Works' (BBC Books). A collection of artefacts such as large sets of teeth, toothbrushes, toothpaste containing fluoride and appropriate leaflets. You may be able to borrow some, or all, of these from your local Community Dental Health Service, who may also be willing to send a member to talk to the children.
Group activities: 1 Paper and writing materials for a letter; appropriate materials for making 3D tooth fairies to stick to the letters (see diagram). These might include: old-fashioned wooden pegs for bodies, pipe cleaners for

Group activity 1
Some children may manage to write just one or two rules and may need help with their tooth fairy model. Others may be able to list several rules, for example regular cleaning, using fluoride toothpaste, eating a healthy diet, drinking milk, making regular visits to the dentist for a check-up, and so on.

Group activity 2
All the children should be able to do this activity, although some will write shorter poems or draw pictures.

arms, gauze, net, cellophane or acetate (for wings), matchsticks and tiny gold and silver stars (for wands), lace, chiffon or coloured lining fabric (for dresses or shirts and trousers), wool or raffia (for hair), sequins and/or glitter (for decoration), adhesive. **2** Poem, as for the Main activity; writing and drawing materials.

PREPARATION
Get in touch with your local Community Dental Health Service to find out if they can help with resources or personnel. If they agree to send someone, make sure that you talk to them about the age of the children and how they are going to present what they say. You should also look at any resources or paperwork in advance to make sure that they are suitable and check if you need to augment it in any way.

BACKGROUND
Although the health of children's teeth has greatly improved in recent years, oral hygiene is still not as universal and meticulous as it could be. There are families where not every member has an individual toothbrush and where cleaning teeth is not part of an everyday routine. Although children need to be made aware of the importance of caring for their teeth and oral hygiene, the subject should be approached in a sensitive way. When you are six it is not always up to you whether you have your own toothbrush or not.

Fluoride toothpaste has been a major factor in the reduction of dental cavities and most brands of toothpaste now contain fluoride. The current advice is that teeth should be brushed regularly and kept clean, but not after every meal. The acid produced after eating in the localised area round the teeth etches the enamel, and brushing at that time may cause extra wear. It is best to clean teeth before breakfast and before going to bed, or at least an hour after eating. Eating crunchy foods does nothing to help clean the teeth, although eating a piece of cheese after a meal does help, as cheese contains a substance that neutralises the acid that causes tooth decay.

STARTER
Reading the Pam Ayres poem 'Oh I wish I'd looked after my teeth', with the whole class gathered around you, would be a stimulating way to start this lesson. A discussion about the best way to look after teeth can then take place without personalising it.

MAIN ACTIVITY
Gather the children around you and ask them all to give you a big smile so that you can see their teeth. Smile back! Ask the children why teeth are important and what we do with them. (We need them to chew our food, but they also help us to form our words properly and keep the shape of our mouths.) Ask: *Does anyone know what we need to do to help keep our teeth and gums really healthy?* (Clean them regularly with fluoride toothpaste, eat a healthy, balanced diet (including milk), don't suck sweets last thing before you go to sleep at night and so on.) Show the children the resources that you have and, with the large teeth and toothbrush, demonstrate how to clean the teeth properly (working up and down and getting right to the back teeth).

Discuss with the children how looking after the teeth and eating a healthy diet can help to prevent tooth decay. Ask if any of them have been to the dentist and what the dentist did. *Did they look carefully at all your teeth and tell you how to look after them?* Try to instil the idea that going to the dentist is a good thing and is a vital part of looking after their teeth.

Most children will have had a good experience at the dentist and may have been given a badge and a picture to colour to show how good they have been. Some children could recount such visits, but nip any horror stories in the bud! Ask the children if any of them have started to lose their baby teeth. Remind them that the new teeth that come through when the baby teeth have gone have to last them for the rest of their lives and need to be taken care of. If you have a visitor from the Community Dental Health Service allow time for him or her to talk to the children and answer questions before you move on to the Group activities.

GROUP ACTIVITIES

1 Write individual letters to the Tooth Fairy telling him or her about the rules for keeping teeth and gums clean and healthy. Before they begin ask the children to remind you of the things you have talked about in the main lesson and some of the rules they will need. Ask the children to make and stick a 3D model of a tooth fairy onto the corner of their letter. The letters could then form the basis of a class display. Tell the children that the Tooth Fairy doesn't like collecting decayed teeth!
2 Read the Pam Ayres poem again and ask the children to write a funny poem about looking after teeth.

ASSESSMENT

Check the children's work to find out if they have understood how to take care of their teeth and gums.

PLENARY

Ask the children to tell you some of the ways in which they can help to keep their teeth and mouths healthy. Ask some of the children to read their letters or poems.

OUTCOME

- Can describe the care needed to keep teeth and gums healthy.

LINKS

Literacy: writing a poem, writing sets of rules, writing a letter.

ENRICHMENT
Lesson 6 □ Skin care

Objective
- To know that the skin needs to be kept clean for good health.

Vocabulary
- Skin, hygiene, health, clean, wash, bacteria, germs

RESOURCES

Main activity: A flipchart, board or large sheet of paper to note points from the discussion; a washing-up bowl of warm water, soap, a clean white towel or paper towel; class display of toiletries; pomander (see Preparation, below) made from a small orange studded with a quantity of cloves and tied with a length of ribbon.
Group activities: 1 Simple reference books and CD-ROMs, paper and pencils, drawing and collage materials. **2** Writing materials.
Plenary: Flipchart, large sheet of paper, scissors, felt-tipped pens

PREPARATION

You will need to make the pomander (see diagram below) about two weeks before the lesson. This gives the pomander time to dry out a bit before use. It will last for several years once it has thoroughly dried out.

Push some cloves into the rind of an orange, trying to cover the whole surface. In a small bowl, mix together 2 tablespoons of orris root, and add some cinnamon, nutmeg and lemon or orange oil. Then roll the orange around in the mixture. Next cut a piece of ribbon, about 1m in length. Place the middle of the ribbon at the top of the fruit, and tie it round the package as if you were tying a parcel. Tie a bow at the top so that the pomander can be hung from it.

BACKGROUND

The dangers of a lack of hygiene, and of passing bacteria from one person to another, are well known, particularly in relation to touching others or handling food. A recent survey has shown that, in spite of all the reminders, a high proportion of people still do not wash their hands after visiting the toilet. It is therefore very important that children, from a young age, are made aware of the dangers. Germs are easily passed from one person to another through touching each other with unwashed hands. We can also harm ourselves by putting dirty hands into our mouths and ingesting bacteria that can cause a range of illnesses. Unwashed skin begins to smell and can become infected and sore.

STARTER

Gather all the children around you and ask: *Who thinks they know why it is important to keep clean?* In this way you will find out about the children's own ideas and be able to build on them during the discussion.

MAIN ACTIVITY

Talk to the children about the dangers of a lack of hygiene and the importance of regular bathing and washing. Tell them about some of the possible results of not keeping clean, building on some of the things they have mentioned in the Introduction. As well as leaving germs on our dirty hands and maybe getting an upset stomach, we would also become very smelly if we didn't wash. Eventually our skin would become infected and sore.

Show the children the pomander, pass it around and let them smell it. Ask: *What do you think it is?* Explain that long ago people didn't know about the benefits of washing properly and keeping clean, so everyone was very smelly. Rich people carried pomanders, like this one, around with them so that they had something nice to smell instead of the horrible smell of other people and the dirt everywhere. Tell the children that, at that time, people also used perfumes to try to make them smell better, but perfume is not enough to make you smell nice if you are dirty.

Show the children the collection of toiletries and explain that we still use perfumes today, but that they smell much nicer when put on to a clean body. Ask the children if they recognise any of them and what they are used for. Ask: *Who knows why we should be particularly careful to wash our hands thoroughly after visiting the toilet?* Tell the children that they might get sick from the germs on their hands if they put them in their mouths, and that if they touch other people they might spread the germs and make them sick too.

Ask the children to mime how they would wash their hands. Then use the bowl of water, and the soap to show the children how to wash their hands really well and dry them thoroughly on the towel. Remind them that washing properly all over every day is the best way to keep our skin clean and healthy and help prevent germs from spreading.

GROUP ACTIVITIES

1 Put the children into groups of about four and ask them, using reference books and CD-ROMs, to find out about people who need to have really clean hands to do their work. (People who handle food, for example on the delicatessen counter in the supermarket, butchers, bakers, cooks, waiters,

Differentiation
Group activity 1
To support children, ask them just to label their drawing with the occupation of the person and tell you why it is important for them to keep their hands clean. Other children may be able to write a little more about the people that they have chosen.
Group activity 2
This activity will be accessible to all the children.

doctors, nurses.) Each group could select one or two of these people, make a large drawing or collage of them and write a sentence or two about why they need to have particularly clean hands.

2 Remind all the children about the discussions in the Main activity and ask them (in groups of about four, with one child in each group acting as scribe) to think of, and write down, as many sensible hygiene rules as they can. Tell them that they will then, as a class, decide which are the most important rules and turn them into a class display.

ASSESSMENT
During the Plenary session, note which children understand the link between hygiene and health. Are the rules that they have come up with sensible and relevant?

PLENARY
Talking to the whole class, ask the children to read out the rules that they have written in their groups. Make a note of these on a large sheet of paper or on a whiteboard. Read them through again with the children and talk about which are the most important. (The health and hygiene ones should come before the ones about keeping our work clean, for example.) Number the rules in order of importance. Cut the sheet up to separate the rules and stick them, in order of importance, onto a fresh sheet to display in the classroom or re-order them on the whiteboard.

OUTCOME
● Can describe how to care for the skin and keep it clean.

LINKS
Literacy: writing rules.

ENRICHMENT
Lesson 7 ● Wash those hands!

Objective
● To know that the skin needs to be kept clean for good health.

RESOURCES
A bowl or plastic tank of water per group of six, sufficient white paper towels for each child to have one.

MAIN ACTIVITY
Try to do this activity at the end of the morning when hands are likely to be grubby! Put the children into groups to share a bowl or tank of water, making sure they have at least one clean white paper towel each. Tell them that they are going to see how dirty their hands are. Ask them to wet their hands in the water, then wipe them thoroughly on the paper towel. Spread out the towels and look at the resulting dirt. Remind them that it is nearly lunchtime and that they are just about to handle food. Ask: *What should you be sure to do before you go to lunch? Why?* Ask them to talk in their groups about all the things they, and other people do, where having dirty hands could cause problems (preparing, cooking and eating food; putting dirty hands in the mouth; doing work that needs to be kept clean such as sewing or drawing). Tell the children that each group is going to report back on their discussion to the whole class.

ASSESSMENT
During the Plenary session, as the groups of children report to the class, note those who understand that the skin gets dirty and why it needs to be kept clean for good health.

Differentiation
The main part of this activity is accessible to the whole class.

PLENARY
Ask each group to report on their discussion to the whole class. Take this opportunity to reinforce the hygiene rules they created in Lesson 6.

OUTCOME
● Understand how dirty the skin gets and why it needs to be kept clean.

Lesson 8 ● Safety with medicines

Objective
● To know that people who are ill take medicines to help them.

Vocabulary
medicine, drugs, better, well, adult, dangerous, bottles, packets, difference, syringe, disease, illness, safety

RESOURCES
Main activity: A collection of empty pill and medicine bottles and packets; sweet packets, tubes, boxes and wrappers (including throat 'sweets'); syringes without needles (different sizes, if possible); one or two pills that look rather like sweets.
Group activities: 1 Several empty pill bottles and packets, sweet wrappers, packets, tubes and boxes for each group of four; two large sheets of paper or small hoops for each group to sort onto or into. **2** Writing and drawing materials.

BACKGROUND
From a young age children need to be introduced to the fact that medicines are drugs. They are used to make you better when you are ill, or keep you well if you have a condition such as asthma, diabetes or epilepsy. Children should understand that they must only ever take medicines (drugs) from a known and trusted adult. They must also understand that they should never eat anything that they find if they don't know where it has come from, even if it looks very like sweets. It is sometimes thought that young children should not be introduced to syringes but, unfortunately, syringes are found regularly in some school grounds and playgrounds. Children need to be made aware that they should never touch these, that they are very dangerous and that, if they do see them, they should tell an adult at once. On the other hand children may have to go to the doctor for an injection, either for an illness or an immunisation, and a fear of syringes may turn this into a much more traumatic and stressful experience than it should be. It is therefore also important to show them, and tell them about, the beneficial uses of syringes.

STARTER
Ask the whole class if they know what medicines are. You will then be able to judge what level their understanding is at and build on their ideas without reinforcing misconceptions.

MAIN ACTIVITY
Ask the children when you should take medicines. *What sorts of things do you take medicines for? Does anyone sometimes have a headache and Mummy or Daddy gives you something to make it better? Who has ever had medicine for a cough? Does anyone have to take medicine all the time to keep them well?* (This may create a good opportunity to talk sensitively about people who need to stay on medication for long periods in order to feel well, such as asthmatics or diabetics.)

Ask the children to tell you who should give them medicine. Stress that they should never take medicine from anyone except an adult that they know and trust, or a doctor or nurse. Explain that medicines are drugs that people take when they are ill to make them better, or to keep them well. Add that if they are taken at the wrong time, they can also be dangerous. Show the children the syringes (without needles) and ask: *Can anyone remember going to the doctor or nurse to have an injection? Can you remember what it was for?* Explain to the children that injections can only be given by a doctor or nurse – or a parent at home (to a diabetic child, for example) – to treat, or to stop us catching, an unpleasant disease. Make sure that the children understand that if anyone shows them a syringe, or if they see one anywhere other than at a doctor's or a hospital, they should tell a grown up straightaway. Schools sometimes use syringes as instruments in science or the water tray; the children should know that this is fine.

Show the children the collection of pill bottles and sweet wrappers. Hold up one or two of each and ask the children if they can tell the difference. Show them the tablets that look like sweets and explain that they are not sweets, but strong medicines that could be dangerous for children. Make sure they understand that they should never eat things they find, even if they look like sweets, but should take them to a grown-up. Look at some of the medicine boxes, bottles and wrappers in detail with the children and read out some of the warnings on them. Point out that, although they are called 'sweets', the things that people suck for sore throats are actually medicines and should only be taken by adults. Now look at some of the sweet wrappers and boxes and show the children that the same warnings do not feature on these.

GROUP ACTIVITIES

1 Ask the children (working in groups of about four) to sort the packages, bottles and packets in front of them into two sets – one set of medicines and one of sweets. Children could then write a sentence individually to say why they should always take medicines only from a trusted adult.
2 Working as individuals, ask the children to design a package for a medicine, showing quite clearly that it is a medicine and warning people of the dangers of not following safety rules.

ASSESSMENT

Look at the sets when the groups have finished sorting and talk to the children. Note which children know that medicines can be dangerous unless taken under adult supervision, and that people should only take medicines to keep them well or make them better.

PLENARY

Ask the children to tell you when it is safe to take medicines. (When they are ill or to keep them well). *Who should give you medicine? What should you do if you find some pills or medicines?*

OUTCOMES

● Know that medicines are drugs that can be dangerous if they are not taken as instructed.
● Know that children should only take medicines under adult supervision.
● Can explain that people take medicines to keep them well or make them better.

Lesson 9 ▪ Hazard symbols

RESOURCES ◉

Main activity: A collection of empty and well-rinsed household substance containers and packets, including some products that are used in the garden.
Group activities: 1 A copy of photocopiable page 28 (also 'Hazard symbols –1' (red), available on the CD-ROM) for each group of three; a collection of labels from household substance and chemical bottles and packets which contain hazard and warning symbols; the collection of bottles and packets used in the Main activity; scissors, adhesive, writing and drawing materials.

Vocabulary
● substances, household, dangerous, safe, poison, chemical, container, harmful, irritant, toxic, highly flammable

2 A copy of photocopiable page 29 (also 'Hazard symbols –2' (red), available on the CD-ROM) for each child; writing and drawing materials.
ICT link: 'Hazard symbols' interactive, from the CD-ROM.

PREPARATION
Main activity: Make sure that the empty household substance containers have been thoroughly rinsed.
Group activities: 1 Ensure that any hazard symbols cut from packets have no residue of the substance on them.

BACKGROUND
Every year many children end up in hospital, and some die, from touching or swallowing household and garden chemicals and substances. It is therefore important that children are made aware of these dangers and recognise some of the substances involved. The main symbols that children should be able to identify and understand at this stage are:

 Harmful or Irritant: This will damage the skin and is harmful when swallowed. The substances are usually dilute acids or alkalis.

 Toxic: This is used on all poisonous substances. Bleach, cleaning fluids, weed killers and insecticides would be included in this group.

 Highly flammable: This symbol appears mostly on liquids but is also used on some solids and gases that ignite quickly. Included in this group are methylated spirits, turpentine, white spirit, lighter fuel and firelighters.

STARTER
Remind the children about what they learned in Lesson 8: that medicines can be dangerous if we take them when we don't need them. Tell them that there may be other things in their houses that are very dangerous, and that it is important that children know never to touch or play with these.

MAIN ACTIVITY
Ask the children: *Does anyone know what a household substance or household chemical is? Can anyone name one?* If the children are able to name some and you have them, point these out in the collection.

Look at the rest of the collection with the children and ask them if they recognise any of the bottles or packets. *Do you have any of these at home? What are they for? Why is it important that they are kept somewhere safe?* Tell the children that these substances are dangerous and that they should never play with them or handle them. Explain that these items should be kept in a very safe place, away from children, babies and pets.

Point out the hazard symbols (see diagram from the CD-ROM) and read some of the hazard warnings on the packets and bottles. Tell them that sadly many children and babies become ill and end up in hospital because they have swallowed or touched household substances or chemicals. *Can anyone think of good, safe places where dangerous things like bleach, toilet cleaner or weed killer could be kept, away from children?* (A high cupboard which is out of the reach of children, a locked cupboard or a locked shed.)

GROUP ACTIVITIES
1 Organise the children into groups of three. Give each group a copy of the sheet of hazard symbols on photocopiable page 28 and a collection of labels from bottles. The children should cut out the symbols from the photocopiable sheet and then sort the labels, into the correct groups, to match with the symbols. Then ask each child to choose one of the symbols

and stick it in their books (or on a sheet of paper). They should then find one or two things from the collection of bottles and packets that carry that symbol, draw these, and write underneath their drawing what they are.
2 Give the children copies of photocopiable page 29 and ask them to sort the listed items according to whether they are 'harmful' or 'not harmful' and then to explain, in writing, where these items could be stored. Remind them that they talked about good places to store harmful substances in the Main activity.

ICT LINK 🔘
Children can use the 'Hazard symbols' interactive to match different symbols with their definitions.

ASSESSMENT
Ask the children to name a range of dangerous household substances. Use their work to assess whether the children are able to suggest suitable places to store dangerous substances so that they are kept safely, away from children and pets.

PLENARY
Talk to the whole class about what they have learned. Ask the children to tell you about some of the ways in which household substances are dangerous. (They are poisonous, they can damage your skin, they may catch fire.) Read out some of their suggestions for keeping dangerous substances out of the reach of children, babies and pets.

OUTCOMES
● Can identify dangerous household substances.
● Can suggest ways in which dangerous household substances might be kept away from children.

Lesson 10 ▸ Exercise diary

Objectives
● To know that regular exercise is needed to maintain good health.
● To know the difference between exercise and inactivity.

Vocabulary
exercise, energetic, active, inactive, regular, muscle, fit, abdominal

RESOURCES 🔘
Main activity: The hall, large PE equipment.
Group activities: 1 A copy of photocopiable page 30, (also 'Exercise diary' (red), available on the CD-ROM) for each child; pencils, coloured highlighter pens. **2** Writing and drawing materials.

BACKGROUND
The human body is designed to be active and needs regular exercise in order to maintain good health. Children are becoming less active and their overall health is suffering as a consequence. This is not only due to the popularity of activities such as watching television and sitting for long periods, playing computer games, it is also because children are often driven to and from school and kept indoors because of parents' fears for their safety. PE at school may be the only regular physical activity some children get. Muscle tone is lost when there is insufficient use (this includes the heart). Sufficient, regular exercise also helps to burn off any excess calories.

STARTER
Remind the children about the lessons on moving their bodies that they had in Year 1/Primary 2 Ask them what they can remember. Ask: *Does anyone know what 'exercise' means and what it does for our bodies?*

MAIN ACTIVITY
Before you begin the physical part of the lesson, talk to the children about

Differentiation ◉
Group activity

To support children give them a copy of 'Exercise diary' (green), from the CD-ROM, which asks them to draw pictures of their weekly exercise activities.

To extend children, give them 'Exercise diary' (blue), from the CD-ROM, which includes additional columns for recording the amount of time spent exercising per week and asks them to calculate the total time spent exercising per week.

the fact that the body is designed to be active and that we need to take regular exercise in order to keep healthy. Tell them that we need to use our muscles to keep them strong. Ask: *What sort of things we are do to exercise our bodies? What sort of exercise do you enjoy?* (running, cycling or skating, for example). Find out whether the children think they have any exercise at school. Do they realise that the various aspects of school PE are exercise? Ask whether they think they are getting exercise when they are out on the playground. (Only if they are moving about.)

Begin the physical part of the lesson with a vigorous warm-up, asking the children to change the way they are moving and the parts of the body they are using when you call out: *Change!* Ask the children to stop once they are well warmed-up, and to close their eyes and think about their bodies. *What is different about your body since you started moving? Are you warmer, are you out of breath, do you feel thirsty, do you feel more energetic than when you started the lesson?*

Move on to the large apparatus, asking the children as they work to think about the muscles that they are using and developing. Stop the class occasionally and ask individual children to say which muscles they have been using (leg, arm or abdominal). At the end of the lesson, ask the children if they know the difference between being active and inactive. Ask them to tell you some of the inactive things that they do regularly. (Watching television, playing on the computer, working at their desks, sitting quietly listening to a story.)

GROUP ACTIVITY

Give each child a copy of photocopiable page 30. Ask them to complete their own exercise diary for one week, including all the exercise they get both at home and at school. Remind the children what exercise is and help to get them started by mentioning a few possibilities such as walking, cycling or swimming. Talk to them about the fact that exercise needs to be regular in order to be properly beneficial and ask them to highlight with a coloured highlighter pen any forms of exercise that they do regularly (such as school PE).

Lesson 11 ◘ Adults and babies

Objectives
● To know that animals (including humans) produce young which grow into adults.
● To know that different animals mature at different rates.

Vocabulary
young, grow, care, rate, mature, produce, live birth, mate, womb, offspring, hatch, dependent, independent

RESOURCES ◉

Main activity: If possible, obtain butterfly and moth larvae or pupae and observe them in the classroom as they develop and emerge. (See Preparation and Background.)

Group activities: 1 Pictures of animals and their babies (or use the resources on photocopiable page 31, (also 'Adults and babies –1' (red), available on the CD-ROM); reference books, dictionaries and CD-ROMs; a copy of photocopiable page 32 (also 'Adults and babies – 2' (red), available on the CD-ROM) for each child, pencils. **2** A copy of photocopiable page 33 (also 'Adults and babies –3' (red), available on the CD-ROM) for each child, reference materials as for Group activity 1, pencils.

ICT link: 'Adults and babies' and 'Caring for children' interactive activities, from the CD-ROM.

PREPARATION

Main activity: Butterfly rearing kits can be obtained from, Small-Life Supplies, Station Buildings, Station Road, Bottesford, Notts, NG13 0EB (www.small-life.co.uk.). The kits include caterpillars, feeding kits and an observation chamber. You could also visit a local, butterfly park, if available.

Group activities: 1 If you use the photocopiable (page 31), photocopy one sheet for each group (enlarge to A3, if possible). Cut the symbols into separate cards and laminate for durability.

BACKGROUND
Animals vary greatly in the amount of time taken for embryos to mature in the womb or egg (from a few weeks for mice to 21 months for elephants), but there is also great variation in the degree of maturity of the young. Kangaroos, for example, give birth to tiny immature creatures that instinctively work their way up the mother's fur into the pouch where they latch on to a nipple and the rest of their development takes place. Baby mice and the young of many other rodents are born pink, blind and hairless, and take time to develop and grow their first coats. Similarly, baby birds are born without their feathers. All these creatures are totally dependent on the care and protection of their parents. Human babies too, although more developed at birth than the creatures mentioned above, rely on adults for everything in order to survive.

In contrast, the young of animals such as horses and deer are able to get to their feet and run almost immediately after birth. This is necessary for their survival in the wild, a world of predators and prey, although they too rely on their mothers for protection and food. The young of most cold-blooded creatures are born fully mature, able to take care of themselves from the moment of birth and generally require no further help from their parents. This applies to creatures such as snakes, lizards, turtles, crocodiles (although some mother crocodiles carry their young down to the water in their mouths when they have hatched), and most fish and crustaceans. Most insects are independent from the time of hatching, although in some instances the mother offers protection for a time - spiders may carry their hatchlings on their backs for a short time after they emerge from the egg.

Young children find it fascinating to observe a butterfly or moth caterpillar changing into a pupae and subsequently emerging (a very different form of growing and maturing from humans). This can be done very easily in the classroom.

STARTER
With the children around you, remind them of what they learned about animals in Year 1/Primary 2. Say: *Can anyone tell me about some of the things we learned about animals and their babies, and the ways in which humans (we are animals too) grow and change as they get older?*

MAIN ACTIVITY
Ask the children to think about humans and some other animals such as birds, insects, dogs or cats. Remind them that all animals, including humans, are similar in that they all have babies that grow up, grow old and eventually die. Now ask the children to think very carefully. Ask if they can tell you about some of the similarities and differences between this process in humans and in other animals. (Some lay eggs, some give birth to live babies; some are independent at birth and some need to be cared for.) Most animals grow up much more quickly than humans and don't need care for very long.

Humans live longer than most animals, although there are some creatures, such as tortoises, parrots and elephants, that may live as long, or longer, than humans. Ask: *Can anyone tell me about the very different ways that butterflies and frogs grow and develop into adults from the way in which humans grow and get old?* (Their parent lays eggs, they then hatch into caterpillars or tadpoles, butterflies change into pupae and emerge as butterflies, tadpoles grow legs and their bodies change.) Humans are born as babies, with their legs and arms in place, they then grow bigger and develop into adults.

Show the class the butterfly kit (if you have one) and tell them that they are going to watch the caterpillars grow and change into pupae, and that the pupae will eventually split and butterflies will emerge. This will only

Differentiation
Group activity 1
For children who need support, use 'Adults and babies -2' (green), which contains a selection of familiar animals. To extend children, use 'Animal and babies -2' (blue) which contains a more unusual selection of animals and asks them to find two other animals whose babies have a special name.
Group activity 2
To support children use 'Adults and babies- 3' (green), which contains a smaller selection of animals to sort. Children may need help in reading the sheet and some may prefer to work in pairs, to find information. 'Adults and babies -3' (blue) extends the children by including a wider and more complex range of animals.

take a few weeks and the caterpillars do not need their parents to look after them while all this happens. Set aside time every few days for the class to look at the butterfly observation chamber and note any differences. Keep a close eye on it yourself, particularly when the butterflies are due to emerge. Hopefully this will happen when the class is in session – the children's excitement and amazement will make all the effort worthwhile!

GROUP ACTIVITIES

1 Organise the children into groups of about four and give each group a set of cards with pictures of adults and babies (possibly cut from photocopiable page 31). Remind them that they matched some adults and babies in Year 1/Primary 2 but that today they are going to match more unusual babies to their parents. Ask them to match each baby to its parent. Then give each child a copy of photocopiable page 32 and ask them to complete it by finding out the special names of the baby animals. They should use the reference materials to help them.

2 Give each child a copy of photocopiable page 33. Explain the three groups that the circles represent and ask the children to complete the sheet by copying the name of each animal into the correct circle. Encourage them to use the reference materials.

ASSESSMENT

Use the children's work to assess their understanding.

ICT LINK

The children can use the 'Adults and babies' interactive, from the CD-ROM, to match baby animals to their parents and the 'Caring for children' interactive, from the CD-ROM, to sort babies into groups according to how much care they require.

PLENARY

Discuss with the children, what they have learned, during the lesson. Review the 'Adults and babies - 2' sheet. Ask the children to tell you the names of the babies, as you read out the adults' names. *Did anyone find a really unusual baby name? Can you tell me some of the similarities/ differences, in the way that human and other animal babies grow?*

OUTCOMES

● Can compare the growth of some animals with that of humans.
● Can match parent to offspring.

LINKS

Unit 2b, Lesson 25, Frog wheel

Lesson 12 ▸ Caring for children

Objectives
● To know that young humans need care while they are growing up.

RESOURCES

Pictures of parents, babies and children, flipchart or board, a parent with children of different ages who is willing to talk to the class.
ICT link: 'Caring for children' interactive activity, from the CD-ROM.

MAIN ACTIVITY

Ask the class: *How many things do parents need to do for their children, as they are growing up?* (Feeding, keeping warm, keeping clean, cuddling, talking to them.) Ask a parent, with older and younger children, to visit the class and talk about the things he or she does to care for children of different ages.

Differentiation
All the children can take part in this activity.

Before the visit, help the children to prepare sensible questions. Ask the visitor to include, in their talk, the aspects of care, beyond looking after their child's physical needs, such as, encouraging them to talk and read books.

ASSESSMENT
During the Plenary session, note those children who contribute sensible suggestions for the list.

ICT LINK
The children can use the 'Caring for children' interactive, from the CD-ROM, to sort babies into groups according to how much care they require.

PLENARY
Ask the children to tell you some of the ways in which parents care for young humans as they are growing up. List these on the flipchart. Encourage the children to talk about types of care that are not just physical. Help the children to complete the list.

OUTCOME
● Can describe some of the ways in which young humans need care as they grow up.

Lesson 13 ▪ Assessment

Objectives
● To assess whether the children can sort food into different groups.
● To assess whether the children can identify dangerous household substances.

RESOURCES
Assessment activities: 1 A copy of photocopiable page 34 (also 'Assessment -1' (red), available on the CD-ROM), for each child; writing materials. **2** A copy of photocopiable pages 35 and 36 (also 'Assessment- 2' (red) and 'Assessment - 3' (red), available on the CD-ROM) for each child; scissors, adhesive. **3** A copy of photocopiable page 37 (also 'Assessment - 4' (red), available on the CD-ROM).
ICT links: 1 'Keeping healthy –1' and **2** 'Keeping healthy –2' interactives, from the CD-ROM.

STARTER
Remind the children what they have been learning about in this unit.

ASSESSMENT ACTIVITY 1
Give each child a copy of photocopiable page 34 and read through the sheet with them. Ask them to look at the pictures of different foods and copy the name of each food into the correct food group. Then ask them to write a sentence about why it is necessary to eat a balanced diet.

ANSWERS
Fruit and vegetables: lettuce, apple, tomatoes, cabbage.
Meat, fish, eggs and dairy produce: cooked chicken, cheese, eggs, fish, sausages.
High energy: chocolate bar, packet of crisps, bag of sweets.
Cereals: packet of cereal, spaghetti, loaf of bread.
For the writing activity, accept any answer that indicates an understanding that a balanced diet is needed for health and well-being.

ICT LINK
Children can use the 'Keeping healthy –1' interactive, from the CD-ROM, to sort food into types by dragging and dropping the pictures of food into boxes.

LOOKING FOR LEVELS

Most children should be able to categorise the foods correctly. Some may have difficulty in recognising that the bread is made from cereal. Some may put the sausages under 'High energy foods'; these children need to be questioned as to their reason for doing this. If they recognise that sausages are very high in fat, this is an acceptable reason. If they also realise that the sausages could be listed under 'Meat, fish, eggs and dairy produce' this indicates a higher level of understanding. Some children will show a clear understanding of the need for a balanced diet, while others will have difficulty explaining this.

ASSESSMENT ACTIVITY 2

Give each child a copy of photocopiable pages 35 and 36 and explain the pictures to them. Ask them to cut the pictures out and stick those that could be dangerous into the high cupboard out of the reach of children, and those that are safe into the low cupboard.

ANSWERS

High cupboard: bottle of pills, bleach, medicine, aerosol, firelighters, weed killer, white spirit, blister pack of pills.
Low cupboard: lemonade, cereal, spaghetti, jar of jam, tin of beans, apple, oranges, basket of pegs.

ICT LINK

Children can use the 'Keeping healthy – 2' interactive, from the CD-ROM, to sort the hazardous and non-hazardous items into high and low cupboards.

LOOKING FOR LEVELS

Most children should complete the sheet successfully. Less able children may have difficulty in distinguishing between the bottles of liquid and may not recognise the dangers of aerosols. More able children could be asked to try and add more items to each cupboard.

ASSESSMENT ACTIVITY 3

Give each child a copy of photocopiable page 37 and ask them to list as many differences as they can between babies and toddlers.

ANSWERS

For example: can/can't walk; can/can't talk; can feed self /needs feeding; only drinks milk/eats solid food; needs a nappy/can use toilet; has little hair/ lots of hair; stays at home/goes to playgroup; can't dress self/dresses self.

LOOKING FOR LEVELS

Some children may only be able to think of two or three differences. Most children should be able to think of four or five and some children should be able to complete the sheet and perhaps add one or two extra differences.

Giant face

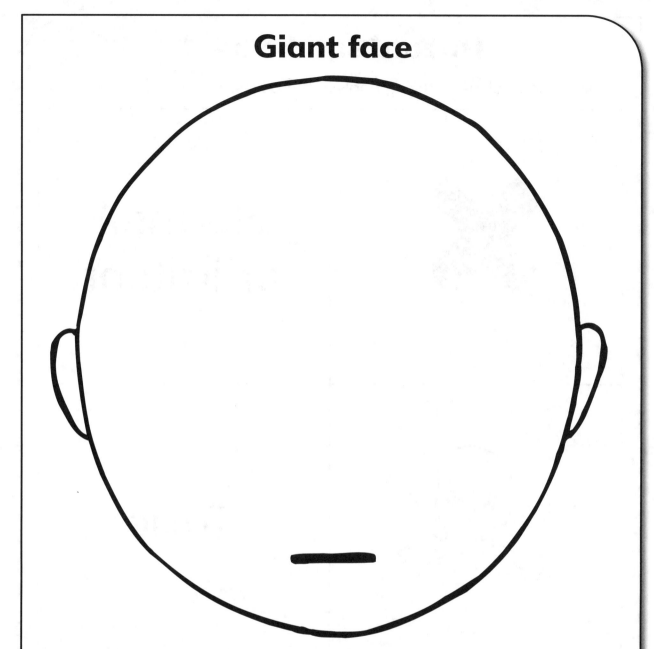

■ Write your food words under the headings on the tongue.
■ Cut out the tongue and stick it into the mouth.

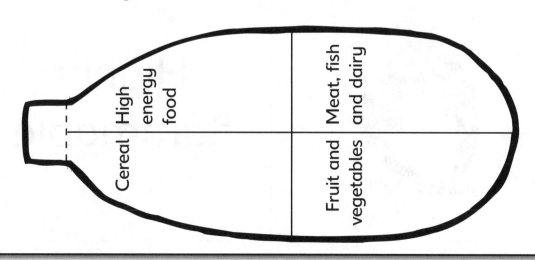

Hazard symbols – 1

■ Match your labels to the symbols in the boxes.

	Harmful or irritant
	Toxic
	Highly flammable

Illustration © Ann Kronheimer

Hazard symbols – 2

Bleach
Milk
Cereals
Lemonade
Washing powder

Weed killer
Oven cleaner
Spray furniture polish
Toothpaste
Sugar

◀ Sort the products above into the correct box.

HARMFUL	NOT HARMFUL
Harmful or irritant	
Toxic	
Flammable	
Where could these products be stored safely? _____ _____ _____	Where could these products be stored? _____ _____ _____

Exercise diary

Day	At school	At home
Monday		
Tuesday		
Wednesday		
Thursday		
Friday		
Saturday		
Sunday		

◼ Highlight with a coloured pen the exercise you do regularly.

My favourite sort of exercise is _____

_____

Adults and babies – 1

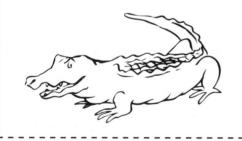

PHOTOCOPIABLE

Adults and babies – 2

The adult is a:	The baby is called a:
swan	
deer	
frog	
goat	
bear	
tiger	
horse	
goose	
lion	

◪ Fill in the blank box with the name of one more adult creature whose babies have a special name.

Adults and babies – 3

◾ Some babies need caring for completely. Their parents do everything for them.

◾ Some babies only need feeding and protecting.

◾ Some babies are completely independent and may never see their parents.

Care for completely	Feed and protect

◾ Copy the name of each animal into the correct circle.

human	frog
dog	goldfish
deer	cow
horse	kangaroo
cat	ladybird
elephant	monkey
robin	snake
butterfly	mouse

Completely independent

PHOTOCOPIABLE

Assessment – 1

lettuce

cooked chicken

chocolate bar

packet of cereal

loaf of bread

cheese

eggs

packet of crisps

apple

sausages

fish

spaghetti

tomatoes

cabbage

bag of sweets

◧ Write the name of each food in the correct box.

Fruit and vegetables	Meat, fish, eggs and dairy produce

Cereals	High energy foods

◧ Using the back of this sheet write about why it is important to eat a balanced diet.

Illustration © Ann Kronheimer

◪**SCHOLASTIC**

Assessment – 2

A very high cupboard with a lock, out of reach of children.

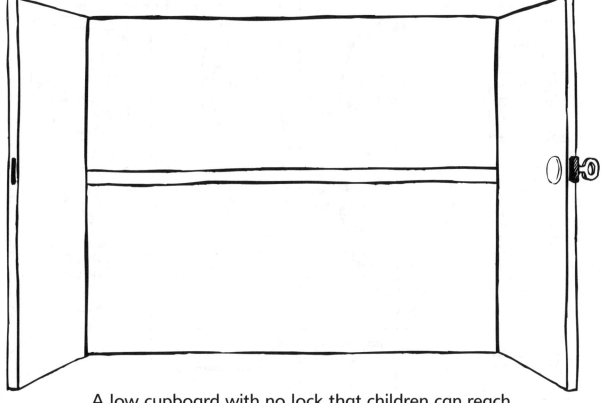

A low cupboard with no lock that children can reach.

Illustration © Ann Kronheimer

PHOTOCOPIABLE

Assessment – 3

◼ Cut out the pictures and put each picture in the right cupboard.

◢SCHOLASTIC

Illustration © Ann Kronheimer

Assessment – 4

◼ List five differences between babies and toddlers.

1 _____

_____

_____

2 _____

_____

_____

3 _____

_____

_____

4 _____

_____

_____

5 _____

_____

_____

CHAPTER 2 Plants and animals

Lesson	Objectives	Main activity	Group activities	Plenary	Outcomes
Lesson 1 Animals and plants	• To know the difference between an animal and a plant.	Distinguish between plants and animals.	Complete a sheet with differences between plants and animals. Make a mismatch book.	Discuss the differences identified between plants and animals.	• Can distinguish between plants and animals.
Lesson 2 On the farm	• To know the difference between an animal and a plant.	Farm or park study.		Look at the similarities and differences between plants and animals.	• Can describe differences between animals and plants.
Lesson 3 Living things	• To sort living things into groups of animals and plants.	Sort pictures of animals and plants and give reasons.	Play animal and plant card games. List and write	Discuss the differences between plants and animals.	• Can sort living things into animal and plant groups.
Lesson 4 Plant groups	• To know that plants can be separated into groups (flowering and non-flowering). • To practise close observation skills.	Look at a range of different flowering and non-flowering plants.	Make a mushroom spore print. Make an observational drawing of a flowering plant.	Discuss and sort flowering and non-flowering plants.	• Can compare plant structures. • Can identify a fern and a flowering plant. • Can make detailed observational drawings.
Enrichment Lesson 5 Broad leaf or conifer?	• To know that trees can be separated into groups (broad-leaved and conifer).	Compare broad-leaved trees and conifers.		Talk about broad-leaved trees and conifers.	• Can tell the difference between a broad-leaved tree and a conifer.
Lesson 6 Let's find out about plants	• To know how to use secondary sources to find out about plants.	Use reference materials to find out about a particular type of plant.		Children present the information they have found.	• Can present information gained from a secondary source.
Lesson 7 Wildlife in the locality	• To know the names of some of the plants and animals in the local environment.	Visit the local environment and look for things moving and growing.	Make a class reference book of plants or animals. Find out more about some of the things seen.	Look at the class reference book.	• Can recognise some of the plants and animals in the local environment.
Lesson 8 Life processes in the locality	• To relate life processes to animals and plants found in the local environment.	Look for evidence of feeding or nesting (life processes) in the environment.		Talk about what was seen on the walk.	• Can identify life processes occurring in the environment.
Enrichment Lesson 9 Flower jigsaw	• To know that plants in the local environment are similar to each other in some ways and different in others.	Compare similarities and differences in plants.	Compare flowers. Make a cut-and-paste jigsaw of three plants.	Talk about similarities and differences in plants.	• Can identify the parts of common plants. • Can compare some common plants.
Lesson 10 Habitats	• To know that the local area is divided into different habitats. • To know that there are differences and similarities between habitats.	Conduct a habitat survey of the local area (grassland, pond, wood, garden). Compare how much sun, shade or wind each gets. Make a habitat map.	Make a drawing, painting or collage to add to the habitat map. Write a description of, or poem about, a habitat.	Discuss the habitats on the class map.	• Can identify different habitats in the environment. • Can describe some features of different habitats in the environment.
Lesson 11 Habitat investigation	• To know some of the plants and animals in a named habitat.	Look at a habitat in detail and record results.		Groups report on the different habitats.	• Can identify some plants and animals found in a particular habitat.
Lesson 12 What will we find?	• To make predictions about what might be found in a different habitat. • To design a simple chart for collecting information.	Use information from Lessons 10 and 11 to make predictions of what might be found in a different habitat.	Design a chart to take out in Lesson 13. Use reference materials.	Discuss the children's charts.	• Can use previously gathered information to make predictions. • Can design a simple chart.
Lesson 13 Were we right?	• To investigate a different habitat, testing predictions made.	Visit different areas and test predictions.		Discuss what the children found.	• Can make observations to test predictions. • Can describe how two habitats differ.
Enrichment Lesson 14 Picture sentences	• To know that living things in a habitat, depend on each other.	Look at the relationships between plants and animals.	Make a habitat display. Draw pictures to show relationships.	Use the habitat display to talk about the different relationships .	• Can give examples of how living things depend on each other.

Lesson	Objectives	Main activity	Group activities	Plenary	Outcomes
Enrichment Lesson 15 Animal disguises	• To know that some animals use camouflage to help them survive in a habitat.	Discuss origins of, and reasons for, camouflage.	Make camouflage pictures . Describe, or write a poem about camouflage..	Discuss effective camouflage.	• Can explain how camouflage helps animals to survive in a habitat.
Enrichment Lesson 16 Hide it!	• To understand how camouflage works.	Groups camouflage an object on the school field		Discuss how camouflage works.	• Can use camouflage to hide an object.
Enrichment Lesson 17 Tree slider	• To know that plants and animals change in appearance and behaviour with the seasons.	Discuss a year in the life of a tree and its inhabitants.	Make a 'tree' slider of the changing seasons.. Make a zig-zag book .	Talk about how things change through the year and how living things depend on each other.	• Can describe how some animals and plants change through the seasons.
Enrichment Lesson 18 Caring for habitats	• To know ways in which the environment can be cared for.	Review the habitat visits to consider examples of pollution or abuse and how they could be stopped.	Write a newspaper report about the state of a habitat. Make a set of rules and a poster about protecting the environment.	Discuss ways to care for the environment.	• Can identify habitat damage • Can explain how habitat damage affects things living there. • Can suggest ways to care for the environment.
Enrichment Lesson 19 Plant and animal care	• To know about caring for living things indoors.	Discuss caring for plants, a fish tank, or for pets at home. Care for plants grown from seeds.	Write a simple instruction booklet about caring for a pet. Care for a coleus plant as it grows.	Discuss caring for plants and animals.	• Can describe how to look after living things in the classroom and at home.
Lesson 20 From flowers to seeds	• To know that flowering plants produce seeds.	Examine flowers to find pollen and identify the seed-case.	Look for different seed-heads and make an observational drawing. Set and care for seeds	Look at the drawings and discuss the seed-heads.	• Know that seeds come from flowering plants.
Lesson 21 A fruity array	• To know that there are many different types of fruits and seeds.	Look at, and compare, a range of fruits and seeds.		Talk about fruits and seeds.	• Know that there are many different kinds of fruits and seeds.
Lesson 22 How many seeds?	• To know that different fruits contain different numbers of seeds.	Examine and count the seeds in the seed-heads of different plants.		Discuss the variation in the numbers of seeds produced by plants.	• Know that different fruits contain different numbers of seeds.
Lesson 23 Fair test	• To plan and carry out a simple fair test with help. • To investigate the effect of water on seed germination and seedling growth.	Investigate the germination of seeds and the growth of seedlings. Plan, a fair test to see if all seedlings need water.	Groups set up the test with each group using different seeds. Write up the investigation.	Discuss how the test was set up and kept fair. Decide when to check the pots for progress.	• Know that seeds and seedlings need water to germinate and then grow.
Lesson 24 Light for growth	• To plan and carry out a simple fair test, with help • To investigate the effect of light on seedling growth.	Investigate the growth of seedlings. Plan a fair test to see if all seedlings need light.		Review what is needed to make a fair test and compare the plants.	• Know that seedlings need light for healthy growth.
Lesson 25 Frog wheel	• To know that animals reproduce and change as they grow older.	Use a Big Book to talk about the life cycle of a frog.	Make a frog wheel to show a frog's life cycle. Use secondary sources to research the life cycle of other small creatures.	Discuss the life cycle of a frog.	• Can describe how some animals change as they grow up.

Assessment	Objectives	Activity 1	
Lesson 26	• To assess whether children know that living things in a habitat depend on each other. • To assess whether the children recognize the difference between animals and plants.	Link the various dependencies between plants and creatures in a habitat.	

SC1 SCIENTIFIC ENQUIRY

Germination experiments

LEARNING OBJECTIVES AND OUTCOMES
- To ask questions and decide how they might find out the answers.
- To recognise when a test or comparison is unfair

ACTIVITY
Children are asked questions to help them devise a fair test to find out whether all plants need water and light to grow. They learn that to make a test fair, only one thing can be investigated at a time and all the other factors in the investigation must remain the same. They record their investigation on a simple sheet.

LESSON LINKS
This Sc1 activity forms an integral part of Lesson 23, Fair test.

Lesson 1 ▪ Animals and plants

Objective
- To know the difference between an animal and a plant.

Vocabulary
animal, plant, alive, living, breathe, feed, grow, reproduce, die, similarities, differences

RESOURCES ●
Main activity: Flipchart or board, a healthy pot plant, a small animal (borrow a pet for the day if you do not keep animals at school, or use one of the children instead).
Group activities: 1 A copy of photocopiable page 69 (also 'Animals and plants' (red), available on the CD-ROM) for each child, writing and drawing materials. **2** Thick paper or thin card (A4 size) to make the mismatch book, drawing and colouring materials, stapler, scissors.

PREPARATION
Write the questions listed on the right on the flipchart.

BACKGROUND
Plants and animals have many similarities as well as differences. Children at Year 2/Primary 3 should have enough experience of animals to appreciate that most have eyes and ears and can feel, taste and smell. Animals and plants both reproduce but in different ways. Animals lay eggs or have babies whilst plants reproduce either seeds or spores. Some, like the strawberry plant, reproduce by sending out runners to root and grow into new plants. New plants can also be grown from cuttings taken from a mature plant.

In Year 1/Primary 2 children looked at how plants and animals both need water. Animals also need food but plants make their own food through the process of photosynthesis. All animals depend ultimately on plants for their food. Many feed directly on plants, while animals that are higher in the food chain eat the plant-eaters.

Animals are obviously more mobile than plants but plants do move as they grow. Even some cut flowers may be seen to turn towards the light.

Children may say that animals breathe and plants do not. Plants also need to take in air but they do not breathe in and out visibly as mammals do.

STARTER
Remind the children that they learned about caring for plants and animals in Year 1/Primary 2. Show them the healthy plant and animal to help them remember.

MAIN ACTIVITY
Working with the whole class, look carefully at the plant and ask the children

Can it see?
Can it talk(make a noise)?
Can it hear?
Can it feel?
Does it eat?
Does it need water?
Can it move?
Does it have babies or lay eggs?
Does it have roots?
Does it live forever?

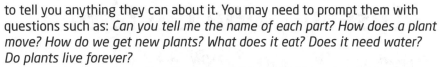

Differentiation 💿
Group activity 1
To support children, give them 'Animals and plants' (green), from the CD-ROM, which asks them to draw features that distinguish animals and plants. To extend children, use 'Animals and plants' (blue), which asks them to suggest some similarities as well as differences between animals and plants
Group activity 2
Some of the children should be able to measure and cut their own pages but others may need help to do this or have the pages photocopied for them.

to tell you anything they can about it. You may need to prompt them with questions such as: *Can you tell me the name of each part? How does a plant move? How do we get new plants? What does it eat? Does it need water? Do plants live forever?*

Then look at the animal and ask the children what they know about it, using similar prompt questions. You may also ask: *Can it speak or make a noise? What does it eat? Does it need water?*

Ask the children questions from the flipchart list and tick or cross the prepared columns for the plant and the animal as appropriate. Talk about the questions and help the children to decide what main differences they can see between plants and animals. There are, of course, many differences, but the obvious ones for children at this stage are probably those linked to the senses and movement. Some children may understand that animals need food, while plants are able to make their own. There are also many similarities, and some children may be able to start thinking of these. (Plants and animals both need water and air, they grow and go through a life cycle.)

GROUP ACTIVITIES

1 Give each child a copy of photocopiable page 69 and ask them to complete it by writing or drawing five things that distinguish plants and animals.
2 Make a mismatch book. Each child will need two sheets of thick paper or thin card. These should be roughly A4 size. Divide each page into three equal sections on both sides (see diagram, opposite).

Some children may be able to do this for themselves, but you may prefer to mark one page and photocopy it before giving it to the children. Fold each page in half to make a book. On the first page the children should draw a plant, and on the fifth page a tree, keeping the flower or head of the tree in the top section of the page, the stem or trunk in the middle section, and the roots in the bottom section. On page three they draw a boy or girl and on page seven an animal or bird. This works best if the animal is two-legged, such as an ostrich, so that the head can be kept in the top section, the body in the middle section and the legs and feet in the bottom section. Staple the book together with a staple through each section, then cut each page along the lines into the three sections. The sectioned pages may then be turned to make 'mismatch' creatures which are part-plant and part-animal. The drawings must be positioned similarly on each page.

ASSESSMENT
Check the children's work in Group activity 1 to assess their understanding.

PLENARY
Go through some of the work that the children have done in Group activity 1, pointing out some of the differences between plants and animals that they have listed. Remind the children about the questions they answered in the Main activity. *Were there any similarities?* Have fun looking at some of the mis-match books!

OUTCOME
● Can distinguish between plants and animals.

Lesson 2 ▪ On the farm

Objective
● To know the difference between an animal and a plant.

RESOURCES
Access to a farm (or wildlife park), camera.

MAIN ACTIVITY
Visit a farm and look at the plants and animals there. (You will need to follow your LEA guidelines before arranging a farm visit.) Point out that cows give milk, sheep provide wool and hens lay eggs. Wheat, oats and corn are grown as food for humans and other animals.
If you are visiting a wildlife park, look for animals and their babies, plants in enclosures or gardens, trees in the parkland. Compare the differences between the plants and animals.
    Back in the classroom the children can record their experiences in various ways, focusing on the differences between the plants and animals that they have seen.

ASSESSMENT
Use the children's work to assess their understanding of the differences between plants and animals.

Differentiation
Children may record their observations in different ways. Some may write their own account, while others may contribute pieces of writing or pictures to a group or class book, or simple captions for photographs.

PLENARY
Discuss similarities and differences. Animals and plants are both found on a farm, or in a park. Animals need to be fed and looked after. Plants need care but make their own food. Both plants and animals need water. Animals move around the farm or park, but plants stay in the same place. Both plants and animals grow and reproduce, and so on.

OUTCOME
● Can describe differences between animals and plants.

Lesson 3 ▪ Living things

Objective
● To sort living things into groups of animals and plants.

Vocabulary
plant, animal, kingdom, similarities, differences

RESOURCES ◉
Main activity: Pictures of plants and animals (including mammals, insects, fish, birds and molluscs), two large PE hoops, two large labels.
Group activities: 1 Animal and plant cards made from the pictures on photocopiable pages 70 and 71 (also 'Living things –1' (red) and 'Living things – 2' (red), available on the CD-ROM; see Preparation, below). **2** A copy of photocopiable page 72 (also 'Living things – 3' (red), available on the CD-ROM) for each child; pencils.

PREPARATION
Make enough sets of cards from photocopiable pages 70 and 71 to have one set between two. Enlarge the sheets to A3 if possible. When coloured and laminated these will make a useful resource for several activities. Write 'Animal' on one label and 'Plant' on the other; use these to label the hoops.

BACKGROUND
Many children will think that the animal kingdom consists only of mammals. This activity will help them to understand that insects, spiders, fish, reptiles, birds and humans are all part of the animal kingdom, as well as helping them to sort animals from plants. At this stage they do not need to be able to name individual species, although some interested children may become quite knowledgeable in certain areas.

STARTER
Working with the whole class, remind them of what they learned in Lesson 1. Look at a picture of a mammal and a plant and ask the children to say which is the animal and which the plant. Can they say how they know which is which?

MAIN ACTIVITY
One at a time, look at the other pictures you have and ask the children to decide whether they are plants or animals. Ask for reasons for their decisions. Put each picture in the appropriately labelled hoop. Gradually build up two sets, one of animals and one of plants. Discuss similarities and differences. All animals need to eat and have senses. They do not all have legs (compare a snail and spider) but they can move. Plants have stems and leaves and are usually green and may also have flowers and fruits.

GROUP ACTIVITIES
1 Divide the children into groups of four or six and give each group two sets of cards made from the pictures on photocopiable pages 70 and 71. Suggest that they use the cards to play Snap, or a matching game like Pelmanism, where they match any two animal cards or any two plant cards. Before they can keep them, the children need to say whether their cards are 'plants' or 'animals'.
2 Give each child a copy of photocopiable page 72. Explain that they should write the names of the animals in the gaps and add why they are animals. They then list the plants and write about why they are plants.

ASSESSMENT
Observe the children as they play the games, particularly Pelmanism. Are they able to match things from the same kingdom? Use the work from Group activity 2 to assess their understanding.

PLENARY
Review the pictures sorted in the Main activity or some of the writing done in Group activity 2 and discuss the fact that each one belongs to either the plant or animal kingdom. Draw out the fact that although members of each kingdom may look very different from each other, they still have things in common.

OUTCOME
● Can sort out living things into animal and plant groups.

Differentiation
Group activity 1
Children who need support can use 'Living things -1' (green) and 'Living things -2' (green) from the CD-ROM, which contain a smaller selection of animals and plants.
Group activity 2
Support children by giving them 'Living things -3' (green). The children need to pick just two animals and two plants and they are not required to provide reasons for their choices.
    To extend children, use 'Living things 3' (blue), which asks them to identify all the living things on the sheet provide reasons for their choices.

Lesson 4 ▪ Plant groups

RESOURCES
Main activity: Two or three examples of different flowering plants, two or three ferns, moss; pictures of plants, including a flowering plant (showing seed-heads if possible).
Group activities: 1 A large open mushroom for each group of three, empty margarine pots or similar, white paper, fine hairspray or pastel fixative, magnifiers.
2 Flowering plants, drawing and colouring materials, large sheets of paper, fern leaves, small garden sprayer or diffuser containing suitable non-clogging paint.
Plenary: Seeds to match one of the flowering plants.

Objectives
● To know that plants can be separated into groups (flowering and non-flowering).
● To practise close observation skills.

Vocabulary
fern, flowering, non-flowering, seeds, spores, fungi, gills, reproduce, leaf, flower, stem

BACKGROUND

There are a huge variety of plants on the Earth and, like animals, these can be divided into groups. Green plants which produce flowers and then seeds, are perhaps the most familiar. Some plants however do not have flowers – conifers produce cones that bear seeds and ferns develop tiny spores (asexual reproductive cells) usually on the underside of their leaves. Some plants have become highly adapted to their habitats – cacti have spines that are really leaves adapted to lose as little water as possible in the hot dry climates they inhabit.

Many children will be familiar with mushrooms but may not realise that they are not plants. They belong to a separate group called fungi, which reproduce by dispersing millions of tiny spores.

STARTER

Gather all the children together and remind them of the things they learned about plants in Year 1/Primary 2. Using a picture, or a flowering pot plant, rehearse the names of the different parts of a plant (leaf, flower and stem).

MAIN ACTIVITY

Ask the children to look carefully at the plants you have collected. Look at each one in turn, starting with a flowering plant. Invite one child to point to and identify the different parts – leaf, flower and stem. Ask: *How do we get new plants from this one?* (Seeds develop that will grow into new plants in the right conditions.) Look at another flowering plant and invite a different child to find the same features on the new plant. Depending on the season you may have a plant with some seed-heads on, otherwise use a picture showing the seed-heads or fruits on a flowering plant. Ask: *Why do plants produce fruits and seeds?* (In order to reproduce.)

Look next at a fern. Ask the children which parts they can identify. Ask: *Where are the flowers? Do you think this plant ever has flowers?* Some children, who have not seen ferns before, might think that it does but that they are not out yet. Ask them to look closely to see if they can see any sign of buds forming. You will then need to tell them that this is a special type of plant that does not have flowers, but instead produces tiny spores on the underside of its leaves. Show the children the underside of a fern leaf and talk about how these spores, like seeds, will grow into new plants. Ask the children to sort your small collection into flowering and non-flowering sets.

GROUP ACTIVITIES

1 Show the children a mushroom. *Ask: are mushrooms plants?* Explain that they actually belong to the fungi family. Tell them that mushrooms use spores to reproduce and that the spores are hidden in the gills under the cap. Sort the children into groups of three and encourage them to use a magnifier to look closely at the gills of their mushroom. Tell them that the spores are difficult to see, but there is a way of getting them out so that you can see them. Remove the stem from an open-capped mushroom and place the mushroom, gills down, on a clean piece of white paper. Carefully cover it with a margarine pot or similar so that it is not disturbed and leave it somewhere warm and safe overnight. Next morning, lift the mushroom very gently to reveal the pattern of the gills outlined in tiny spores that have fallen from the cap during the night. A gentle spray of pastel fixative or light hairspray will help to preserve the print.

2 Allow the children to choose to draw either a fern leaf or a flowering plant. Suggest that they draw just part of the plant – a leaf, a flower or seed-head – very carefully, rather than trying to draw the whole thing. If you have a good supply of fern leaves then try placing the leaves on paper and spraying over them using a hand sprayer or diffuser with suitable paint: this can produce some very effective patterns. Move the leaves and spray again with a different colour. Large sheets done in this way provide an interesting

Differentiation
All the children can take part
in these activities.

backing for a display. Make sure the children are well protected and
supervised when spraying – it may be better to do this activity outdoors!

ASSESSMENT
Observe the children as they sort the plants into sets. In Group activity 2, as
the children are working, ask them to tell you the difference between a fern
and a flowering plant.

PLENARY
Gather together all the plants you have been using and ask for a volunteer
to come and sort them into sets of flowering and non-flowering plants. *Can
anyone remember what some of the non-flowering plants are called?*
(Ferns) Ask the children if they can tell you the main difference between the
two groups of plants that they have been looking at. (One has flowers, the
other doesn't.) Ask the children: *How do the ferns reproduce?* Talk about the
spores, how tiny they are and how they are produced in vast quantities.

Look at the seeds from which a pot plant might grow. These may be quite
small too, but will still be much bigger than the spores produced by the ferns
or the mushroom. Look at one of the mushroom spore prints and ask a child
from one of the mushroom groups to explain what they have been doing.
How are the mushrooms similar to the ferns? (They both produce spores
instead of seeds.)

OUTCOMES
- Can compare the structure of different kinds of plants.
- Can identify a fern and a flowering plant.
- Can make an observational drawing showing some detail.

LINKS
Art: observational drawing.

ENRICHMENT
Lesson 5 ▪ Broad leaf or conifer?

Objective
- To know that trees can be
separated into groups (broad-
leaved and conifer).

RESOURCES
Small pieces or branches from various conifers and cones. (Beware! Do not
use yew, as this is highly poisonous.) Small pieces or branches from broad-
leaved trees such as oak, ash, horse chestnut or whatever is available
locally; fruit or seeds (or pictures of these) from the selected trees.

MAIN ACTIVITY
Look at the specimens and compare and contrast them. Talk about the fact
that the broad-leaved trees are a different type of flowering plant. Look at
the fruits or seeds from these trees and compare them with the cones.
Discuss the fact that most conifers are 'evergreen' and what this means.
Introduce the word 'deciduous' and explain what it means. Go outside and
see if you can find examples of conifers and broad-leaved trees in the
locality. Can the children distinguish between the two?

ASSESSMENT
Show the children a piece from a conifer and a piece from a broad-leaved
tree and ask if they can name the group to which each belongs.

Differentiation
All the children can take part
in these activities.

PLENARY
Talk about the two groups of trees you have been looking at and sort the
pieces of plant material into two sets. Discuss the fact that there are many
different groups in the plant kingdom and these are just two of them.

OUTCOMES
● Can tell the difference between a broad-leaved tree and a conifer.

Lesson 6 ▪ Let's find out about plants

Objective
● To know how to use secondary sources to find out about plants.

RESOURCES
Reference books, CD-ROMs, posters and videos about plants; writing and drawing materials, tape recorder and tapes, OHP and transparencies, OHP pens.

MAIN ACTIVITY
Ask the children if they can remember the names of the groups of plants they looked at in previous lessons. Remind them that there are lots of different groups and that they are going to try to find out as much as they can about another group. Show them pictures of cacti, carnivorous plants, climbing plants and so on from the reference materials and ask them find to out as much as they can about a particular group (their choice or yours).

Work could be presented as a booklet, a newsletter for a gardening club, an audio-tape or a series of slides on an OHP.

ASSESSMENT
Assess the quality of the work produced.

Differentiation
Some children may need to work together and contribute to a group booklet.

PLENARY
Ask different children or groups of children to tell or show the rest of the class what they have found out.

OUTCOME
● Can present information gained from a secondary source.

Lesson 7 ▪ Wildlife in the locality

Objective
● To know the names of some of the plants and animals in the local environment.

Vocabulary
environment, collect, sample, flora, fauna, specimen, minibeast

RESOURCES
Main activity: Reference materials, clipboards, paper, pencils, plastic trays, pooters, small paintbrushes, bug boxes, white trays, magnifiers, empty containers for collecting small creatures, cameras.
Group activities: 1 Specimens collected during the Main activity, magnifiers, reference materials; materials to make a class book: paper, treasury tags or laces. **2** Reference materials including CD-ROMs.

PREPARATION
Take a walk around your own locality, or the area you are planning to use, to identify some of the common flora and fauna that the children are likely to find. In most cases the emphasis will be on trees and flowers, rather than animals, since creatures are often quite difficult to spot. Make sure that these species are well represented in your reference materials.

BACKGROUND
At this stage, children should begin to learn the common names of some of the flora and fauna that are found in their locality. They should be able to name, for example, an oak tree or a dandelion.

STARTER
With the whole class, use some of your reference materials to look at pictures of plants and animals that you might expect to find in the locality.

MAIN ACTIVITY

Talk about what the children might expect to see in the local area. Look at the pictures and talk about where the children might see these things. *Can you name any of them? Where might you look for them?* Tell the children that you are all going outside to see how many plants and animals you can identify. Talk about the need to take care of the environment and advise them to collect any samples very carefully. They should take only one leaf from each tree, preferably one that has fallen off. If there are lots of flowers of a particular kind then, again, they may take one, but if there are only one or two then they should draw them or take a photograph. Small creatures, such as snails, might be gently collected and returned to the environment as soon as they are finished with, but make sure that the children know how to use a pooter or paintbrush to collect minibeasts safely.

If the children can name the tree, plant or animal they see, they may not need to collect that particular item, but just make a note or drawing to show that they have seen it. They will need to make sketches or take photographs of any animals, such as rabbits, cats or dogs, since it is obviously not easy to collect them! Divide the children into groups of three or four and provide each group with a clipboard, a plastic tray and any other collecting equipment you think they may need. Go outside and see what you can find.

GROUP ACTIVITIES

1 Back in the classroom, each group should use reference materials to identify any samples brought back. As items are identified, label them and lay them out on the table. Compare the findings of each group. Ask the children to draw pictures of their finds and collect them together in a class book which could then act as a reference book for other classes, or be used as a comparison for the next year. Any photographs taken could also be used. Make the book with loose pages held together with treasury tags or laces so that extra pages can be added if more things are found.

If you do this lesson in the autumn you could stick dried leaves from the trees directly into the book. If you mount these on cards and cover them with sticky-backed plastic they will last for several years. Make sure that any small creatures are returned to their habitats as quickly as possible and that any pots are washed before they are put away.
2 Ask the children to use reference materials, including CD-ROMs, to discover more about some of the samples found in the Main activity and add this information to the class reference book.

ASSESSMENT

Use the children's work to assess their knowledge. During the Plenary session ask them how they would use the class reference book, or how other people could use it. Note those children who can identify pictures of things found in the area.

PLENARY

Look together at the book the children have compiled. Hold up some of the leaves, flowers or creatures that they have included and ask if they can recognise and name any of them. Talk about how they might use the book to identify what things are. Suggest that the book can be added to each time one of the children finds something new in the area.

OUTCOME

● Can recognise some of the plants and animals in the local environment.

LINKS

Literacy: producing a book and organising entries in alphabetical order.

Lesson 8 ▫ Life processes in the locality

Objective
● To relate life processes to animals and plants found in the local environment.

Differentiation
All the children should be able to take part in this activity, although some may need occasional reminders of what they are looking for.

RESOURCES
Pictures of the flora and fauna found in Lesson 7, the class reference book made in Lesson 7.

MAIN ACTIVITY
Talk about some of the flora and fauna previously found. Can the children remember where they were found? *Did the animals move? How fast? Where were they going? Where did they live? What were they eating? Where were the plants found - in the Sun or in the shade? Where did they seem to grow best? Were there any seeds or new plants?* Go outside again and retrace your steps from Lesson 7, but this time look for seed-heads or baby plants and for signs that plants are growing healthily or struggling (on the side of a path or near a playground). *Are there any baby creatures about?* Look especially for caterpillars or other grubs that will change into moths or butterflies. Can they see holes in leaves where creatures may be feeding?

ASSESSMENT
Note those children who contribute sensibly to the Plenary session.

PLENARY
Talk about what you saw on the walk. *Did you see evidence of animals eating plants? Were there any signs that plants or animals were reproducing themselves?* (Baby creatures, seeds, young plants.) *Did you find any nests or homes?*

OUTCOME
● Can identify life processes occurring in the environment.

Lesson 9 ▫ Flower jigsaw

Objective
● To know that plants in the local environment are similar to each other in some ways and different in others.

Vocabulary
leaves, flowers, stem, arrangement, florets, similar, different, variety

RESOURCES ◉
Main activity: Sufficient dandelions, daisies or buttercups, with leaves, for each pair or group of three to have one of each type. Try to obtain one complete plant of each type to show how the leaves are arranged, otherwise use pictures of whole plants. Substitute similar flowers if these are out of season. If you have difficulty finding wild plants locally you could use something like a primula and a pot chrysanthemum. Try to include some of the plants identified by the children in Lesson 7 Wildlife in the locality.
Group activities: 1 Writing and drawing materials; flowers for each group (different from those used in the Main activity). If possible, try to find multi-headed flowers such as rosebay willow herb or wallflowers (to challenge children, try hyacinths or bluebells). **2** A copy of photocopiable page 73 (also 'Flower jigsaw' (red), available on the CD-ROM) for each child, scissors, adhesive, colouring materials.
ICT link: 'Flower jigsaw' interactive, from the CD-ROM.

BACKGROUND
The Earth holds an enormous variety of plant life. As with animals, many plants have basic similarities but are infinitely different. In this lesson the aim is to encourage children to look more closely at plants within their environment. This should enable them to see how plants are often quite similar (they have leaves, stems, flowers and so on), but different in the way that the flowers are formed or leaves are shaped and arranged on the stem.

STARTER
You can use almost any flowers for this lesson but, for ease of explanation, buttercups, dandelions and daisies are being used as examples. Working with the whole class, hold up a daisy. Ask: *Can anyone remember the name of this plant?*

MAIN ACTIVITY
Give each pair or group of three a daisy, a buttercup and a dandelion. Ask them to look closely at the daisy. *What colour is it? What are these called?* (Petals.) *What shape are they?* Ask the children to draw the shape of the petals in the air. Now look closely at the buttercup. *What colour is it? What shape are the petals? How is it the same?* (Both flowers have petals and a yellow bit in the centre.) *How is it different?* (The petals are a different colour and shape. A daisy has lots of petals while a buttercup usually has just five.) Now look at the leaves on the daisy.

Show the children the whole plant, or a picture of the plant growing. *What colour are the leaves? What shape are they? Where are they found on the plant?* (Daisy leaves are usually clustered around the base of the plant with the flowers on straight stems above the rosette). Compare these with the leaves on the buttercup. *What colour are they? What shape are they? Can you draw those in the air? Where are they found on the plant?* (Again there may be a rosette of leaves around the base, but other leaves on the stem below the flower. This will depend on the species of buttercup you have. Some types grow quite tall while others put out runners and are lower-growing).

Look now at the dandelion and compare it to the other two plants. The flower is the same colour as the buttercup but it has lots of petals like the daisy. (The 'petals' of a dandelion are actually individual florets, but children at this stage do not need to know this). *The leaves are long, a bit like the daisy, but with a jagged edge, more like the buttercup. They are arranged at the base of the plant like the daisy.* Ask the children: *Do all three plants have leaves?* (Yes.) *Do all three have flowers?* (Yes.) *Do all three have stems?* (Yes.) If possible, go outside to find some of the growing plants and notice how the leaves are arranged.

GROUP ACTIVITIES
1 Give each group another quite different flower to compare with the buttercup, daisy or dandelion. *Does it have just one flower on a stem like the daisy?* Can they identify the petals and say how they are different from the flower they looked at in the Main activity? Ask them to look at the leaves. *What shape are they? How are they arranged on the plant?* Ask the children to draw pictures of each plant and list the similarities and differences. They could press examples of their flowers to add to their work at a later date.
2 Give each child a copy of photocopiable page 73. Ask them to cut out the pieces and stick them on another sheet to make three different flowers.

ICT LINK 💿
Children can use the 'Flower jigsaw' interactive, from the CD-ROM, to complete the flower jigsaws on screen.

ASSESSMENT
During the Plenary session, note the children who are able to compare the flowers and tell you some similarities and differences. Use the children's work from the first Group activity to assess their understanding.

PLENARY
Ask some of the groups to explain where they found the petals and leaves on their new flower and how they were the same or different from the one

in the Main activity. Ask the children to tell you some similarities that are usually found in flowering plants. *Can you tell me some things that might be different? How do we tell one flower from another?* Say that plants are a bit like people. We all have eyes, noses and mouths but they are all a little different in shape, colour or arrangement so we can tell people apart.

OUTCOMES
- Can identify the parts of common plants.
- Can compare some common plants.

LINKS
Art: observational drawing.

Lesson 10 ▪ Habitats

Objective
- To know that the local area is divided into different habitats.
- To know that there are differences and similarities between habitats

Vocabulary
habitat, environment, Sun, shade, picture map, identify, specimen

RESOURCES
Main activity: Access to a range of wildlife habitats, flipchart or board, clipboards and pencils for each group of three, a copy of photocopiable page 74 (also 'Habitats' (red), available on the CD-ROM) for each group (plus a few extra), a camera, a prepared display board (see Preparation, below), marker pen or chalk.
Group activities: 1 Drawing, painting and collage materials. **2** Writing materials or access to a word processor.
Plenary: Pieces of grey or black net (optional).

PREPARATION
Visit the area you intend to use to make sure that there are different habitats and that they are safely accessible to the children. Stick large sheets of paper together to cover a display board.

BACKGROUND
At this stage it is important that the children begin to learn how to channel their curiosity, investigate in a more systematic way and begin to look for cause and effect. All schools are surrounded by different habitats, although some are obviously richer and more diverse than others. You may be lucky enough to have a wildlife area that you can use but, if not, a log pile takes up little space and can easily be created in a corner of the school field or playground. A small pond can be made in an old sink or baby bath. If you have a school field, try to arrange for one corner of the grass to be left uncut. You will quickly develop a habitat for grasses, insects and wild flowers.

If none of these options are open to you, churchyards or local cemeteries are often excellent wildlife havens. Local parks are also a possibility if they are not too well-manicured. Children begin to appreciate that plants and animals live in particular places and may be well adapted to certain conditions. At Year 2/Primary 3 it is quite acceptable for the children to use the common names for things - you may even have regional variations in the names of some plants or animals. The children may find some plants or animals that cannot easily be identified. Encourage them to classify these as 'flying insect', 'aquatic insect', 'climbing plant' and so on.

STARTER
Remind the children that in Year 1/Primary 2 they learned that a habitat is a small part of the environment and is home to particular plants and animals. They looked at a tree and some of its inhabitants.

Differentiation

For children who need support, use 'Habitats' (green), from the CD-ROM, which includes a simplified version of the recording sheet.

To extend children, use 'Habitats' (blue), which includes additional habitat features for the children to consider.

MAIN ACTIVITY

Tell the children that you are going to go outside into a particular area and look for different habitats. Ask if they can think of habitats (places) they might look for. (Sunny or shady places, wet or dry places, places with thick vegetation or very little cover, places with rotting vegetation, hedges, ditches, trees, walls, seashore and so on.) Make a list on the flipchart of some of the habitats you might find in your area.

Divide the class into groups of three or four and give each group a copy of the record sheet on photocopiable page 74 (on a clipboard) and explain to them how to fill it in. In the 'habitat' column they write a very brief description of the habitat (woodpile, corner of field under big tree, pond, and so on). Read through the other columns with them and say that they can just put a tick or a cross, or write something such as 'some shade' or 'very wet'. In the 'plants' and 'animals' columns the children should just note any obvious ones that they recognise. Tell them that you have some extra sheets if they run out of space.

Go outside to the chosen area and explore. As the children are working, take photographs of the habitats they are recording. Back in the classroom, gather the children around the prepared display board and, in a suitable place, mark a significant landmark such as a school wall or fence, a gate or a big tree. Ask the children to say where the habitats they looked at are in relation to this landmark and mark them on the display in order to create a rough map of the area. Don't worry about scale or accuracy, just make sure that the habitats are in roughly the right place.

GROUP ACTIVITIES

1 Ask each small group to do a painting or small collage that could be put on the picture map to illustrate a habitat. Some children might like to draw or paint pictures of other significant things and these could also be included on the map. Add any photographs that are available.

2 Ask the groups to write or word-process a short description of or poem about a habitat, using the information from their record sheets. Encourage the groups to choose different habitats (or choose for them) so that all are covered.

ASSESSMENT

Use the work from Group activity 2 to assess the children's understanding. In the Plenary session, note those children who contribute sensibly to the discussion.

PLENARY

Look at the picture map you have created and discuss the features of each habitat. *Was it wet, dry, windy? Can you decide from which direction the Sun was shining? Which areas were in the shade?* (If you have some grey or black net you could, at this point, cut out pieces and stick these over the shady areas to represent the shade.)

OUTCOMES

● Can identify different habitats in the environment.
● Can describe some features of different habitats in the environment.

LINKS

Geography: creating simple maps.
ICT: word processing.

Lesson 11 ▪ Habitat investigation

Objective
● To know some of the plants and animals in a named habitat.

RESOURCES
Collecting equipment such as plastic bags, plastic pots, pooters, small soft paintbrushes, white trays, nets (pond or sweep), magnifiers; a stereo microscope (if available), clipboards, camera, reference materials.

MAIN ACTIVITY
Look together at some of the equipment they are going to use and remind the children how to use it. Divide them into their groups from Lesson 10. Tell them not to share pooters and to decide within their groups who will be responsible for each piece of equipment to ensure that nothing is lost or left behind. Remind them to collect any specimens with great care, to make a note of familiar things on their clipboard rather than collecting unnecessary samples, and to pick only one flower and one leaf when there are plenty of plants. They should make a sketch or take a photograph of unusual things that can't be collected.

Go out and spend time looking for living things in a particular habitat. Different groups could study different habitats within the same area (under the hedge, on the playing field, in the shade, in the log pile, or any others identified in Lesson 10).

Add the lists of any plants and animals that are found to each area of the picture map or make separate group booklets to go with the display.

Differentiation

All the children should be able to take part in this activity.

ASSESSMENT
During the Plenary session note those children who can name some of the living things found in a particular habitat.

PLENARY
Ask the groups to report back on what they found. Look at the lists. *Were any things common to every habitat?* (There may have been some grass in each one.) *Was there a habitat that had very different things in it?* (Perhaps a pond.)

OUTCOME
● Can identify some plants and animals found in a particular habitat.

Lesson 12 ▪ What will we find?

Objective
● To make predictions about what might be found in a different habitat.
● To design a simple chart for collecting information.

Vocabulary
habitat, specimen, example, prediction, conditions

RESOURCES
Main activity: Reference materials, writing materials.
Group activities: 1 Paper, pencils, rulers. **2** Reference materials, including CD-ROMs.

BACKGROUND
The children studied one particular habitat in Lesson 10 and 11. If it is not possible to go to a completely different location for this lesson, ask the children to study a different habitat within the same area.

Children will begin to understand that, although habitats vary infinitely, some of the variations may be very subtle. (A habitat in light shade or sunlight.) Some species of plants and animals may occur in both.

STARTER
Remind the whole class of what they did in Lessons 10 and 11.

MAIN ACTIVITY

Show the children the collection of appropriate reference books. Tell them that this time, before they go out to look at a different habitat, they are going to try to predict what they might find there. Ask the children to think about what they might find in a very wet area such as a pond. (Frogs, tadpoles, fish, water plants.) Take some suggestions and then ask one of the children to check on the display made in Lesson 10 to see if these are correct. Ask: *Where else might I look to find out what might live in this sort of habitat?* (Reference books or CD-ROMs.) *Can anyone find a book from the collection that might be helpful?*

Now suggest a different type of habitat, perhaps a damp, dark place. *What would you expect to find there?* (Woodlice or slugs but no flowers.) Again consult the display and find any suitable reference books. Continue in this way until you feel that the children understand. Ask the children to work in the same groups as in Lesson 10 and allocate each group a 'new' habit to look at. Ask them to think about the kinds of plants and animals they might find there and make a list of their predictions on a flipchart or white board. Explain that it is not always necessary for them to identify particular species. They may predict 'no flowers' or 'some flowers', but should be able to predict 'frog' or 'tadpole' in a pond habitat.

GROUP ACTIVITIES

1 Working in their groups, or individually, ask the children to design a simple chart that they can take out with them to test their predictions. It should list the animals and plants that they think they will find, with a column to say whether they found them or not.
2 Tell the children to check relevant reference materials to familiarise themselves with the new plants and animals they have predicted they might find. This will enable them to recognise them if they do find them.

ASSESSMENT

Use the work to assess their ability to design simple charts and make sensible predictions.

PLENARY

Ask the children to show their charts and say how they plan to use them. Look at the lists of creatures they have predicted that they may find and ask the rest of the class if they agree or have any other suggestions. Ask the children why they have predicted finding certain things. (The type of habitat: it is damp and dark so we might find woodlice and slugs; it is hot and dry with long grass so there might be grasshoppers.)

OUTCOMES

- Can use previously gathered information to make predictions.
- Can design a simple chart.

LINKS

Maths: designing simple charts.

Differentiation
Group activity 1
Some children may find it easier to try out ideas on a board, white board or flip chart before committing these to paper. Some may make only a few predictions and limit themselves to more obvious things.
Group activity 2
Some children may prefer to do simple drawings or make a few notes to help them remember particular features.

Lesson 13 ▪ Were we right?

Objective
- To investigate a different habitat, testing predictions made.

RESOURCES

Collecting equipment such as plastic bags, plastic pots, pooters, small soft paintbrushes, white trays, nets (pond or sweep); magnifiers, a stereo microscope (if available), a camera, reference materials, the children's own charts on clipboards.

Differentiation
Some children may look for
fewer and more obvious
things and may prefer to work
as a group, with one member
marking up a group chart.

MAIN ACTIVITY

Visit the 'new' habitat from Lesson 12 and look for plants and animals. The
children should check finds against those they predicted, making a note of
any unexpected finds. Collect some samples carefully and take these back
to the classroom to look at in more detail, using magnifiers or a stereo
microscope if you have one.

ASSESSMENT

During the Main activity, note which children are able to use their charts to
check their predictions. In the Plenary session ask children to describe
differences between the two habitats they have looked at.

PLENARY

Gather the children together and ask which groups found the things they
had predicted they would. *Did any group find everything they predicted? Did
any group find something totally unexpected?* Ask the children what they
based their predictions on. *How did the new habitat differ from the last one
you studied?*

OUTCOMES

- Can make observations to test predictions.
- Can describe how two habitats differ.

Lesson 14 ▶ Picture sentences

Objective
- To know that living things
in a habitat depend on each
other.

Vocabulary
depend, rely, survival, food,
shelter, support

RESOURCES 💿

Main activity: Depending on the area you are visiting, you may find extra
adult help useful.
Group activities: 1 Drawing and painting materials, fine string, white
cotton thread, black tissue, black paint, small egg boxes, pipe-cleaners,
collage materials including feathers, green paper, old socks or tights,
polystyrene packing chips, rope or twine, scissors, adhesive. **2** A copy of
photocopiable page 75 (also 'Picture sentences' (red), available on the CD-
ROM) for each child; simple reference books.

PREPARATION

For Group activity 1 you may wish to make the spider's web before the
lesson if you think this is beyond the children's capability.

BACKGROUND

At this stage children do not need to know about food chains but they
should be aware of some of the ways in which living organisms depend on
each other. The dependency between plants and animals is often a two-way
process. Plants provide food for animals but, in return, they may rely upon
animals to disperse their seeds or carry their pollen from one flower to the
next. In some cases animal droppings not only help to spread the seed but
also provide a rich seed bed in which the new plants can grow.

STARTER

Remind the children about the work they did in Year 1/Primary 2 when they
looked at the things living in a tree and how they depended on each other,
or the tree, for their food and shelter.

MAIN ACTIVITY

Ask the children to think about their own families. Their home is their
habitat and the members of most families depend upon each other. They
depend on mum or dad to provide food and shelter. Mum or dad may rely on

Differentiation
Group activity 1
All the children can contribute to Group activity 1. Some children may be able to help make labels.
Group activity 2
To support children, use 'Picture sentences' (green), from the CD-ROM. This sheet includes the words that children need to draw as prompts. To challenge children, use 'Picture sentences' (blue), which includes an extension question about how plants and animals depend on each other.

them to play with their little brothers or sisters while they are busy. The children may even rely on an older brother or sister to take them to and from school. *Are there any other ways in which the people (the family) living in that particular habitat rely on each other?* (You may have to tread carefully here with regard to the family backgrounds of some of the children.)

Ask the children to think of some of the things that they found when they were looking at particular habitats in the last few lessons. *Can you think of any ways in which the plants or animals there depended on each other? Do any of the animals eat each other? Might the plants be used for nests, for bedding, or for supporting a web?*

Go outside to look for evidence of plants or animals depending on each other. Look for holes in leaves or ragged edges that show where they have been eaten. Look for twigs supporting spiders' webs or leaves that have little clusters of eggs on the underside. *Are there any flies trapped in the webs?* You may find empty, broken snail shells left by thrushes, or pine-cones nibbled to the core by squirrels. You may find some ivy or honeysuckle which is using a tree to support its upward climb. *Can you see bees or other insects visiting flowers?* The plants provide nectar, but in return depend on the insects to carry pollen from one flower to another. Some relationships may not be so beneficial. Aphids and other such insects may damage plants by sucking their sap or introducing disease, but the aphids also provide a food source for many small birds, such as blue-tits, and ants harvest the sticky honeydew they secrete.

GROUP ACTIVITIES
1 Make a habitat display. In one corner of the room, or on a display board, make a large spider's web from fine string. Make spiders from balls of black tissue, or small egg boxes painted black, with pipe-cleaner legs. Wrap balls of black tissue in white cotton thread to represent captured flies. Cut out giant leaves from green paper and cut holes in the middle or from the edge as if they have been eaten. Stuff old (but clean!) tights or socks to make caterpillars and put these on the leaves. Attach leaves to rope or twine to make a climbing plant. Make a collage picture of a bird (using feathers) eating the caterpillars. Paint some big flowers, using pipe cleaners with pieces of packing material on the ends for the stamens, then make a bee to visit the flower. Be sure to represent any particular evidence you found on the walk. Add labels to show the interdependence of the plants and animals. (For example, the spider needs the tree from which to hang its web.)
2 Give each child a copy of photocopiable page 75 and ask them to complete it using drawings to finish the sentences. The answers are: 1. A (bee) takes pollen from flower to (flower); 2. A spider eats up the (insects); 3. A (squirrel) in the tree eats the berries and scatters the (seeds); 4. A (caterpillar) eats holes in the leaves.

ASSESSMENT
Use the photocopiable sheet from Group activity 2 to assess the children's understanding. Note those children who contribute new ideas in the Plenary session.

PLENARY
Use the habitat picture to talk about the different relationships between the plants and animals. Ask the children if they can suggest others which might have gone on the display. (Ants and aphids, climbing plants and so on.)

OUTCOME
● Can give examples of how living things depend on each other in a habitat.

LINKS
Art: models and collage.

ENRICHMENT
Lesson 15 ▪ Animal disguises

Objective
● To know that some animals use camouflage to help them survive in a habitat.

Vocabulary
camouflage, hide, hunt, prey, predator, disguise, protect

RESOURCES
Main activity: Pictures of camouflaged animals (leopards, tigers, stick insects, caterpillars, frogs, toads); camouflage clothing or pictures of soldiers or tanks in camouflage.
Group activities: 1 Thick paper, cardboard tubes, paint, adhesive. **2** Writing materials.

BACKGROUND
Animals adopt camouflage for various reasons. It allows them to merge with their surroundings and hide from predators or, in some cases a predator may use camouflage to gain advantage over its prey. Leopards become almost invisible in dappled shade; plaice are mottled to look like the seabed and caterpillars can be indistinguishable from the twigs. Most animals are camouflaged to match the surroundings in which they are usually found.

Some animals, like chameleons or people, can change their colouring (or clothing) to match whatever surroundings they happen to be in. All of the above are examples of camouflage by colouring but some animals, such as the stick insect, are also camouflaged by their shape.

STARTER
Show the children the camouflage clothing or pictures of soldiers in camouflage. Ask: *Why do soldiers wear camouflage?*

MAIN ACTIVITY
Many children will be able to tell you that soldiers wear camouflage so that they can't be seen, or so that they can move about without being seen. Look at the soldiers' clothing and talk about what it is like. *Why is it patterned like that?* (Random shapes merge with the light and shade better than regular angular shapes.) *Why have those colours been used?* (They blend with wooded landscapes.) *Would the same colours be used if the soldiers were in the desert or in snow?* (Desert camouflage is a mixture of sandy colours, and whites and greys are used in snowy areas.) Explain that people probably learned how to use camouflage from animals. Some animals need to hide from their enemies (predators), or sometimes they need to hide from other animals that they are hunting (prey). Look at some pictures of well-camouflaged animals. *Can you spot the animal? Why is it camouflaged? Is it hunting or being hunted?*

GROUP ACTIVITIES
1 Give each child a large sheet of thick paper and ask them to paint it in any pattern they choose (stripes, spots, random blobs, checks, and so on). Tell them to cover the whole page. Cut the paper in half and tell them to draw the shape of an animal, fish, bird or insect on the back of one of the pieces and then cut it out. Stick the animal on to a small card roll or small box and then stick this to the other half of the painted paper so that the camouflaged animal is mounted slightly away from the camouflaged background. *Which patterns act as the best camouflage?*
2 Choose an animal and ask children to do a piece of writing to say how camouflage helps it to survive in its habitat.

Differentiation
Group activity 1
All children should be able to take part in Group activity 1.
Group activity 2
In Group activity 2, some children may find a word list helpful. Others may like to present their writing in the form of a poem.

ASSESSMENT
Use the children's work from Group activity 2 to assess their understanding.

PLENARY
Look at the pictures made by the children in Group activity 1 and decide

which sort of pattern makes the best camouflage. Ask some of the children to read out their writing or poems. Ask: *How does camouflage help animals to survive in a habitat?*

OUTCOME
● Can explain how camouflage helps animals to survive in a habitat.

LINKS
Literacy: writing poems.

ENRICHMENT
Lesson 16 ● Hide it!

Objective
● To understand how camouflage works.

RESOURCES
Garden netting, twigs and branches, hay or straw; four stage blocks or other large objects - one for each group. If you are in a 'brick' environment, you may wish to use old sheets that the children can paint appropriately.

MAIN ACTIVITY
Take the children out on to the school field, by a hedge if possible. Divide them into four groups and give each group the task of camouflaging their object, using the netting and any other suitable materials they can find. When they have finished, take them all some distance away and ask if they think the objects are well camouflaged. Invite another class to come and see if they can spot the objects.
If you have a military base nearby you may be able to persuade someone to come and show you some real camouflage netting.

ASSESSMENT
Observe the children as they carry out the task to see who has grasped the idea of making the object blend into the background. Note those children who give sensible answers in the Plenary session.

PLENARY
Ask the children how camouflage works. *Why do some animals find it useful or even necessary?*

Differentiation
All the children can take part in this activity.

OUTCOME
● Can use camouflage to hide an object.

ENRICHMENT
Lesson 17 ● Tree slider

Objective
● To know that plants and animals change in appearance and behaviour with the seasons.

Vocabulary
change, hibernate, camouflage, migrate, dormant

RESOURCES
Main activity: Pictures of trees to act as a stimulus.
Group activities: 1 Thin card, writing and drawing materials, adhesive, sticky tape, scissors, rulers. **2** Stiff paper or card, reference materials, writing and drawing materials. 'Tree slider' diagram, available on the CD-ROM.

PREPARATION
Make a 'tree slider' as an example to show the children in Group activity 1 (see diagram below).

BACKGROUND
The behaviour or appearance of many plants and animals is affected by climate or day length. Most plants do not grow in the cold dark days of winter so there are no tender shoots available for slugs, snails and insects

to eat. Animals that depend on such things for food are therefore at risk. Some are able to migrate to a warmer climate and some hibernate. Others rely largely on fat which they have stored up during summer and autumn. In plants the seasonal changes are marked by changes in appearance, while in animals changes in behaviour are most noticeable.

In spring we see new plant growth, while birds sing their best songs and display their finest feathers in an effort to find a mate. Many animals produce their young at this time to coincide with the new plant growth or increased insect activity. In summer, plants continue to grow and animals rear their young, sometimes producing a second brood. The birds that migrated to warmer climates during the winter return to nest and raise their families.

STARTER
Remind the children that, in Year 1/Primary 2, they looked at how plants and animals change through the seasons.

MAIN ACTIVITY
Ask the children: *Can you tell me what a year in the life of a tree would be like?* (Buds appear in the spring and then the leaves and flowers come out. There are lots of green leaves in the summer and in the autumn the fruits ripen, the leaves change colour and fall off. In the winter it looks dead.)

Establish how the children think the changes in the tree affect the creatures which live in it? Ask: *What happens to the tree in the spring?* (New shoots and blossom.) *What might like to eat the fresh new leaves?* (Insects such as caterpillars or leaf miners.) *What might visit the blossom looking for food?* (Insects, including bees.) Remind the children of Lesson 14 Picture sentences. *Can you remember how the insects are helping the tree?* (They are helping to pollinate the flowers.) *What other animals might visit*

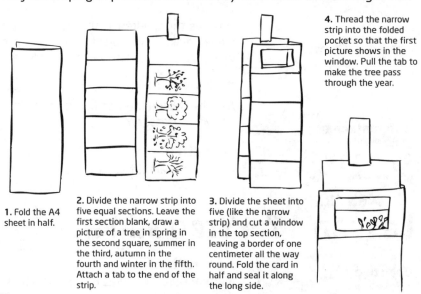

4. Thread the narrow strip into the folded pocket so that the first picture shows in the window. Pull the tab to make the tree pass through the year.

1. Fold the A4 sheet in half.

2. Divide the narrow strip into five equal sections. Leave the first section blank, draw a picture of a tree in spring in the second square, summer in the third, autumn in the fourth and winter in the fifth. Attach a tab to the end of the strip.

3. Divide the sheet into five (like the narrow strip) and cut a window in the top section, leaving a border of one centimeter all the way round. Fold the card in half and seal it along the long side.

the tree in the spring? (Birds, butterflies or moths.) *Why do they need the tree?* (Birds might build a nest in its branches or in a hole in the trunk, or they might just come to eat the insects feeding on the leaves. Butterflies or moths lay eggs under the leaves that provide a food source for the emerging caterpillars.) *What happens to the tree in the summer?* (It continues to grow larger). The fruits start to grow and so do the insects, if they are not eaten first!) *What season comes next?* (Autumn.) *What happens then?* (The fruits ripen and the leaves change colour and fall off.) *Who eats the fruit?* (Birds, insects, squirrels; sometimes humans and other animals if the fruit falls to the ground.) *How does this help the tree?* (It can help to scatter the seed over a wider area.) *What happens next? What season will it be?* (It is winter and the tree becomes dormant.) *What do you think happens to all the things that were living in the tree?* (Many will die off in the cold but eggs laid in the autumn will remain over winter to hatch in the spring. Some creatures will burrow deep into the bark and hibernate. Birds will get food where they can. Squirrels will rely on their fat reserves and hidden food stores.) *Is this where the story of the tree stops?* (No, next it is spring and the story starts all over again.)

GROUP ACTIVITIES

1 Show the children how to make a simple slider and demonstrate how it works. The children may find it easier to create the window if they cut from the edge of the card, cut out the window and then mend the original slit with a small piece of adhesive tape. Give each child a piece of thin A4 card and a second strip that is slightly narrower than the folded card (see instructions on the previous page).
2 Tell the children to choose a living thing, perhaps a hedgehog, and use reference materials or previous knowledge to make a zig-zag book about a year in its life. Ask them to include information on how it is affected by other animals or plants (lack of slugs and snails for food in the winter).

ASSESSMENT

Use the children's work from Group activity 2 to assess their understanding.

PLENARY

Ask some children to demonstrate their tree sliders. Ask others to tell their 'Year in the life of...' stories. Talk about how things change through the year and how living things depend on each other.

OUTCOME

● Can describe how some animals and plants change through the seasons.

LINKS

Technology: making a slider (following instructions).

Differentiation

Group activity 1
All the children can attempt Group activity 1, but some may need a little help with measuring, cutting and folding. Some children may be able to follow the diagram on page 58, (also available on the CD-ROM).

Group activity 2
Children who need help with reading may work better with a partner who can help them in Group activity 2. To challenge children, encourage them to add more detail and information to their booklets. They may decide to present their work as a conventional booklet if this allows them more space.

ENRICHMENT

Lesson 18 ▪ Caring for habitats

Objective

● To know ways in which the environment can be cared for.

Vocabulary

care, pollution, damage, conservation, destroy, save, wildlife, litter, hazard, risk, graffiti

RESOURCES

Group activities: 1 Writing materials, use of a computer. **2** Writing and drawing materials, poster-sized paper.

BACKGROUND

Much of the damage done in the local environment is caused more by thoughtlessness than by deliberate malice. Graffiti is unsightly but may not cause any actual damage to wildlife (unless they are unfortunate enough to be caught in the spray). More damage is caused by people carelessly breaking branches, or dropping litter which are real hazards for small creatures. Broken glass can act as a magnifier and cause grass fires, as well as being a danger to the bare feet of larger animals. Discarded fishing lines and nets are hazardous for water birds and fish.

STARTER

Ask the children if they know of any areas in the neighbourhood that are not cared for, or an area that is well cared for. (Some villages enter 'best-kept village' competitions and are very well-cared for. Some urban areas have 'clean-up' campaigns to improve the area.)

Differentiation

Group activity 1
Support children by asking them to just list some of the things they saw. As extension, ask children to make some suggestions for improving the area (providing extra litter bins, emptying them more frequently, and so on).

Group activity 2
All the children should be able to make a poster in Group activity 2, but some children may need to work together to make a group set of rules.

MAIN ACTIVITY

Go back to visit one of the areas you have used previously in this unit. *Is there any graffiti?* Look for damage to trees and bushes. *Are there any broken branches, or is litter stuck in the branches? Are there any uprooted plants? Are the paths trampled at the edges or are they overgrown?* If there is a pond or stream, ask: *Is it covered in oily scum or is it full of litter? Have people been riding bikes or motorcycles and churning up the ground? Is there any rubbish tipped in the hedge? Are any litter bins provided? Are they used and, if they are, are they emptied regularly?* Look for evidence that paths have been cleared or pavements mended; hedges or grass cut. *Can you find any other ways in which the area is being cared for?*

Back in the classroom discuss with the children what they have seen and how it might affect the wildlife living in the area. *What could happen to a damaged tree?* (Broken and damaged trees may die and no longer provide food or shelter for animals.) *Why are discarded cans, bottles and plastic bags dangerous for animals?* (Small creatures may get trapped, or cows might eat them and die.) *Why do we need to keep streams and ponds fresh?* (Oily scum prevents oxygen entering the water and this can harm any life there. Chemicals can poison it. Trolleys tipped into the water may trap other rubbish that rots and poisons the water.)

GROUP ACTIVITIES

1 As individuals, ask children to write a newspaper report about the state of the area you visited. It may be quite negative if there is a lot of litter or damage, or it may be a very positive report if it is a well-kept area. Your local newspaper might be interested in printing some of these reports.
2 Write a set of rules for caring for the environment, such as: Always put litter in the bin. Don't break fences. Don't draw graffiti. Don't break tree branches. Keep to the paths. Don't pick wild flowers. Help plant trees. Treat wildlife with respect. Each child could make a poster to publicise one particular rule for a class display. A local shop may be interested in displaying some of these.

ASSESSMENT

Use the children's written work to assess their knowledge and understanding.

PLENARY

Talk to the children about what they saw on their visit. Ask one or two to read their reports. Discuss with the children ways in which they can help to care for the environment. Do they all obey the rules they have listed?

OUTCOMES
- Can identify ways in which a habitat is damaged.
- Can explain how habitat damage affects things living there.
- Can suggest ways to care for the environment.

LINKS
Literacy: writing for a purpose (report).

ENRICHMENT
Lesson 19 ▪ Plant and animal care

Objective
- To know about caring for living things indoors.

RESOURCES

Main activity: A small collection of plants to make a display in the classroom (try to include a rubber plant or something similar that needs dusting), a small watering can, a soft cloth for cleaning the leaves of larger plants, plant nutrient, paper and pencil.
Group activities: 1 Copies of commercial 'How to care for' booklets for pets;

Vocabulary
care, depend, responsible, needs, injection, grooming, exercising, worming, vet, nutrient

writing and drawing materials. **2** Coleus seeds, compost, plant pots, newspaper, water, labels, plant nutrient, trays to stand pots in.

BACKGROUND
Even young children should learn that if we choose to own or keep another living thing then we must accept responsibility for it and take care of it. It is important that children realise that caring for a living thing is an ongoing responsibility and should not be taken lightly.

STARTER
Ask which children have pets at home and what they do to help look after them.

MAIN ACTIVITY
Talk about how the children care for their pets at home. Do they help with feeding, grooming or exercising, or is it left to Mum or Dad? If you have a school pet, how is that cared for? Do they take turns to clean out the rabbit or the fish tank, or is it always left to one person? Talk about how important it is to take your turn with duties like these. If animals are in a cage they have no way of finding their own food and water and rely on their owners for their food, drink and well-being.

Look at the display of plants and ask the children how they would care for them. *What do they need?* (Water, light, warmth, but not too much of any.) *What about the plants with big broad leaves? What happens if they get dusty?* Explain that if they were outside in their normal habitat, the rain would clean the leaves. The leaves need to be clean to absorb the sunlight that the plants need to make their food and grow. Explain that when we are keeping plants indoors we need to help them keep clean by wiping the leaves with a damp cloth from time to time. They also need a little nutrient occasionally (be careful not to call it food). Talk about how the children can help to keep the display of plants looking fresh and healthy. Put the children in pairs and make up a rota so that everyone takes a turn to look after the plants. Make a list of the tasks involved.

GROUP ACTIVITIES
1 As individuals, design and write a simple instruction booklet for someone looking after a particular pet. Look at some commercially produced leaflets to see the sort of information that is important. Don't forget that caring may also include worming, getting the appropriate injections and perhaps even insurance.
2 Working in pairs, sow Coleus seeds and care for the plants as they grow. Coleus seeds germinate well and produce plants that vary widely in colour and pattern. They do flower but are grown mostly for the colour of their leaves. The children could grow them to give as presents for some special occasion or to sell at a school fair. Sow one or two seeds in each small pot, or sow a number in a larger pot and separate them into individual small pots when the seedlings are big enough to move. They need careful handling to ensure that the delicate new shoots and roots are not damaged. Choose whichever method you think the children will best cope with. Continue to grow the plants, perhaps transferring them to even bigger pots as they grow.

ASSESSMENT
Use the children's work from Group activity 1 to assess their understanding. Observe children as they care for their coleus plants or the class display. Note those children who remember their tasks and those who need to be reminded.

Differentiation
Group activity 1
Some children may need to work in a group to produce a group booklet, with each child doing one page. Some children will be able to produce a detailed booklet on their own.
Group activity 2
All the children should be able to participate in Group activity 2.

PLENARY
Ask some children to read each other's instruction booklets and explain how to care for a pet. Look at the display of plants or the growing coleus plants and discuss how they have benefited from the care they have received.

OUTCOME
● Can describe how to look after living things in the classroom and at home.

LINKS
Literacy: writing for a purpose (booklets).

Lesson 20 ▪ From flowers to seeds

Objective
● To know that flowering plants produce seeds.

Vocabulary
seed, pollinate, fertilise, produce, germinate, grow, seed-head, stamens, pollen, ripe, reproduce

RESOURCES
Main activity: An example of a flower and its seed-head (perhaps a rose and rose hip), a cotton bud.
Group activities: 1 Magnifiers, drawing materials, a selection of flowers and seed-heads, available according to season (wallflowers, daffodils, busy lizzies, marigolds, buttercups, rape, sweet peas); small knives for cutting open the seed-heads (the ASE publication *Be Safe!* lists flowers and plants that should be avoided because of their toxicity). The developing seed-heads can be seen best as the flowers begin to die so try to find stems with a mixture of flowers, dying flowers and seed pods. **2** Plant pots, seeds, compost, labels, newspaper.

BACKGROUND
Not all flowers will automatically produce fruit. This depends on whether the flower was pollinated and then fertilised.

Flowers are produced to attract insects, who carry pollen from one flower to another. This is pollination. Pollen grains (which are the male gametes) then grow down through the stigma to fertilise the ova in the ovary of the plant, which is usually found at the base of the flower. As the flower dies, the ovary can be seen to swell with the developing seeds. Children of this age do not need to understand the process of pollination and fertilisation, but it is helpful for them to know that pollen plays a part in the development of seeds. If the subject is introduced the correct terminology should be used to avoid the danger of children developing misconceptions.

STARTER
Ask the children if they know how we get new plants. Remind them about the seeds they grew in Year 1/Primary 2 and ask if they can remember what happened.

MAIN ACTIVITY
Working with the whole class, look at a flower and a dead flower head, such as a rose (Rosa Rugosa -a single, bright pink rose, is useful for showing both stamens and ovary). Try to obtain several examples to pass around the class. Look at the petals and the centre of the flower. You may be able to gather a little pollen from the stamens on a cotton bud to show the children. Explain that pollen has to be taken from one flower to another, usually by insects or the wind, in order to help them produce seeds. Ask the children to look carefully at the bulge behind the flower head and explain to them how this swells into a seed-case. Look further down the stem where the flowers have already died and fallen off and point out that the swelling is much bigger. Ask: *What do you think is inside the case?* Cut the seed-head in half and show the children what is in there. Ask: *Why do plants produce seeds?* (In order to reproduce themselves.) Take the opportunity to reinforce the safety

Differentiation
These activities should be accessible to all the children.

message that they should never eat any seeds or fruits unless they are told that it is safe to do so by a responsible adult.

GROUP ACTIVITIES

1 Working alone or in pairs, give the children examples of other flowers, with both developing and fully developed seed-heads. Ask them to look for a developing seed-head. They should then carefully cut a ripe seed-case open, look for the seeds inside and make an observational drawing.
2 Working in small groups, take some seeds from one of the seed-heads and set them in a pot of compost. Label the pot with the date of sowing and the variety of plant, if known. Ask the children if they can remember how to care for them. (Keep the seeds warm and damp and you should have some success with germination whatever the time of year.) This will help the children to see that new plants do begin to grow from the seeds produced by flowering plants. Further growth of the plants will depend on the time of year and the type of seeds chosen. If the seeds are of a size that can be counted, the children could keep a record of the number sown and see if they all germinate and form new plants.

ASSESSMENT
During the Plenary session ask the children if they can explain where seeds come from, and why seeds are necessary.

PLENARY
Look at some of the drawings the children have done. Ask them to describe the flower they have drawn and where they found the developing seed-head. *Were all the plants similar or were some of the seed-cases different shapes?*
Ask: *What will the seeds grow into if you plant them?* Help the children to understand that the seeds will grow into plants similar to those from which the seed came.

OUTCOME
● Know that seeds come from flowering plants.

LINKS
Art: observational drawing.

Lesson 21 ◗ A fruity array

Objective
● To know that there are many different types of fruits and seeds.

RESOURCES
A selection of different fruits such as apples, crab apples, pears, peaches, mangoes, papaws, blackberries, raspberries or rose hips; knife.

MAIN ACTIVITY
Look at an apple. *Where are the seeds?* Cut the apple in half and look for the seeds. Look at different fruits and their seeds and compare the shapes and sizes of the seeds. Explain to the children that the fruits of some plants are attractive to certain animals. When the animals eat the fruits with the seeds in them they help to disperse the seeds. (Beware! Some fruit, such as blackberries, may stain.) Reinforce the warning that children should not eat any berries or fruits that they find.

ASSESSMENT
During the Plenary session ask the children why plants produce fruits.

Differentiation
All the children can take part in this activity.

PLENARY

Discuss the fact that each type of plant produces its own particular fruit containing seeds. Ask the children why they think some seeds are hidden within fruits. Discuss fruits being attractive to animals and that they help to disperse the seeds by eating the fruits and discarding the seeds.

OUTCOME

● Know that there are many different kinds of fruits and seeds.

Lesson 22 ▪ How many seeds?

Objective
● To know that different fruits contain different numbers of seeds.

RESOURCES

A collection of fruits or berries such as rose hips, apples, pears, sweet peas, peas, runner beans, broad beans, sycamore seeds, rape or shell-on peanuts; knives, paper, pencils, clear adhesive tape.

MAIN ACTIVITY

Working in pairs, give the children different fruits to investigate. Help them to cut the fruits in half and look for the seeds inside. Encourage them to remove the seeds carefully and place them, in a row, on a piece of paper. Cover each row with a strip of clear adhesive tape. Count the seeds and record the type of plant and number of seeds by the side of each strip. Use the information to produce a simple graph. *Which plant produces most seeds?* Avoid plants that have a large number of very small seeds that are impossible to count.

ASSESSMENT

Ask the children to tell you, from their graph, which fruit has the most seeds and which the least.

ICT LINK 💿

The children could use the graphing tool, on the CD-ROM, to create a block graph or pie chart.

PLENARY

Discuss the variation in the numbers of seeds produced by different plants. Ask the children if they have any ideas why some fruits (such as a peach) have only one seed whilst others have many. (Where there is only one seed it tends to be covered in a very hard shell and for this reason it is often discarded rather than eaten with the fruit. Seeds from other fruits may actually be chewed and digested and therefore plants need to produce a greater number of seeds to ensure that some will germinate.)

Differentiation
Some children could collect information from other groups and begin to think about the average number of pips, for example, in an apple.

OUTCOME

● Know that different fruits contain different numbers of seeds.

Lesson 23 ▪ Fair test

Objective
● To plan and carry out a simple fair test with help.
● To investigate the effect of water on seed germination and seedling growth.

RESOURCES 💿

Main activity: Flipchart board or whiteboard.
Group activities: 1 Two small plant pots for each group of three or four; compost, water, measuring jugs, newspaper; plant labels (lolly sticks), some marked with coloured tape to indicate the dry pots; two plastic trays labelled 'Wet' and 'Dry' to hold the pots; a variety of seeds such as broad beans,

sweet peas, French marigold or radish. **2** A copy of photocopiable page 76 (also 'Fair test' (red), available on the CD-ROM), for each child; pencils.

PREPARATION
Spread some compost out on a tray and leave this in a warm place for two or three days until it is really dry. You will need enough compost to fill half the number of plant pots. Wrap some coloured tape around half of the plant labels so that the pots that are to be kept dry can be distinguished easily.

BACKGROUND
Children at this stage will need lots of help to plan a fair test, and the quality of their thinking and answers will depend greatly on the quality of the questions they are asked.

Make sure that when you are talking to the children you distinguish carefully between seeds that are germinating and seedlings that are growing. Seeds do not grow. They contain sufficient nutrients to sustain them while they germinate and they do not technically begin to grow until they produce their first pair of true leaves and start to photosynthesise. The children do not need to know the details of this but it is helpful if they develop the correct vocabulary.

Make sure that the children know to wash their hands well after handling compost and that any cuts must be covered before they start.

STARTER
Working initially with the whole class, remind the children of what they learned in Year 1/Primary 2 about plants needing water and light.

MAIN ACTIVITY
This lesson will need to be revisited over the next few weeks to make observations.

Ask the children: *What do plants need in order to grow well?* Write 'water' and 'light' on the flipchart. Then ask: *Do all plants need these things? How could we find out?* Explain that, to make a test fair, we can only investigate one thing at a time and we have to keep all the other factors in our investigation the same. *This time we are going to investigate if seeds need water to germinate. We are going to work in groups and each group can test a different kind of seed. Each group is going to set two pots of seeds and give one pot water but keep the other pot dry.* Ask: *What will we need to keep the same to make our test fair?*

Look first at the word 'light' on the flipchart. Ask: *How can we make sure all the pots get the same amount of light?* (Put them in the same place.) *What else will we need to keep the same?* (Some children may volunteer things such as: the same sort of plant pots, the same sort of compost, the same number of seeds, set them at the same time, keep them all warm.) As the children make suggestions add them to the list on the flipchart. If suggestions are not forthcoming ask questions such as: *Do you think it matters if we use a different sort of compost in each pot? Will it make a difference if we give some seeds a lot of water and some just a drop?*

Strictly speaking, it is not necessary for the amount of water given to be exactly the same. However, as part of the process of getting the children to understand what a fair test is, it may be a good idea to decide on an equal amount of water for each group to give to their pot. Remember seeds do not respond well to being drowned! How much water you give will depend on the atmosphere and the heat of the classroom. The compost only needs to be kept damp, and you may need to water every day or just alternate days. With the children, feel the compost each day and decide whether to water or not. You may also need to adjust the amount of water you are giving as the investigation progresses, but talk about this and make sure that each group does the same thing.

GROUP ACTIVITIES

1 Divide the children into groups of three or four. Give each group two plant pots, some dry compost and some damp compost and one variety of seed. Fill one pot with dry compost, one with damp compost, and label the pots with the name of the group, the name of the seeds, and whether the pot is to be kept wet or dry. Place all the pots in the wet tray or the dry tray. Water the 'wet' pots using the measured amount of water. (Keep them separate to avoid the dry pots getting watered unintentionally.) Revisit the activity at sensible intervals to check progress.
2 Give each child a copy of photocopiable page 76 to write a simple structured plan of the investigation, completing all but the last section of the sheet. Keep the children's sheets safe so that you can give them out for completion at the end of the investigation.

ASSESSMENT

Observe how well the children handle the equipment as they set up their investigation. Use the record sheets from Group activity 2 to assess their understanding.

PLENARY

Revise with the children how they set up the investigation and how they tried to keep the test fair. Ask: *What do you think will happen?* Decide together when the pots are to be checked for progress. You will need to gather the children together for a short time to review their observations at least once each week until the end of the investigation (three or four weeks). You will need a longer session in the final week to compare the plants, draw some conclusions and allow the children to complete their sheets. You should have some reasonably healthy plants in the pots that have been watered, but no growth in the dry pots. Tip the dry pots out on some newspaper to see if you can find the seeds. Unless they have become damp they should be the same as when they were planted. Ask the children why they think they have not germinated. (Seeds need water to germinate.)

OUTCOME

● Know that seeds and seedlings need water to germinate and then grow.

LINKS

Literacy: writing for a purpose.

Lesson 24 ▪ Light for growth

RESOURCES

Two small plant pots of a similar size for each group of three or four; compost, a variety of seeds such as broad beans, sweet peas, French marigold and radish; water, measuring jugs, newspaper, plant labels (lolly sticks), a copy of photocopiable page 76 (also 'Fair test' (red), available on the CD-ROM) for each child.
  Each group should set their seeds two weeks before this lesson and keep the compost moist so that they have healthy seedlings to work with. Set a few pots yourself for emergency replacements!

MAIN ACTIVITY

Plan a fair test to find out if seedlings need light in order to grow well. Each group sets two similar pots with seeds. Both are given water as needed but one pot is placed in a light place and the other in a dark place. Make observations every other day and record these on photocopiable page 76.

ASSESSMENT
Observe the children as they set up the investigation. Use their recording sheets to assess their understanding.

PLENARY
Review what is needed to make a fair test. At the end of the investigation, compare the plants grown in the dark with those that have been in the light.

OUTCOME
● Know that seedlings need light for healthy growth.

Differentiation
All the children can take part in the investigation but some may need help with recording.

Lesson 25 ◗ Frog wheel

Objective
● To know that animals reproduce and change as they grow older.

Vocabulary
change, mature, grow, metamorphosis, adult

RESOURCES
Main activity: A Big Book version of 'Tadpole Diary' by David Drew (Rigby) or other pictures showing the life cycle of a frog.
Group activities: 1 Paper plates, split pins, scissors, drawing materials. **2** Reference materials including CD-ROMs (the Insect Lore catalogue contains quite a good selection of appropriate reference materials on this subject, available from Insect Lore, PO Box 1420, Kiln Farm, MK19 6ZH; Tel 01908 563338; www.insectlore-europe.com).

BACKGROUND
Bear in mind that it is illegal to buy frogspawn or to take it from the wild. It can be taken from a garden pond with the owner's permission. It needs to be kept in a cool place away and from direct sunlight. If you can't get pondweed, watercress is a good substitute food for the tadpoles. As they begin to grow legs they will need extra protein to help their development. They can be given raw meat, but this has hygiene implications and you may find that giving them a little flaked fish food is preferable. At this stage, they will also need a rock or stone so that they can climb out occasionally.

   As soon as the tadpoles become froglets they need to eat insects and should be returned to the pond from whence they came.

STARTER
Remind the class about the work they did on ageing in Year 1/Primary 2. They talked about how people change as they grow older, and that adults can have babies which in turn grow up and have babies of their own. They may also have cared for some tadpoles and watched them change.

MAIN ACTIVITY
Look at the big book 'Tadpole Diary', or the pictures. If the children cared for tadpoles last year, ask them what they can remember. Look at how the tadpoles develop. *What do the tadpoles look like when they first emerge from the spawn?* (Very small with external gills.) *Which legs grow first?* (The back ones.) *How are they different from the front legs?* (The back legs are much longer and stronger.) *How does the shape of the head and body change? What happens to the tail?* (The head and body become longer and more frog-like and the tail gradually disappears, as it is absorbed back into the body.) If you have tadpoles in the classroom, relate these stages of development to them and ask the children: *What stage are they at now?*

GROUP ACTIVITIES
1 Make a 'frog wheel' using paper plates. Each child will need two paper plates and a paper fastener. Divide each plate into six sections (some may need help with this) and from one section of one plate cut a window. On the other plate, draw one stage of the frog's life cycle in each section. (1.

frogspawn, 2. tadpole with gills, 3. tadpole without gills, 4. tadpole with back legs, 5. tadpole with back and front legs and reduced tail, 6. froglet.) Fasten the two plates together with a split pin through the middle so that the top plate can be turned to show the stages of the life cycle in succession (see diagram below).

2 Work in small mixed-ability groups to use reference materials to find out simple facts about the life cycle of other animals such as moths or bees.

ASSESSMENT
During the plenary, check that children can explain and have drawn the life cycle stages in the correct order.

PLENARY
Select children to explain how their frog wheels work. Revise the stages of the frog life cycle. Emphasise that it is only when the frogs are fully grown that they spawn. Ask the groups to share their findings about the life cycle of other animals. Discuss how animals change as they grow older and reiterate that it is only when they are fully grown that they have babies.

OUTCOME
● Can describe how some animals change as they grow up.

LINKS
Literacy: using secondary sources.
Unit 2a, Lesson 11, Adults and babies.

  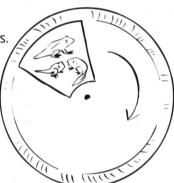

Lesson 26 ▸ Assessment

Objective
● To assess whether children know that living things in a habitat depend on each other.
● To assess whether the children recognise the difference between animals and plants.

RESOURCES
Assessment activity: A copy of photocopiable page 77 (also 'Assessment' (red), from the CD-ROM) for each child; writing materials.

STARTER
Remind the children of some of the work they have done in this unit. Revise some of the vocabulary learned.

ASSESSMENT ACTIVITY
Give each child a copy of photocopiable page 77 and ask them to complete it. Check they understand what each creature is.

ANSWERS
1. pollinate
2. food
3. shelter or food
4. plants
5. birds or hedgehogs
6. insects
7. prey (mice, voles and so on)

LOOKING FOR LEVELS
Most children will be able to answer the questions correctly. Some may answer 'food' for a number of answers, which may show a lack of understanding. Some children will answer the questions on the blue sheet correctly and may be more specific in their answers, for example, listing such things as mice, voles and shrews for the food owls hunt for at night.

Animals and plants

■ Draw or write five things in each shape to show how animals and plants are different.

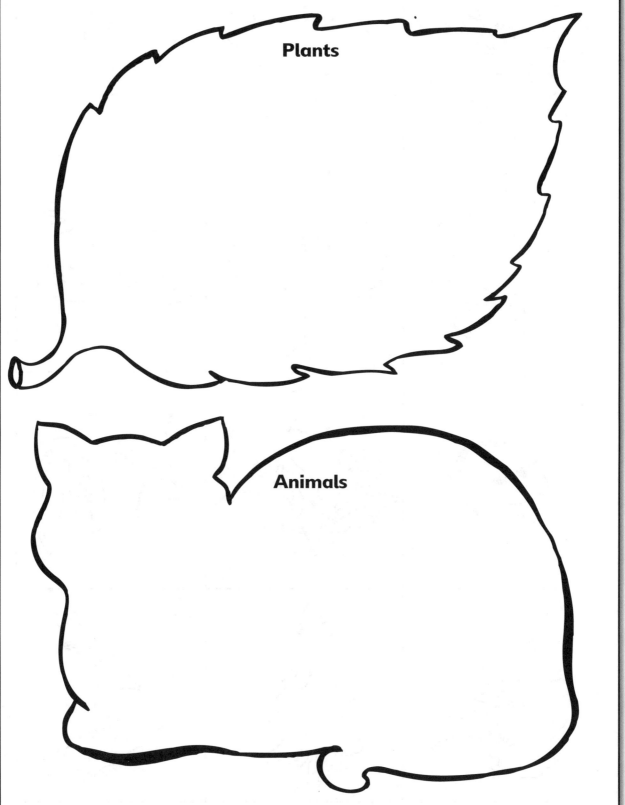

Plants

Animals

Illustration © Ann Kronheimer

Living things – 1

■SCHOLASTIC

Living things – 2

Illustration © Ann Kronheimer

Living things – 3

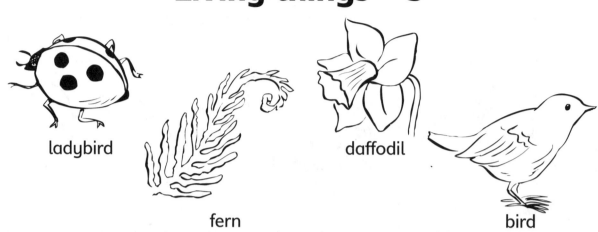

ladybird

fern

daffodil

bird

The _____ and the _____ are both animals
because...

_____

_____

_____

_____

The _____ and the _____ are both plants
because...

_____

_____

_____

_____

■SCHOLASTIC

Illustration © Ann Kronheimer

Flower jigsaw

■ Cut out the pieces and stick them together to make three different flowers. Colour them in the correct colours.

PHOTOCOPIABLE

Habitats

Habitat	wet	dry	sunny	shady	plants	animals
1.						
2.						
3.						
4.						

Picture sentences

- Draw pictures in the boxes to complete each sentence.
- Add your own examples at the bottom of the page.

A [ ] takes pollen from  to [ ]

A  eats up the [ ]

A [ ] in the tree eats the  and scatters the [ ]

A [ ] eats holes in the

A [ ] _____ [ ]

A [ ] _____ [ ]

Fair test

What are you trying to find out?

What do you think will happen?

What equipment will you use?

What do you need to keep the same to make the test fair?

What did you find out?

Assessment

1. Flowers need bees and other insects to _____ them.

2. Ladybirds need aphids for their _____.

3. Birds need trees and hedgerows for _____.

4. Snails, slugs and caterpillars need _____ to eat.

5. Snails, caterpillars and slugs may be eaten by _____.

6. Spiders need to catch _____ in their webs for food.

7. Owls hunt for _____ at night.

Illustration © Ann Kronheimer

CHAPTER 3 Variation

Lesson	Objectives	Main activity	Group activities	Plenary	Outcomes
Lesson 1 Spot the difference	• To understand that plants may vary even though they are the same species. • To practise skills of observation and recording.	Observe and compare differences between two plants of the same species.	Collect leaves showing variations.	Describe and discuss variations.	• Can understand that there are variations in plants even within the same species.
Lesson 2 Shell observations	• To know that there are variations even within the same species. • To practise observation skills.	Observe and compare differences between shells from the same animal species.	Make observational drawings and plaster casts of shells to show variation.	Describe and discuss variations.	• Can understand that there is variation even within the same species. • Can make close observations and record them both in writing and pictorially.
Lesson 3 Cats and dogs	• To know that there are variations even within the same species. • To practise observation skills.	Look at pictures of cats or dogs and compare varieties.	Draw and describe an animal from a photograph. Compare drawings with a partner's and list differences. Make a collage to show variation among cats or dogs.	Describe and discuss variations.	• Can understand that there is variation even within the same species. • Can make close observations and record them both in writing and pictorially.
Lesson 4 Changing faces	• To know that there are variations between humans. • To practise observation skills.	Observe similarities and differences between members of the class.	Write a description of a classmate. Change the appearance of a face template.	Read out descriptions for classmates to guess who the subject is.	• Know that there are variations between humans • Can make close observations.
Lesson 5 Similarities and differences	• To know that plants have similarities and differences.	Observe and compare similar plants of different species. Make a list of similarities and differences.	Compare pictures of other similar plants. Make an observational drawing of a leaf or flower.	Discuss similarities and differences between plants.	• Know that there are similarities and differences between plants.
Lesson 6 Measuring hand spans	• To understand that some differences between humans can be measured. • To make measurements using non-standard or standard units. • To make suggestions about fair testing.	Take hand measurements by drawing around the hand onto graph paper. Discuss what is meant by a fair test.	Take hand measurements using hand prints. Take foot measurements to find out whether the child with the widest hand span also has the longest foot.	Discuss results and which method of measuring was the most accurate.	• Know that some differences between humans can be measured. • Can make measurements using non-standard or standard units. • Can make suggestions about fair testing.
Lesson 7 Spot the insect	• To know that animals can be sorted into groups.	Sort animals into main groups, giving reasons.	Sort out a set of insect pictures giving reasons for sorting. Make a collage picture of an animal for a class picture. Decide which group it belongs to.	Discuss the characteristics of the collage animals and which groups they belong to.	• Can sort animals into groups giving reasons for their groupings.
Lesson 8 Animal factfinders	• To know how to use secondary sources to find out about a wide range of animals.	Prepare a presentation on an animal using research.		Children present the information they have found.	• Can use secondary sources to find out facts about animals. • Can present information about animals obtained from secondary sources.
Lesson 9 Check your facts!	• To confirm information they have read about animals by observing them.	Make a list of questions and observations to investigate with small creatures such as snails, slugs and worms.		Children explain what they were looking for and what they found.	• Can observe animals guided by information that they have read.

Assessment	Objectives	Activity 1	Activity 2
Lesson 10	• To assess if the children are able to identity differences between an animal and a plant. • To assess if the children can sort animals into groups.	Answer questions about plants and animals.	Draw and write the names of animals and plants found in the local environment. List similarities between plants and between animals.

SC1 SCIENTIFIC ENQUIRY

How do we make a fair test?

LEARNING OBJECTIVES AND OUTCOMES

● To make simple comparisons.
● To make measurements using non-standard or standard units.
● To recognise when a comparison is unfair.
● To know the importance of collecting evidence from observations and measurements when answering a question.

ACTIVITY

Children are asked to measure their hand-spans, suggesting how they can do it in a fair way so that the data collected is as reliable and accurate as possible.

LESSON LINKS

This Sc1 activity forms an integral part of Lesson 6, Measuring hand spans

Lesson 1 ▪ Spot the difference

Objective
● To understand that plants may vary even though they are the same species.
● To practise skills of observation and recording.

RESOURCES

Main activity: Access to a patch of simple flowers such as buttercups or daisies; magnifiers; collection of similar shapes, such as triangles, with different dimensions; digital camera; drawing materials.
Group activities: 1 Collected examples of leaves from different individuals of the same species; flower presses or sheets of absorbent paper and suitable weights such as heavy books; card; adhesive; clear sticky plastic or laminate. **2** Pictures of different varieties of the same plant.
Plenary: Whiteboard.

BACKGROUND

No two living things will be exactly the same - even organisms within the same species! While two flowers or leaves will look similar there will be subtle differences in the size or shape of the petals, the number of indentations in the leaf or the pattern of veins. Various factors may influence the differences between the plants in a patch of buttercups growing on the edge of a field, for example. Some may be in the sun for longer during the day; some may have access to more moisture if they are growing nearer to a ditch and so on.

STARTER

Look at the collection of triangles and talk about the fact that although they are all triangles, they are different sizes. Some are long and thin, some have a right angle (square corner) etc. Tell the children that individual plants vary, even though they are the same species. For example, pine trees growing on a rocky mountainside will be small and less robust than pine trees growing in good soil. Trees that are exposed to high winds mainly from one direction will grow bent, away from the wind. The trees themselves may be stunted and their needles smaller. Plants of the same species will vary widely depending on whether they are in the sun or in the shade, how much moisture they have and so on.

MAIN ACTIVITY

Take the children outside to look at patches of the same plant. Ask the children to look carefully at two plants and compare them. How many

Differentiation
All the children should be able to participate in Group activity 1, though some may need help with their labels.
In Group activity 2, some children may need help with their bar chart. Other children may be able to record their finding using a computer programme.

differences can they find? *Are the leaves different in shape or size? Are the flowers the same size? Do they all have the same number of petals? Are the flowers on one plant bigger than on the other? Is one flowering more profusely and so on?* Use a magnifier to look at patterns of veining. Do drawings or take photographs of particular plants. Take a leaf and flower from separate plants that show some differences for comparison back in the classroom. Revise the rules of responsible collecting.

GROUP ACTIVITY

1 Ask the children to collect examples of leaves showing variations from different plants of the same species. Back in the classroom, allow the children to press the leaves in a flower press or by placing them under heavy books between two sheets of absorbent paper. Allow the leaves to dry for about 24 hours then let the children stick them onto card and label them. Laminate the cards to make a reference resource.

2 Make a collection of pictures of different varieties of the same plant. Fuchsias, marigolds, daffodils and penstemons are examples of plants that vary widely in leaf shape, flower shape, colour and number of petals. Ask the children to find and list as many differences as possible. They should then choose one difference, such as colour or number of petals and make a simple bar chart. Use the pictures, lists of variations and bar charts as the basis for a class display.

ASSESSMENT

Use the children's records to assess how well they have understood. During the Plenary note those children who have grasped the concept that there is variation between individual members of the same species of plants.

PLENARY

Look at the leaves the children have collected. Can they describe the differences they have observed in either leaves or flowers? Project any photos that you have taken on to a whiteboard and discuss the variations.

Look at the lists of differences between the plants from Group activity 2 and remind the children that all the plants are the same species even though they are different in lots of ways.

OUTCOME

● Can understand that there are variations in plants even within the same species.

LINKS

Maths: bar charts.

Lesson 2 ▪ Shell observations

Objective
● To know that there are variations even within the same species.
● To practise observation skills.

RESOURCES

Main activity: Collection of sea shells, garden snail shells including different varieties such as roman snails and banded snails, or several types of bi-valve mollusc or cone shells; magnifiers; whiteboard or flipchart.
Group activities: 1 Collection of shells as in main activity. **2** Plaster of Paris, paints.

BACKGROUND

No two living things are exactly the same. Even when members of a species appear to be identical there will be subtle differences when they are observed closely. Variations can be caused by differences in habitat as well as genetic differences within a population and between populations.

STARTER
Ask three boys and three girls to come out to the front of the class and ask: *What similarities can see between these children?* (all the children - boys and girls have faces, ears, eyes). *How can we tell them apart?* (Differences in height, hair, colour of skin).

MAIN ACTIVITY
Explain that animals of the same species are just like humans in that, although they are basically the same, they have variations that make them different from each other. Using a collection of shells, ask the children what is the same about them all. (They are all shells and they all come from the same type of land (snail shells) or sea creature.) Look for differences between them. With garden snails look for stripes, the number of turns in the spiral and differences in colour. With other molluscs such as cockles or scallops, count the ridges and observe variations in colour both inside and outside the shell. Tell the children that the variations between members of the same species can often be very subtle and that they must observe very carefully. Make a list of all the differences that the children find.

GROUP ACTIVITIES
1 Ask the children to make careful observational drawings of two shells of the same species, such as two razor shells or two cone shells. They should use coloured pencils to record variations in colour and pattern and clearly label other observed differences such as the number of bands, spiral turns and so on.
2 Let the children make plaster casts of two shells (different varieties of the same species) and paint them to show the variations.

ASSESSMENT
Note those children in the Plenary who can describe the variations they have observed and understand that there are differences between individuals of the same species.

PLENARY
Ask the children to describe the variations they have observed. Check these against the list made during the Main activity. *Are there any to add to the list?* Make sure that the children understand that the shells all come from the same species of creature and that they have been finding variations within that species.

OUTCOMES
● Can understand that there is variation even within the same species.
● Can make close observations and record them both in writing and pictorially.

Differentiation
Group activity 1
Most children should be able to carry out the activity, although some may need help in the prompt questions to guide them when making their observations.
Group activity 2
All the children should be able to take part in this activity, although some will find a greater number of and more subtle variations to paint on their casts.

Lesson 3 ▪ Cats and dogs

RESOURCES
Main activity: Pictures of cats or dogs, domestic and wild; whiteboard or flipchart.
Group activities: 1 Pictures from the collection in the main activity, writing and drawing materials. **2** Magazines and catalogues containing pictures of dogs or cats.

BACKGROUND
There is a very wide variety of breeds of cats and dogs. Some have evolved naturally but many have been bred for specific purposes such as hunting

Objective
● To know that there are variations even within the same species.
● To practise observation skills.

Differentiation
In Group activity 1, some children may only be able to draw their pet and may give you a verbal description. All the children should be able to take part in Group activity 2.

dogs, lap dogs and sheep dogs. The differences between varieties that have evolved naturally will have been strongly influenced by such things as habitat and availability of prey. These naturally evolved differences will include such things as colour of coat, level of camouflage, speed, ability to climb trees and whether the animals live alone or in packs. Differences arrived at by breeding can also be very marked – compare a huge St. Bernard to a tiny dachshund!

Cats also vary significantly. There are huge differences between those that have evolved from the common ancestor and remain wild, such as lions or leopards, and domesticated cats - but they are all still cats. Even among domestic cats there are many differences in hair length, colour, size, shape of head and length of tail.

STARTER
Ask the children if any of them have a pet dog or cat at home. Ask the children to describe their pet. *Are they all the same? Are they different colours? Have they got long or short ears? Have they got pointed noses?* Do any children know the name of the breed of their pets, for example Alsatian, Spaniel, Collie or Siamese? Tell the children that these are different varieties of dog or cat but that they are all the same species.

MAIN ACTIVITY
Look at the photos of dogs or cats. Ask the children if they know the name of any of the varieties. Make lists on the board or a chart of the names of the varieties and all the differences that the children can think of. Prompt them if they forget a significant category such as colour of fur/hair. *How are they the same? How are they different?* Choose two examples. List the differences on the board. Talk about why such extreme variation occurs (see Background). Talk about how some dogs are bred for working for example sheep dogs, guard dogs and guide dogs.

GROUP ACTIVITIES
1 Ask the children to draw a picture of their pet or a dog or cat from the picture collection and to write a short description of it. They can then compare their drawing with a partner's and list the differences between the two.
2 Ask the children to cut pictures of dogs or cats from magazines and make large class collage to show variation.

ASSESSMENT
Note those children who can describe the differences between the animals. Use the children's writing and lists from Group activity 1 to assess their level of understanding.

PLENARY
Discuss the children's written work from Group activity 1 and use it to reinforce the children's understanding that there are both obvious and subtle differences between different varieties of the same species. Talk about the variety of animals in the collage but that they are still all dogs/cats.

OUTCOME
● Can understand that there is a great variation of animals even in the same species.

Lesson 4 ▪ Changing faces

Objective
● To know that there are variations between humans.
● To practise observation skills.

RESOURCES 💿
Main activity: Flipchart or whiteboard.
Group activities: 1 Writing materials. **2** Copies of photocopiable page 91 (also 'Changing faces' (red), available on the CD-ROM), acetate sheets, felt pens or markers

BACKGROUND
In Year 1/Primary 2, children looked at obvious similarities between themselves and other animals and between each other. They discussed the fact that humans usually have two arms, legs, eyes, ears and so on. They looked at eye, hair and skin colour. Some of the characteristics they observed could be changed or may change with age. For example, hair colour and style can easily be changed; skin colour may be altered by sunbathing or cosmetics; lines and wrinkles appear; peoples' shapes may alter as they put on or lose weight and, as they grow older, the way they move may change. In some extreme cases the shape of facial features and other body parts could be changed by plastic surgery. However, they are still basically the same as other humans.

STARTER
Remind the children about the work they did in Year 1/Primary 2 about the similarities and differences between humans and between humans and other animals.

MAIN ACTIVITY
Make a quick list on the flipchart or whiteboard of the things most humans have in common – two eyes, a nose, a mouth, two ears, legs, arms and so on. Ask the children to look at each other carefully. Ask: *Is every child's nose exactly the same? Are your eyes the same colour or shape? Are your mouths and lips the same?* Ask the children to hold out their hands. *Everyone has two hands but are yours the same size and shape as your neighbour's? Are your fingernails the same shape? Are your feet the same size and shape?* Ask two or three children to say a simple nursery rhyme. *Did they all sound the same?* They each had a voice but each had a different sound. *Do they sound the same when they laugh? Can the children suggest any other similarities between humans to add to the list but describe how they may vary?* For example, we walk upright but people can often be recognised by their particular walk; we use language to communicate but our voices sound different; we have a sense of humour but may not all laugh at the same joke; we need to eat but don't all like the same food, and so on. Emphasise that basically we are all the same but at the same time we are very varied.

GROUP ACTIVITY
1 Working in pairs, ask the children to write a short description of each other.
2 Give each child a copy of photocopiable page 91 together with two or three acetate sheets. Place the acetate sheets over the photocopied page and invite the children to alter the appearance of the head using coloured markers. They could change the appearance by adding make-up or wrinkles, and by changing the style and colour of the hair. If the acetates are removed, the basic head with eyes, nose and mouth, remains the same.

ASSESSMENT
In the plenary, note those children who were able to describe their partner sufficiently well for other children to recognise them.

Differentiation
Some children may find it helpful to have a list of words such as long, short, wide, thin, colour and so on to help with their descriptions. Some may need to draw rather than write about their partner. Other children may be able to put their description into verse.

PLENARY
Ask some children to read out their descriptions of their partners. Can the other children recognise them from the description? Talk about how some things in our appearance or character can be changed and, indeed, may change over time, but how others cannot.

OUTCOMES
● Know that there are variations between humans
● Can make close observations.

Lesson 5 ▪ Similarities and differences

Objective
● To know that plants have similarities and differences.

RESOURCES
Main activity: Two pot plants of different species with evident similarities and differences, for example: geranium and osteospermum (cape daisy), Busy Lizzie and flowering grass, penstemon and patio rose (be careful not to choose plants that may be poisonous or irritant); whiteboard or flipchart.
Group activities: 1 Seed catalogues, gardening books or magazines, writing materials. **2** Drawing materials including coloured pencils, the two pot plants used in the main lesson, hand lenses.

BACKGROUND
There is a very wide variety of plant life but many are made up of the same basic parts such as roots, stems, leaves, flowers and seeds. In some these may be greatly modified and almost unrecognisable. For example, petals may be fused into bell-shaped flowers and leaves may be modified, such as the spines on cacti. A potato is a modified stem designed as a food store for the plant. This can be demonstrated by leaving a potato in the light. The potato will turn green, because of the presence of chlorophyll, whereas a root would not. Virtually all green plants, including trees and grasses, are flowering plants even though at times the flowers may be very insignificant and difficult to spot.

STARTER
Remind the children of the work that they did in Lesson 1 Spot the difference, where they looked at the differences between two plants of the same species. Explain that in this lesson they are going to look at similarities and differences between two plants of different species.

MAIN ACTIVITY
Show the children the two plants you have chosen. Ask them to tell you about the differences between them. For example, the colour and shape of the flowers, leaves and stems, the number of petals, the scent, the feel of the leaves and so on. Use a flipchart or white board divided into two columns headed 'Differences' and 'Similarities' and list the children's suggestions in the first column. Prompt the children with any differences they have missed. Repeat the activity but this time look for similarities and list them in the second column. Talk to the children about the fact that almost all green plants are made up of the same basic parts but that they may look very different, from huge trees to tiny little daisies. Looking again at the lists and ask the children if there are more similarities or differences. *Would the lists be different if two different plants were compared?* If possible, go outside and find a tree. Compare this in terms of similarities and differences with one of your pot plants.

GROUP ACTIVITIES

1 Use pictures of plants from seed catalogues, gardening books or magazines to compare other pairs of similar plants such as peas and beans. Ask the children to choose two plants and make lists under the headings similarities and differences. When they have completed their lists, ask them to compare them with the lists made in the Main activity.
2 Ask the children to make careful observational drawings of a leaf or flower from each plant noting the different size, shape and colour. Make sure that the children look carefully before they begin to draw and talk to them about what they see.

ASSESSMENT

During the Main activity and the Plenary note those children who contribute with understanding to the discussion. The drawings from Group activity 2 will give you an insight into the level of children's close observational skills. Even the crudest of drawings may show more observed detail than a more skilled one.

PLENARY

Ask the children what they have learned about the similarities and differences between plants. *Do they all have leaves, stems, flowers and seeds? How did the plants they looked at in the seed catalogues or magazines compare with those in the main activity?* Hold up some of the children's observational drawings and talk about the different shapes that leaves or flowers can take but how at the same time they have similarities.

OUTCOME

● Know that there are similarities and differences between plants.

LINKS

Art - close observational drawing.

Differentiation
Group activity 1
All children should be able to take part in this activity but the range and quality of their observations will differ. Some children may need to tell you about their observations verbally or have help writing them. Other children may be able to compare more than one pair of plants.
Group activity 2
All children will be able to participate in this activity but some children may need to describe their drawing to you.

Lesson 6 ◾ Measuring hand spans

RESOURCES

Main activity: Graph paper (1cm squared), writing materials, whiteboard with prepared bar chart (see Preparation).
Group activities: 1 Paints, painting paper, trays for paint (large enough for children to put their hands in), thin sheet of plastic foam (optional), rulers.
2 Graph paper.

BACKGROUND

At this stage children should be beginning to formalise their observations, for example by measuring accurately and collecting data. These data can then be used to make simple interpretations, which some children find difficult.

PREPARATION 💿

Prepare a simple block graph on a computer, ready to project onto a whiteboard and collect the children's data. Include measurements at two-centimetre intervals along the bottom axis and numbers of children on the other. Alternatively, use the graphing tool on the CD-ROM, to collate the data and convert into a block graph or pie chart.

STARTER

Ask the children to hold up their hands and look at them closely. What can they tell you about them? For example, they have four fingers and a thumb,

Objective
● To understand that some differences between humans can be measured.
● To make measurements using non-standard or standard units.
● To make suggestions about fair testing.

each finger has a nail, one side is called the back the other the palm and so on. Ask the children to compare their hand with that of their neighbour. *Are they the same shape? Are they the same size?* Ask them to put their hands together to compare size. *Does one have longer fingers or wider palms?*

MAIN ACTIVITY

Tell the children that they are going to measure their hands to find which of them has the biggest/smallest hands and whether the longest hands are also the widest. Give each child a piece of graph paper and explain that each square on the paper measures 1cm. Ask them to place their hand (the one they don't write with) flat on the paper and keep it still while they draw round it with the other hand. Make sure they go down between each finger.

Ask some of the children to hold up their drawings to show the rest of the class. Ask the children to compare the drawings. *Are they the same? Has everyone spread their fingers in the same way? Have some spread their fingers really wide while others have kept their fingers closed? If you were to measure these drawings would the measurement be fair? Would the results be accurate? How could you make it fair?* (All children should spread their fingers as wide as possible or keep them closed). Ask the children to draw round their hands again keeping it as fair as possible. Ask: *Would the new drawings give a more accurate comparison? Where would be the best place to measure? Would it be fair if some children measured across the palm while others measured across the span?*

Ask the children to measure their hand by counting the squares across their span. Make sure that they understand that this measurement is in centimetres. Talk about how, if their hand does not measure in complete squares, they should estimate how much of a square is covered to the nearest centimetre. Some children may need help with this. Ask the children to write their measurement in the middle of their drawing then to enter their measurements on the prepared chart. *Who has the widest hand? Who the narrowest?*

GROUP ACTIVITIES

1 Pour a thin layer of paint into a tray so that children can dip their hands in, or place a thin sheet of plastic foam in the bottom of the tray to act like an ink pad. Ask the children to dip their hand in the paint and make a print on the painting paper. Ask them to measure their print with a ruler. Compare this measurement with their drawn span. Which measurement do they think is the most accurate? Ask the children to cut their prints out and mount them (perhaps as a peacock's tail) as a class display.

2 With the children working in pairs within the group, ask them to take their shoes off and each to stand on the graph paper in turn while their partner draws round their foot. They should then measure how long each foot is, by counting the centimetre squares from the end of the big toe to the end of the heel, and write the measurement inside the drawing. *Does the child with the widest hand-span in the group also have the longest foot?*

ASSESSMENT

During the Main activity, note which children can count their squares and take measurements accurately. Also note which children can enter their data on the chart in the correct column without help and use the data to make comparisons. Assess whose level of understanding enables them to recognise what is needed to make the comparisons fair.

PLENARY

Look at the data entered on the chart and ask the children to tell you what it shows. *Who has the widest hand span? Who the narrowest?* From Group activity 1, ask the children to say whether they think that measuring their hand span with a ruler was more or less accurate than counting squares. Ask the children why they think that accuracy is important when taking measurements. From Group activity 2, ask the children to tell the rest of the class if the child with the widest hand also has the longest foot.

OUTCOMES
- Know that some differences between humans can be measured.
- Can make measurements using non-standard or standard units.
- Can make suggestions about fair testing.

LINKS
Maths - measuring.

Lesson 7 ◗ Spot the insect

Objective
- To know that animals can be sorted into groups.

Vocabulary
animal, insect, mammal, fish, bird, reptile, amphibian, warm-blooded, cold-blooded

RESOURCES 💿
Main activity: Pictures or photographs of animals - these should include at least two examples of each animal class: an ant, a butterfly or a bee (insects); a cat, a mouse or a human (mammals); a goldfish, a stickleback or a shark (fish); a robin, a blackbird or an eagle (birds); a frog, a toad or a newt (amphibians); a lizard, a snake or a crocodile (reptiles). You may need to use pictures from reference books in order to get a good range.
Group activities: 1 A copy of photocopiable page 92 (also 'Spot the insect!' (red), available on the CD-ROM) for each child, writing and colouring materials, insect reference books. **2** Collage materials such as pipe cleaners, cotton buds, feathers, shiny paper, gauze, sequins, fabric and so on; adhesive, scissors, soft wire.
ICT link: 'Spot the insect!' interactive, from the CD-ROM.
Plenary: 'Spot the insect!' (green), from the CD-ROM; whiteboard.

PREPARATION
Make a label for each of the animal classes you are going to sort. Prepare a background for a class picture.

BACKGROUND
The animal kingdom can be divided and sub-divided indefinitely, but Year 2/ Primary 3 children do not need to know subtle divisions. They should be able to distinguish between mammals, birds, fish, insects, reptiles and amphibians, but they are likely to classify spiders as insects (both are members of the phylum Arthropoda), rather than arachnids. (Insects have only six legs while arachnids have eight. Insects have a body divided into three distinct parts - head, thorax and abdomen; arachnids have just two body parts.) Use your professional judgement to decide whether your children are ready to sort spiders from insects or whether it is easier, at this stage, to call them all insects. Some teachers prefer to use the term 'minibeasts'.

Some children may confuse whales and dolphins (mammals) with sharks (fish). Many children find these animals fascinating so you may want to help them understand the difference. Whales and dolphins are warm-blooded creatures and need to come to the surface at regular intervals to breathe. They also give birth to live young and suckle them. Fish are cold-blooded and extract oxygen from the water by passing it through their gills; most fish lay eggs.

STARTER
Sit the children in a circle and hand out the animal pictures so that the children can hold them up for all to see. Look at the pictures and ask if the children can name any of the animals.

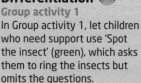

Differentiation
Group activity 1
In Group activity 1, let children who need support use 'Spot the insect' (green), which asks them to ring the insects but omits the questions.

To extend children, use 'Spot the insect' (blue), which includes open-ended extension questions about insect characteristics.
Group activity 2
All the children should be able to take part in Group activity 2.

MAIN ACTIVITY

Look at a picture of a fish. Ask the children: *Where does it live? What is its skin like? How does it move? What do you think it eats? How does it breathe? What is special about its skin? Can you find another fish in a picture?* Find all the pictures of fish, sit those children together and give them the correct label.

Ask: *Can anyone find a mammal among the pictures?* Some children may be able to identify a mammal but, if not, explain that mammals are warm-blooded, are usually covered in hair or fur (even humans, though it is not so obvious) and give birth to live babies. You may need to get the children to look closely at their arms and legs to persuade them that they are covered in hair. *Can anyone find one now?* Identify the rest of the mammals and sit the children with those pictures together with the appropriate label.

Next look at a picture of an insect. Ask: *How do we know it is an insect?* Help the children to recognise that an insect has six legs. Look for the three parts of the body and explain that insects sometimes have wings, but not always. Again, sit the children with the insect pictures together.

Now ask: *Which other animals have wings?* Most children will be able to identify birds. Ask: *What else is special about birds?* Talk about feathers and how the different colours and patterns of feathers help us to identify what sort of bird it is. Group the birds together and give them their label. Say: *Only two groups left! Does anyone know what they are?* Some children may have learned about reptiles from an interest in dinosaurs. *What is special about them?* (They have scaly skins but these are different from the scales on a fish.) Explain that they are cold-blooded and need to lie in the Sun to warm themselves up before they can move very well. Most of them lay eggs and don't look after their babies. Explain that the last group is called amphibians and that they are very special. They can live on land or in water. *Can you remember from Year 1/Primary 2 how frogs go into the pond to lay their frogspawn and how they sometimes spend the winter at the bottom of the pond?* Look again at the groups and help the children to read the labels and name some of the animals in the group. *Can you think of any other creatures that belong to any of the groups?*

GROUP ACTIVITIES

1 Give each child a copy of photocopiable page 92. Ask them to circle or colour all the insects they can find in the picture. Tell them they need to look very carefully. There are ten insects. Ask them to find out the names of some of them and write these on the picture. Ask them to complete the questions if they can.
2 Ask the children to make individual collages of different animals. These could be mounted as part of a class display either as a picture or as separate sets. Try feathers for birds, silver or gold paper scales on fish, cotton bud dragonflies or pipe cleaner insects. Use pieces of soft wire to attach the dragonflies, butterflies and bees to the display so that they appear to hover.

ICT LINK

Children can use the 'Spot the insect!' interactive, from the CD-ROM, to identify the insects in the picture. Each time they click on an insect, it will show the children whether they are correct.

ASSESSMENT

Use the photocopiable sheet from the Group activity 1, to assess children's ability to recognise insects. Ask the children if they can name the group that the animal they made in Group activity 2 belongs to. Note their responses during the Plenary session.

PLENARY
Project the 'Spot the insect' picture on to a whiteboard and ask the children to identify and name the insects. Look at a few of the collages made by the children and talk about some of the characteristics of that creature. (Birds have beaks and feathers, fish have fins and scales, insects have six legs and three parts to their bodies.) Ask a few volunteers to name their favourite animal. Can they say which group it belongs to and why?

OUTCOME
● Can sort animals into groups giving reasons for their groupings.

LINKS
Art: making 3D models and collages.

ENRICHMENT
Lesson 8 ▪ Animal factfinders

Objective
● To know how to use secondary sources to find out about a wide range of animals.

RESOURCES
Reference books, CD-ROMs, posters and videos about animals; writing and drawing materials, tape recorder and tapes, OHP with transparencies and suitable pens.

MAIN ACTIVITY
Working as individuals or pairs, encourage the children to find out about an unfamiliar animal. They could choose an elephant, a crocodile, a shark or an insect, such as a praying mantis or a locust. Their work could be presented as a booklet, a newsletter, an audio tape or a series of slides on an OHP. Tell the children that their presentation should include facts such as which group the animal belongs to, its size, where it usually lives, plus any other interesting information they can find.

ASSESSMENT
Assess the quality of the work produced.

PLENARY
Ask different children or groups of children to tell or show what they have found out.

Differentiation
Some children may need to work together and contribute to a group booklet or presentation.

OUTCOMES
● Can use secondary sources to find out facts about animals.
● Can present information about animals obtained from secondary sources.

ENRICHMENT
Lesson 9 ▪ Check your facts!

Objective
● To confirm information they have read about animals by observing them.

RESOURCES
Paper, pencils, clipboards, reference materials about animals that are likely to be found in the local environment; suitable places for the children to hunt and extra adult supervision.

MAIN ACTIVITY
The children should use secondary sources to find out about one or two animals and make an observation checklist, such as, for snails: *Does the shell always spiral in the same direction? Are they always found in damp places? Do they only eat green leaves? Can the shells be different colours? Are they always the same shape?* The children then go out and make observations to check their research.

Differentiation
Most children will need some help in formulating a list and some will need the list to be made for them.

ASSESSMENT
Note those children who are able to formulate sensible lists of things to look for. In the Plenary session, ask the children to explain their findings.

PLENARY
Ask some children to explain what they were looking for and why they chose those points. Did they find what they were looking for? Did they notice anything else?

OUTCOME
- Can observe animals guided by information that they have read.

Lesson 10 ▭ Assessment

Objective
- To assess whether the children can identify differences between an animal and a plant.
- To assess whether the children can describe similarities between plants.

RESOURCES
Assessment activities: **1** A copy of photocopiable page 93 (also 'Assessment – 1' (red), available on the CD-ROM) for each child, pencils. **2** A copy of photocopiable page 94 (also 'Assessment – 2' (red), available on the CD-ROM) for each child, pencils.
ICT link: 'Animal or plant?' interactive from the CD-ROM.

STARTER
Remind the children that they have been learning about the similarities and differences between plants and animals in this unit.

ASSESSMENT ACTIVITY 1
Give each child a copy of photocopiable page 93 and ask them to complete it. Make sure they understand each question, helping them to read where necessary. Tell them that the answer to each question is either 'plants' or 'animals' (or, once, both).

ICT LINK 💿
The children could complete the assessment using the 'Animal or plant?' interactive from the CD-ROM.

ANSWERS
1. Plants, **2.** Animals, **3.** Animals, **4.** Plants, **5.** Plants, **6.** Plants, **7.** Animals, **8.** Animals

LOOKING FOR LEVELS
Most children will answer about six questions correctly. Some will manage only three or four and others will get them all right.

ASSESSMENT ACTIVITY 2
Give each child a copy of page 94 and ask them to complete it by drawing and writing the names of five plants and five animals that they would find in the local environment and listing five similarities between plants.

LOOKING FOR LEVELS
Most children will be able to list three similarities between both plants and animals. Some may only be able to list one or two while others will give additional examples.

Changing faces

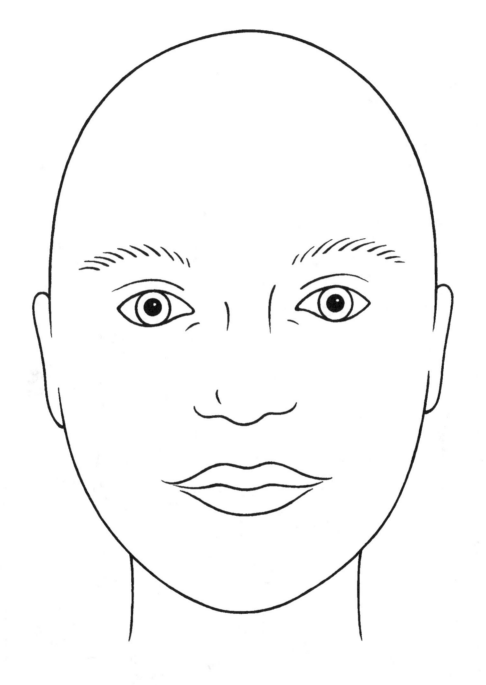

■ Use coloured pens or pencils to change the look of this face.

Illustration © Ann Kronheimer

PHOTOCOPIABLE

Spot the insect!

◀ Put a ring around all the insects you can find in this picture.

◀ There are ten altogether.

How many legs does an insect have? _____

How many body parts does an insect have? _____

Illustration © Ann Kronheimer

Assessment – 1

Write 'plants' or 'animals' in the spaces to make the sentences correct.

1. _____ have leaves.

2. _____ have five senses.

3. _____ eat food.

4. _____ make their own food.

5. Some _____ have flowers.

6. Most _____ produce seeds.

7. _____ can move from place to place.

8. Some _____ eat plants.

Illustration © Ann Kronheimer

Assessment – 2

Draw pictures and write the names of five plants you would find in your local environment.

Draw pictures and write the names of five animals you would find in your local environment.

◀ List five similarities that all plants share.

_____

_____

_____

_____

_____

_____

■SCHOLASTIC

Illustration © Ann Kronheimer

CHAPTER 4 Grouping and changing materials

Lesson	Objectives	Main activity	Group activities	Plenary	Outcomes
Lesson 1 How is it used?	• To know that there Is a range of materials with different characteristics. • To know that materials can be put to different uses.	Review Y1/P2 work on materials and their properties. Group materials and give reasons. Give examples of the uses of some materials.	Identify the properties and uses of some common materials. Investigate rigidity and flexibility by weaving with different 'threads'.	Group materials according to properties.	• Can identify the properties of materials. • Can use the properties to group materials. • Can distinguish between an object and the material it is made from.
Lesson 2 Many materials	• To know that fabrics are made from different materials.	Identify the materials that some fabrics are made from and consider some of their simple properties.		Name natural fabrics and link them to their sources.	• Can name a range of materials that fabrics are made from. • Can link some fabrics to their simple properties. • Can say that natural fabrics come from a plant or an animal and that synthetic fabrics are manufactured.
Lesson 3 Uses of materials	• To know about the everyday uses of some materials.	Identify materials in and around the classroom. Note some of the uses and properties of certain materials.	Prepare to present findings to the rest of the class. Construct a block graph to show the frequency of use of materials.	Present findings.	• Can identify common materials and note the frequency of their use. • Can explain why a material is used for a particular task.
Lesson 4 Where do materials come from?	• To know that some materials occur naturally.	Look at natural materials and link these to where they occur.	Sort materials from living and non-living sources. Understand what needs to be done to natural materials before we can use them.	Identify materials and relate them to their source.	• Can name some naturally occurring materials. • Can distinguish between materials that come from living and non-living sources. • Can describe how some materials are treated before they are used.
Lesson 5 Manufactured materials	• To know that some materials are not natural but are manufactured.	Look at plastics, metal alloys, paper and glass.	Find out how a material is made. Make a zig-zag book. Make a papier-mâché saucer or bowl.	Discuss manufactured materials.	• Can name some manufactured materials. • Can describe how some manufactured materials are made.
Lesson 6 Changing shape	• To know how the application of forces can change the shape of some materials. • To be able to carry out a simple investigation with help.	Bending, stretching, squashing and twisting materials. Investigate elastic bands.	Investigate different widths of elastic. Make pipe-cleaner people.	Discuss results.	• Can identify materials that can be altered in shape by the application of forces. • Can distinguish between materials which are permanently deformed and those that regain their shape.
Lesson 7 Make a cake	• To know that materials often change when they are heated.	Study cooked and uncooked food. Bake cakes.	Make clay thumb pots. Fire these if a kiln is available. Make toast.	Examine the uncooked cake mixture.	• Can describe how some materials change when they are heated. • Can explain how heating can make a material more useful.
Lesson 8 Pop the corn	• To know that materials often change when they are heated.	Make popcorn.		Look at the cooked and uncooked corn.	• Can describe how some materials change when they are heated.

Lesson	Objectives	Main activity	Group activities	Plenary	Outcomes
Lesson 9 Let's cool down	• To know that many materials change when they are cooled.	Observe the effects of freezing on water.	Make jelly. Make ice-lollies.	Examine and discuss the ice.	• Can describe how some materials change when they are cooled.
Lesson 10 Warm it up	• To know that some materials melt and change when they are heated.	Observe ice as it melts.	Candle observation. Make melted chocolate cereal cakes.	Discuss the ice, the candles and the melted chocolate.	• Can describe how some materials change as they melt. • Can describe how some materials change when they are heated.
Lesson 11 The uses of ice	• To know that ice will melt at different rates in different temperatures • To be able to plan and carry out a fair test with help.	Investigate the best place for keeping ice frozen for a long time.	Suck ice to see if it melts more quickly. Find out what ice is used for.	Look at the results and discuss uses for ice.	• Know that the warmer the environment, the quicker ice melts. • Can plan and carry out a fair test with help.
Enrichment Lesson 12 Water and steam	• To know that water turns to steam when it is heated, but the steam turns back to water when it is cooled.	Boil water in a kettle to show water forming on a cold surface.		Discuss what happens when water is heated and when steam cools.	• Can describe what happens when water is heated. • Can describe what happens when steam is cooled.
Enrichment Lesson 13 Things that use heat	• To know that heat is a form of energy and that it may be supplied by several sources.	Look at the uses of heat.	Identify appliances that do and don't use heat. Identify what fuel is used to provide the heat.	Discuss sources of heat energy.	• Know that heat is a form of energy. • Know about different sources of heat energy. • Can recognise different applications of heat in everyday life.

Assessment	Objectives	Activity 1	Activity 2
Lesson 14	• To assess whether the children can suggest everyday uses of some materials. • To assess whether the children know that materials often change when they are heated. • To assess whether children can describe how materials change when they are cooled.	Record the uses of different materials.	Complete sentences about the effects of heating and cooling.

SC1 SCIENTIFIC ENQUIRY

Melting ice

LEARNING OBJECTIVES AND OUTCOMES
- Explore, using the senses, to make and record observations
- Recognise when a test or comparison is unfair.
- Think about what might happen before deciding what to do

ACTIVITY
Children are asked to predict what they think will happen to ice when it is taken out of the freezer and kept in a warm room. They observe what is happening and describe the changes. They are asked to predict what would happen if the water were put back in to the freezer.

LESSON LINKS
This Sc1 activity forms an integral part of Lesson 11, The uses of ice.

Lesson 1 ▪ How is it used?

Objective
- To know that there is a range of materials with different characteristics.
- To know that materials can be put to different uses. ?

Vocabulary
materials, properties, fabric, strong, transparent, opaque, flexible, rigid, elastic, waterproof, attributes

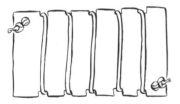

RESOURCES
Main activity: Plasticine, bricks, tiles, stone; a selection of objects made from: wood, rock, metal, elastic, paper, plastic (rigid, sheet and flexible) and glass. Beware of the dangers of broken glass and do not allow the children to handle the glass object you choose. Try to find something that is not easily broken (like a heavy glass bowl).
Group activities: 1 A copy of photocopiable page 118 (also 'How is it used?' (red), available on the CD-ROM) for each child, writing and drawing materials. **2** A 'comb' card for each child (see diagram below), string, scissors, strips of fabric of different weights, lolly sticks, plastic cutlery, plastic and paper drinking straws, lengths of dowel, twigs, feathers, and other flexible materials.

BACKGROUND
At this stage, children should be able to identify and name a range of common materials and their properties and link these to the objects that they are made into (see Resources and Vocabulary, above). They should also be developing an understanding that many materials have more than one useful property. Wood is used for its strength, its insulating properties and because it is relatively easy to cut and shape. Metal is strong, it can be shaped and moulded and conducts electricity. This will lead to an understanding that a material may be chosen for a particular object for one property, and for another object because of a different property. Make sure that the children realise that the term 'material' does not just mean fabric. Many modern synthetic materials are very convincing and it may be difficult for children to sort these from the real thing.

STARTER
Remind all the children of the work they did in Year 1/Primary 2 on materials and their properties. Ask: Can anyone tell me some of the things we learned about materials and the reasons why they are used to make certain things?

MAIN ACTIVITY
Show the children the collection of objects. Lift them up one by one and ask them to say what the object is and what it is made from. Choose one of the objects, such as a metal dinner knife, and show it to the children again. Why is the knife made from metal? Who can tell me what it is about metal that

Differentiation

Group activity 1
Some children will need help to link the uses of the materials to the properties identified. You may wish to put a list of possible properties on a flipchart or whiteboard from which the children can choose.

Group activity 2
All the children can take part in this activity at their own level.

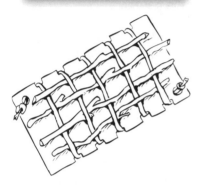

makes a good knife? (It is hard and can be shaped and sharpened so that it will cut.) Repeat this with another object, such as the glass bowl. (Glass is good for bowls because it is transparent - if you have made a beautiful fruit salad you can see the lovely colours through the bowl - it is waterproof, it can be shaped when it is heated.) Stress that these are some of the properties of metal and glass that make them suitable to be made into particular objects. Would a knife made of paper be useful, or a fabric bowl?

Go through the other objects in the same way, choosing different children to come and hold up an object. Ask them to tell you some of the simple properties of the material from which the object is made. Each time, invite the rest of the class to add to the list if they can. After each object has been discussed it can be grouped with other objects that share one or more of the same properties. For example, wood and metal could be grouped together if the main property chosen for both was 'hard'. When all the objects have been considered, look at them again with the children and ask if they could regroup any of them according to other properties.

GROUP ACTIVITIES

1 Give each child a copy of photocopiable page 118 and ask them to complete the sheet. Remind the children of some of the properties of materials identified in the Main activity and ask them to think of as many different uses for each material as they can.

2 As individuals, let the children investigate rigidity and flexibility by weaving with different 'threads': fabric, ribbon, dowel, lolly sticks, twigs, plastic cutlery, feathers and so on. Encourage the children to use the appropriate vocabulary as they are working. Point out that, although most of these are flexible, some materials are more flexible than others - thin twigs and ribbon are more flexible than lolly sticks.

Give each child a comb card and a length of string. Ask them to tie a knot in one end of the string and thread it through one of the holes in the card. Wrap the string around the card to form the warp for weaving. Thread the string through the other hole and tie a knot to secure it. Make sure the string is fairly taut so that the things the children use for weaving do not fall out (see diagram above).

ASSESSMENT

Use the children's work from Group activity 1 to assess the level of their understanding. During the Plenary session, note those children who give correct answers to your questions and contribute well to the discussion.

PLENARY

Shuffle the collections of materials and ask the children to group them again, giving their reasons (properties of the materials) for their choice. Tell the children that the objects may not end up in the same groups as they were in before but, as long as they are grouped according to a common property, this does not matter. Look at some of the children's work and discuss the uses of the materials they have identified. Are the uses sensible, given the properties of the materials involved?

OUTCOMES

● Can identify the properties of materials.
● Can use the properties to group materials.
● Can distinguish between an object and the material it is made from.

LINKS

Art: weaving.
Maths: sorting.

Lesson 2 ▪ Many materials

RESOURCES
A range of fabrics such as wool, cotton, linen, silk, and synthetics such as nylon; a set of labels to attach to the fabrics; if possible, a length of the various threads to go with the fabrics (these can usually be obtained from knitting or craft shops); examples of raw wool, cotton and silk; pictures of sheep being shorn, cotton fields, silkworms and factories making synthetic fabric (optional).

MAIN ACTIVITY
Show all the children the fabrics and tell them the materials that they are made from. Match the fabrics to their appropriate threads. Tell the children that some of the fabrics are made from natural materials and some are made from manufactured materials. Introduce the word 'synthetic' and explain to the children that this word is used for fabrics that are not made from natural materials. Ask: Can anyone think of any animal or plant that we might get natural thread or yarn from? (Sheep, cotton.) Attach labels to the natural wool and cotton fabrics. Carry on in this way until all the natural fabrics have been labelled, telling the children about each plant or animal that the fabric comes from. Show the children the synthetic fabrics and label these, telling them that these are made from threads or yarn that come from oil, and are manufactured in a factory.

Talk to the children about some of the simple properties of the fabrics. Wool keeps us warm, cotton is cool, silk can be made to be warm or cool depending on the thickness of the thread. Natural fabrics are more comfortable, especially in hot weather. Synthetic fabrics are tough, easy to wash and last a long time. It is not necessary for the children to be able to identify specific pieces of fabric but they should know that fabrics can be made from both natural and synthetic materials. As you work through the fabrics, match them to the pictures if you have them.

ASSESSMENT
During the Plenary session, note those children who are able to answer the questions and who show an understanding of the difference between natural and manufactured fabrics.

PLENARY
Ask the children if they can name some of the natural fabrics and link them to the animal or plant that they come from. Who can explain what a synthetic fabric is? Where do they come from?

OUTCOMES
● Can name a range of materials that fabrics are made from.
● Can link some fabrics to their simple properties.
● Can say that natural fabrics come from a plant or an animal and that synthetic fabrics are manufactured.

Lesson 3 ▪ Uses of materials

RESOURCES
Main activity: A classroom and indoor school environment, clipboards, writing materials.
Group activities: 1 Writing and drawing materials, OHP, transparencies and pens; whiteboard, any other resources requested by the children. **2** 1cm squared paper, writing and colouring materials.

Vocabulary
paper, wood, glass, stone, bricks (clay), plastic, metal, materials, uses, properties

PREPARATION
Head a sheet of paper for each group of four with the name of the material they are to look for (see Vocabulary).

BACKGROUND
When children try to identify materials the surface finish can cause confusion – plastic is used to coat metals, for example, and high-gloss paint may hide wood or metal. The children may need help to distinguish this finish from the material from which an object is made.

Groups looking for uses of plastics should also be made aware that sometimes it is only the surface finish of objects that is made of plastic. Plastics can also be made to mimic many other more traditional materials. Tabletops that look like wood may actually be made of plastic, and pipes, windows and doors are now often made from plastic. Modern buildings are likely to have a very high plastic content.

STARTER
Remind all the children about the work they did in Year 1/Primary 2 and how they identified some materials inside and outside the school. Ask: What do we mean by 'materials'? Tell the children that they are going to go on another walk to look at materials in a different way.

MAIN ACTIVITY
Organise the children into groups of four. Give each group a sheet of paper headed with the material they are to look for. Tell them that they are going to look around the classroom and school and focus on a particular material, noting as many different uses as they can. At the end of the lesson they are going to report to the rest of the class not only how many different uses of their material they found, but also say what properties made it the right material for those jobs. They are to count each use only once – don't count every window in the school!

Point out that they need to keep their sheet clean and tidy because other groups will be using it in another activity. (See Group activity 2, below). Choose the materials you allocate to the groups carefully to ensure a range of uses. (Glass, in the school environment, may not yield as many uses as other materials. Stone may be more appropriate in an older school than in a very modern building. If you do choose glass, as it is an important everyday material, you may wish to give that group two materials to survey, such as glass and stone.) Explain that each time they see a different use of their material they must note what it is. Walk around the classroom and school with the children as they list all the uses of their material. Each time they find their material, encourage them to discuss what property or properties made it useful for that particular purpose (for example, wood for doors because it is strong and can be shaped easily, but is not too heavy to open and close as a metal door might be.) Back in the classroom, gather the children together and discuss some of the uses and properties of the materials.

GROUP ACTIVITIES
1 Give the groups time to prepare their presentations. Remind them that they are not only going to tell the class what uses they found for their material but for which property or properties they think it was chosen. The children could decide for themselves how they are going to present their work. (Pictures, words, OHP or whiteboard presentation and so on.)
2 Organise the children into the same groups as they were in for the Main activity and give each group a photocopy of all the groups' sheets. Ask the groups to count the number of different ways each material was used, and to construct a block graph to show the frequency of use of each material.

ASSESSMENT
Observe the children as they prepare their presentations and use their work to assess the level of their understanding. During the Plenary session, note those children who report back effectively and are able to link the use of a particular material to its properties.

PLENARY
Ask each group to give their presentation to the whole class. Discuss the block graphs the children have made and identify such things as the most and least commonly used materials.

OUTCOMES
- Can identify common materials and note the frequency of their use.
- Can explain why a material is used for a particular task.

LINKS
Maths: graphs.

Lesson 4 ▸ Where do materials come from?

Objective
- To know that some materials occur naturally.

Vocabulary
material, natural, manufactured, occurring, source

RESOURCES 💿
Main activity: Materials such as wood, stone, wool, cotton, linen, silk, sand, water, sponge, clay, shell, cork, rubber, coal, metal (gold, silver, copper, tin); labels of the names of each material; pictures of a woodland, sheep, cotton fields, a quarry, a river, a coral reef with sponges and shells, a gold-, tin-, or coal-mine; artefacts made from some of the materials collected (a woollen jumper, shell jewellery, cork mats and so on).
Group activities: 1 A small collection of materials from living and non-living sources for each group (such as woollen, cotton, or silk yarn, natural sponge, cork, wood, shell, clay, stone, sand, metal); writing and drawing materials.
2 A copy of photocopiable page 119 (also 'Where do materials come from?' (red), available on the CD-ROM) for each child, writing materials, reference materials.

BACKGROUND
Children, at this stage, should recognise that some materials occur naturally, while others are manufactured. A distinction needs to be made between manufactured materials such as plastics, that are completely new materials made from another raw material (oil), and natural materials that are sometimes shaped in an industrial or craft process.

Most natural materials can be shaped. Wood can be sawn into shapes in a factory and made into doors, window frames or furniture. Wood can also be carved into sculptures, or artefacts for domestic use. Stone can be cut and finished in a factory into uniform blocks for building or paving, but it can also be sculpted, carved and polished by an individual craftsman. In neither case has the material been through the profound manufacturing process necessary to make plastic out of oil, or glass out of silica. All materials originate from substances occurring naturally on the planet, although children do not need to know this at this stage. Their concept of the difference between natural and manufactured needs to be well-established first. You will need to wash sheep's wool well before the children handle it.

Differentiation 💿
Group activity 1
Some children will need help to distinguish materials from living and non-living sources.
Group activity 2
To support children, use 'Where do materials come from?' (green), from the CD-ROM, which contains a simpler range of material sources to write about. Some children may need to tell you what has been done to the materials rather than write about them.
    To extend children, use 'Where do materials come from?' (blue), which asks the children to use reference materials to find out about plastics.

STARTER

Gather all the children around you and remind them that they talked about natural and manufactured materials, in terms of fabrics, in Lesson 2. Tell them that you are now going to think about some other materials that occur naturally.

MAIN ACTIVITY

Show the children the collection of natural materials one by one, asking them to identify each one if they can. Help them with any names that they don't know or materials they don't recognise. Label each material as it is identified.

Tell the children that each of these materials is natural, rather than manufactured. *Can anyone tell us what those words mean, and the difference between a natural material and one that has been manufactured?* Then show the children the pictures of where the materials occur and ask them to link the two. Start with some fairly easy ones (sheep to link with the wool and woodland to link with the wood). Go through all the location pictures, asking the children to link them to the appropriate material. Help them if they have difficulty.

Talk about where the materials come from. Some children may not be familiar with metal or coal mines. They may not know that cork comes from the bark of cork oaks, or that natural sponges are the skeletons of sea creatures. Discuss the uses of the materials and talk about the fact that, although they are sometimes shaped in a factory or by a craftsperson, they don't have to be 'made' in the same way as materials such as plastic. Wool can be knitted into jumpers or warm hats, shell is sometimes used in jewellery, and wood can be shaped to make spoons or bowls. Show the children the artefacts and put them together with the sample of material from which they are made. Say: *Can anyone see any material that we can use straight away in its natural state without having to do anything to it?* (The sponge, coal and sand.)

GROUP ACTIVITIES

1 Remind all the children that they learned about things that are living and not living in Year 1/Primary 2, and ask them what 'living' and 'not living' mean. Tell them that they are going to sort out materials that come from living things from those that come from non-living sources. Put the children into groups of three or four and give each group a collection of materials. (See Resources.) Explain that you want them to sort the materials into two sets: one where the material comes from a living thing and one where it doesn't. Each child can then choose a material from the 'living' set and draw a picture of where it originates (under the sea, a field of sheep, a woodland and so on).
2 Give each child a copy of photocopiable page 119. Ask the children to complete the sheet by saying which material we get from the various sources and writing about what has to be done to the material before we can use it. The first one is filled in to help them. Remind the children that they can use the reference materials if they need to.

ASSESSMENT

Use the children's work to assess what they have learned. If children explain what they know to you verbally rather than in writing, note whether their explanations are correct.

PLENARY

Go through the collection of materials again, asking the children to identify them and relate them to their sources. Show and read out some of the children's work to reinforce the learning.

OUTCOMES
● Can name some naturally occurring materials.
● Can distinguish between materials that come from living and non-living sources.
● Can describe how some materials are treated before they are used.

Lesson 5 ● Manufactured materials

Objective
● To know that some materials are not natural but are manufactured.

Vocabulary
plastics, paper, pulp, glass, concrete, manufactured, made, raw material, alloy

RESOURCES
Main activity: Glass items, including a tumbler (but don't let the children handle glass objects that are likely to break); as wide a range of plastics as possible (including a transparent plastic tumbler and a plastic sponge); different papers, concrete, metal alloys such as steel or brass; the natural sponge from the last lesson; the fabrics from Lesson 2; pictures of factories, steel works, oil refineries and so on; labels for the sets of materials (plastic, glass, metal alloys, paper, concrete, and so on).
Group activities: 1 Reference materials and CD-ROMs (access to the internet could also prove useful – searching for terms such as 'paper manufacturing' provides a wealth of useful material), writing materials; A5 card for the zig-zag books. **2** Newspaper and cellulose paste (not wallpaper paste which contains fungicide) for papier-mâché, stirrers (wooden spoons or lengths of dowel, for example), 'formers', such as saucers or small bowls, cling film, paint, adhesive.

BACKGROUND
It could be argued that every material on Earth is natural because even materials that we consider to be manufactured come originally from rock or fossil fuel (oil). The distinction we make between made or manufactured and natural relates to the fact that some materials, such as plastics, metal alloys and glass, have to go through a profound manufacturing process, where chemicals are often mixed together in order to create the materials that we use.

Natural materials are sometimes shaped into artefacts and the line between the two is sometimes difficult to draw. Raw clay can be used and shaped straight from the ground, but needs the firing process to make permanent clay artefacts. Glass on the other hand, except for the naturally occurring volcanic glass called obsidian, goes through a profound manufacturing process. Sands (silica) are mixed with differing amounts of other chemicals such as lead, potassium and barium to achieve the desired result in making a range of different types of glass that we use every day.

Unlike alloys, which are a carefully controlled mixture of different metals combined for their various properties, natural metals have usually only to be extracted from the ore and shaped by heat into the desired object. Plastics are manufactured from crude oil (a fossil fuel). Paper (the type that is made from wood) is made by boiling wood chips with chemicals to extract the pulp fibre. The pulp is rinsed to remove impurities and bleached. The pulp is then extracted from the water, more chemicals are added to it and it is pounded to make the paper strong. If you know of any parents who work in a manufacturing industry it might be a good idea to invite them in to talk to the children about what they do.

STARTER
With all the children around you, look again at the collection of materials used in the Main activity from Lesson 4 Where do materials come from? Ask: *What is it about all these materials that is the same?* (They are all natural and have not been manufactured. Many have been shaped, but some, like natural sponge, can be used just as they are.)

MAIN ACTIVITY

Look at the new collection of materials. *Can anyone think why these materials are different from the ones we looked at in the last lesson?* Hold up the objects one by one and ask the children to identify the material that each one is made from. Discuss, in simple terms, what the material originates from and how it is made. (See Background.)

Show the children the pictures of factories, chemical and steel works and link them to the materials in the collection. This would be a good opportunity for a parent in industry (if you have one) to talk to the children.

Tell the children that many materials we use every day, both natural and manufactured, are particularly useful because they can be made into so many things. Show the children the collection of plastic artefacts and ask them to think about the very wide range of objects that can be made from plastic. Match the plastic sponge to the natural sponge, the glass tumbler to the plastic tumbler, and tell the children that plastic is often particularly useful because it can be made to look like, and do, the same job as artefacts made from other materials.

GROUP ACTIVITIES

1 Put the children into groups of four. Ask them to choose one of the materials discussed in the Main activity and use the available reference materials to research how it is made. Make sure that they do not all choose the same material. Each group could then design one or two pages for a class zig-zag book containing information about materials. (If you have a large class you may wish to make two books.)

2 Remind the children about the paper manufacturing process (see Background). Then ask the children, as individuals, to make a saucer or bowl from paper pulp combined with cellulose glue (papier-mâché). Put some glue into a mixing bowl or other large container for each group. Ask the children to tear newspaper into small pieces (roughly 2cm square) and stir these thoroughly into the glue to form a pulp. Cover one side of the saucers or bowls with cling film and press the pulp evenly over the surface to about 0.5cm thick. Leave to dry completely, peel off the cling film and decorate the final artefacts by painting, and then varnishing with diluted school adhesive.

ASSESSMENT

Use the work from Group activity 1 to assess the children's understanding. During the Plenary session note those children who are able to answer your questions.

PLENARY

Show the children the collection of manufactured materials again. Ask them to tell you what they are, and why they are in a collection together. (They are all made or manufactured.) Ask the children to refer to the work they did in Group activity 1 and to tell you some of the things that they have found out about their material. *How is it made? Can you tell me something about the manufacturing process?*

OUTCOMES

● Can name some manufactured materials.
● Can describe how some manufactured materials are made.

LINKS

Literacy: using non-fiction texts.
Art: making a 3D artefact.

Lesson 6 ▪ Changing shape

Objective
● To know how the application of forces can change the shape of some materials.
● To be able to carry out a simple investigation with help.

Vocabulary
stretch, stretchy, push, pull, twist, shape, altered, force, elastic

RESOURCES

Main activity: Elastic bands of various widths (but no really narrow ones that could be easily broken), a sponge, a sheet of A4 paper, a piece of balsa wood, a small saw, a vice, a lump of playdough.
Group activities: 1 Force meters (one per group), rulers, writing materials; uniform lengths of three different widths of elastic (perhaps 0.5cm, 1cm and 1.5–2cm wide) - these should be approximately 50cm in length, knotted to make a loop of about 40cm (one loop of each thickness per group). A copy of photocopiable page 76 from Unit 2b (also 'Fair test' (red), available on the CD-ROM), for each group would be useful if you wish the children to record their investigation. **2** Pipe-cleaners (three for each child), large beads, fabric, wool, scissors, adhesive.

BACKGROUND

Most forces are basically a push or a pull. Children will have learned in Year 1/Primary 2 that they can change the shape of materials or objects by using various types of push (banging, pressing, squashing and rolling). They should also know that pulling, and stretching (a type of pull), will cause materials to change their shape. They need to be made aware that all of the above are types of forces and that use of a force is necessary to effect a change in shape. A twist is a combination of a push and a pull.

The children now need to be made aware that sometimes the force used (cutting or tearing paper, sawing wood) will change the shape of a material permanently, and that sometimes a material can be brought back to its original shape by using another force (rolling play dough back into a ball, unfolding or untwisting paper). Children also need to know that some materials (elastic bands, sponges) go back to their original shape of their own accord, and that this is a very useful property. Rehearse the correct vocabulary with the children as often as possible, complete with a definition. (Use a little more force to stretch the elastic, pull it a little harder.) Be careful not to use words such as 'pressure' and 'power' in a forces context - they have their own, precise, scientific meaning that the children will learn about later. The children simply need to know that they are using a force to change the shape of things.

STARTER

Talking to the whole class, remind the children of the work they did on materials in Year 1/Primary 2. *Can anyone remember some of the materials that could be changed in shape by forces?* (Play dough, paper, pastry, wood.) *What were those forces called?* (Pushes and pulls.)

MAIN ACTIVITY

Tell the children that there is another type of force, called a twist, which can be used to change the shape of some materials. A twist is a mixture of a push and a pull. Take the A4 sheet of paper and twist it into a spill showing the children the movement of your hands as you do so and how the shape of the paper has changed. Can we get that paper back to its original shape? (Yes, if we use a twisting force the other way and then flatten it out, though it will still be a bit creased.)

Do you remember in Year 1/Primary 2 when you changed the shape of some materials by using forces, you could get some of them back to their original shape but some were changed forever, like when you are sandpapering wood, for example? Show the children the wood and the play dough. *When we changed the shape of the play dough by pushing and pulling it, could we get it back to its original shape?* (Yes.) Demonstrate this by changing the shape of the play dough ball and then rolling it back into a ball again. *What about the wood? Could we get the wood back to its original shape after we have cut it with a saw?* (No.) Cut a piece off the wood to demonstrate this. *What did we need to use to change the shape of those materials?* (A force.) *What did we need to use to get the paper and the play dough back to their original shape?* (Another force.) Show the children the sponge. *What do you think will happen if I use a force to squash this sponge so that it is as small as possible and then let go?* (It will go back to its original shape on its own without having to use another force.)

Give each child an elastic band. Warn them that they must only stretch them very gently, because if they are stretched too hard they might fly off and hit someone or break, and this can be very painful. Ask the children to use a force to gently stretch their band. *What can you feel as you stretch the band? Can you feel it pulling on your fingers? What happens when you let* go? Ask them to swap bands with someone who has a different width of band. *Does it take more or less force to stretch (pull) it?* Tell the children that elastic bands (and other sorts of elastic) are materials that are used specially for their elastic (stretchy) properties – they go back to their original shape when they are no longer stretched.

GROUP ACTIVITIES
1 Put the children into groups of four to investigate the force needed to stretch different widths of elastic to a given length. One child holds one end of the elastic loop by the knot; one pulls gently on the other end of the loop with the force meter and reads the results; one measures the elastic loops to ensure that they are all stretched equally and the fourth member of the group records the force meter reading.

The investigation can also be carried out by holding the knotted end of the loop firmly and placing the other end of the loop, hooked on to a force meter, against the end of the ruler. Pulling gently, but firmly, on the force meter, stretch the loop 10cm along the ruler. Record the force needed to stretch each loop the same distance. (When children are carrying out an investigation it is useful for each child to have a specific 'job', so organise the groups accordingly.) Before they start the investigation ask the children to predict which elastic they think will need more force to stretch it, and why. Help the children to organise a fair test. (It may be useful to give the children photocopiable page 76, from Unit 2b, to help with this.)
2 Ask the children, as individuals, to make a pipe-cleaner person, dress it, and give it hair. As the children are doing this ask them to think about the forces they are using to twist the pipe-cleaners into shape (a twist, which is both a push and a pull); to force the head on (push); to cut the fabric and hair (push and pull). As they are working, ask: Could you get the pipe-cleaners back to their original shape if you wanted to? What about the fabric and wool that you have cut?

ASSESSMENT
Observe the groups as they are doing their investigation and note those that have some understanding of the need for a fair test. Also note those children who need relatively little help to organise and carry out their test. Use the children's written work and recording to assess their level of understanding and ability to measure accurately.

PLENARY
Choose some children to report back on their investigation. *How did you make it fair? What were your results? Were the results as you predicted?* Ask some other children to show the class their pipe-cleaner person. *How did you make it? What forces did you use to change the shape of the materials that you were working with?*

OUTCOMES
● Can identify materials that can be altered in shape by the application of forces.
● Can distinguish between materials that are permanently deformed and those that regain their shape.

LINKS
Unit 2c, Lesson 23, Fair test.

Lesson 7 ▪ Make a cake

Objective
● To know that materials often change when they are heated.

Vocabulary
ingredients, heat, heated, cool, cooled, change, irreversible, hygiene

RESOURCES
Main activity: Sufficient muffin cases to cook one cake per child, plus one small cake tin to cook a cake which can be pulled apart during the plenary; enough cake ingredients to fill each case (see recipe on page 120); mixing bowls, spoons, greaseproof paper, kitchen scales, a cooker; an enlarged copy of the recipe (also 'Make a cake' (red), available on the CD-ROM); Marzipan, fondant icing in two colours for decoration (if required); boards, rolling pins, small cutters.
Group activities: 1 Clay, boards, aprons, a kiln (ask your local secondary school to fire your pots if they have a kiln and you do not). **2** Sufficient loaves of sliced bread for each child to have one slice of toast, a toaster, butter or margarine, jam, knives, paper plates.

PREPARATION
Remove one end of each tin completely. Ensure that they are carefully washed and that the rims are free of sharp edges. Line the tins with greaseproof paper.

BACKGROUND
Some of the most effective methods of teaching young children about the ways in which materials can be changed when heated are through cooking and firing clay. The changes are very noticeable, especially when the cooked or fired materials are compared with a sample kept from before cooking or firing. The children need to understand that, as well as producing a profound change that cannot be reversed, heating (as in the case of making pots) often makes the material more useful. Clay is also a good material for demonstrating to children that some changes are reversible and others are not. An air-dried clay pot looks and feels very different from the damp, shiny, plastic clay that they started with, but the addition of water will soon enable them to return the clay to its original plastic state. When the clay is fired in a kiln the change is irreversible and, no matter how much water is added, the fired clay will not return to the original plastic state. Cooked food, especially when several ingredients have been mixed together, is very different in look, smell, taste and texture from the raw foods. Cooking is another irreversible change.

Differentiation
Group activity 1
All the children should be able to take part in these activities at their own level. For Group activity 1, children who need help to read instructions could use 'Make a cake' (green), from the CD-ROM. This version of the recipe includes an illustration for each step.
Group activity 2
In this activity, you may wish some children to write about how their clay or toast was changed by the application of heat, and why the clay was then more useful. Some children may be able to tell you this verbally.

STARTER
Gather the children around you and ask: Who likes cake? Tell them that you are going to bake cakes today, but before you do so you are going to look very carefully at the materials (ingredients) that the cake is made from.

MAIN ACTIVITY
This activity can be done as a whole class, but would work better in groups of about six, if you have sufficient adult help. Pin up the enlarged copy of the recipe and read through the ingredients and quantities required with the children. Make sure that the children have washed their hands and

understand the need to work hygienically. Show them the various ingredients and identify them. *Say: We are going to mix these ingredients together and cook them to make cakes. Who can tell me whether or not they think the ingredients will be changed during the cooking process? Will we be able to get the raw ingredients back, after they have been* cooked or will they be changed forever? Choose children to come out in turns to weigh out the ingredients, put them into the mixing bowl and stir.

Show the children the resulting mixture. *Has it changed at all yet? Will it change more when we cook it? How?* Allow each child to fill a case with the mixture ready to go into the oven, but keep some raw mixture aside to compare with the cooked cakes. Fill the extra tin for use in the Plenary session.

When the cakes have cooled, the children could decorate their own cake with marzipan and fondant icing. They could cut a decoration from fondant icing to give a pretty finish, and take the cakes home as presents.

GROUP ACTIVITIES

1 Give each child a ball of clay and a board to work on. Ask the children to have a good look at and feel their clay. *What does it look like?* (Damp and shiny.) *Can you change its shape with your fingers?* Show the children how to push their thumb into the centre of their ball of clay and gently pinch it round and round to turn it into a small thumb pot. Make several extra pots yourself to compare with the children's pots at every stage of the process from raw clay to a finished, fired pot. When the pots are made set them aside to dry. When air-dried, look at them again. *How have they changed? Do they still feel and look the same? Are they useful as pots yet? Could we get the clay back to how it was before we made the pots?* (Yes, because the clay has not yet been changed forever by the heat in the kiln, which is just like a big, hot oven.)

Take one of the pots that you have made and pour water into it. Show the children how the water soaks into the clay until you can eventually roll it up into a ball again.

Fire the pots, keeping at least one unfired for comparison. When the pots are fired, show them to the children and ask the same questions as before. Demonstrate that the fired pot is now more useful because it will hold water (although it may still be porous) so, if it were a bigger pot, you could keep a plant in it. The unfired one still goes soggy and lets the water straight through. Reinforce the fact that heating the clay, by firing it in a kiln, has changed it forever and made it more useful.

2 Show the children the untoasted bread and ask them how heating it in a toaster (toasting it) will change it. *Has it been changed forever when it is toasted, or can we get it back to the same as it was before we toasted it?* Toast sufficient slices for the entire group to have a piece (but only allow the children to use the toaster under close one-to-one supervision). Ask the group to look closely at their toast when it is done and compare it with a slice of untoasted bread. *How has it changed?* (It has been cooked (toasted) on the outside by the heat of the toaster. It can't be returned to its untoasted state.) Butter the toast and put jam on it for a feast!

ASSESSMENT

Note those children who can describe how some materials are changed when they are heated, and that this can make some materials more useful. Look at the children's writing (see Differentiation) to help you make your judgements.

PLENARY

Look at the spare cooked cake. Pull it apart on a plate and pass it around alongside the reserved raw mixture for the children to compare the two. *Say: Look carefully at both mixtures. How has the cooked one changed? Do you think that we can get the cooked one back to what it was before it was cooked, or into the separate ingredients again?* Make sure that the children understand that it is the cooking process (application of heat) that has changed the ingredients forever.

OUTCOMES
- Can describe how some materials change when they are heated.
- Can explain how heating can make a material more useful.

LINKS
Art: making clay pots.
Technology: food safety and hygiene.

Lesson 8 ▪ Pop the corn

Objective
- To know that materials often change when they are heated.

RESOURCES
Uncooked popcorn, a cooker, cooking oil, a large saucepan with a lid, paper plates or bowls, paper, writing materials.

MAIN ACTIVITY
Show the children the unpopped corn, giving them each a grain to handle. Ask them to tell you how it feels. *Does it smell? Is it hard or soft?* Place some popcorn in the pan, together with a little oil and place it on the cooker. Make sure the lid is firmly on the saucepan. Shake the pan gently now and then as the popcorn cooks to prevent it sticking. Ask the children to listen very carefully. *What can you hear?* (The popcorn can be heard popping as it cooks.) When it stops popping, put a little on a plate for each child and ask them to look carefully at and smell the popped corn, comparing it with how it was before cooking. *How has it changed? Does it smell the same? Does it feel very different? Do you think we could change the corn back to the way it was before we heated it, or do you think that heating has changed it forever?* Children could save some of the corn, both popped and unpopped, stick it to some paper and write a sentence or two about how heating (cooking) the corn has changed it. Have fun eating the popcorn!

Differentiation
All the children should be able to take part in this activity at their own level. In the writing part of the task, more able children should give several ways in which the corn has been changed by heating.
Less confident children may only manage one or two changes and may have to tell you their ideas.

ASSESSMENT
During the Plenary session, note which children are able to answer your questions and know that the material (popcorn) has been changed by heat. Look at the children's work to assess the level of their understanding.

PLENARY
Look at the cooked and uncooked corn again with the children. Ask them to remind you of some of the ways in which the cooking (heating) of the corn has changed it. Ask: Has it been changed forever? Look at some of the children's work and discuss it with them.

OUTCOME
- Can describe how some materials change when they are heated.

Lesson 9 ▪ Let's cool down

Objective
- To know that many materials change when they are cooled.

RESOURCES
Main activity: Ice cube trays or ice cube bags, water in clear plastic jugs, access to the freezing compartment of a fridge or a freezer.
Group activities: 1 An unmade jelly for each group (include a range of

Vocabulary
cool, cooled, cold, change, set, freeze, reversible, irreversible, liquid, solid, dissolve.

different colours, if possible. Agar jellies are available for vegetarians), bowls, spoons; hot - not boiling - water; writing and drawing materials.
2 A well-washed, empty film canister for each child (the transparent kind would be best. You can usually obtain these free from chemists that do their own film processing), a lolly stick for each child, access to a freezer or the freezing compartment of a fridge, water, fruit syrups, empty ice cream containers (to keep the lollies upright while freezing).
Plenary: A tea towel.

PREPARATION
Freeze some water in ice cube trays and bags the day before the lesson in case those prepared during the lesson do not have time to freeze properly before the Plenary session.

BACKGROUND
The children will eventually be expected to know the difference between a reversible and an irreversible change and be able to give definitions. They will also need to know the difference between a solid and a liquid. This lesson is a good vehicle for demonstrating reversible change and liquids changing into solids.

It is worthwhile introducing the correct vocabulary and concepts at this stage, but don't expect all the children to understand or retain them. The main objective of the lesson is that the children should know that some materials change when cooled and that they are able to describe the process.

STARTER
Talk to all the children about what they did in Lessons 7 and 8. Ask them whether they could return the cooked ingredients of their cakes, the popcorn or clay back to their original state.

MAIN ACTIVITY
Remind the children that once the food was cooked and the clay fired they could not get them back to the way they were before. This is called an irreversible change - it can't be changed back. Now we are going to look at some more changes that happen when materials are cooled.

Show the children the ice cube trays or bags and the jugs of water. Ask the children what they would need to do to turn the water into ice cubes. (Fill the trays or bags and put them in the freezer to get really cold.) Invite some children to help you do this and put the trays or bags into the freezer or freezing compartment of the fridge. Ask the children to tell you what they think is happening to the water when it is put in the freezer. *Why is it called a freezer?* If possible, take the ice cube trays or bags out of the freezer during the freezing process so that the children can look at them and see what is happening. Ask: *How is the water changing? What is happening to it?* (It is getting colder and colder and the water is beginning to freeze: it is changing from a liquid to a solid.)

GROUP ACTIVITIES
1 Tell the children that there are some materials that change when they are cooled but that don't actually have to be frozen. Jelly is one of these materials. It needs to be dissolved by adding warm water to it and should then be put somewhere cool to set. (You may need access to a fridge for this.) The children can make jelly in groups of three or four, then write about what they did and what they think will happen as the jelly cools. Encourage them to use as much of the appropriate vocabulary in their writing as they can. You may wish to put a list of words on the board to help them, such as 'warm', 'dissolve', 'cool', 'set', 'liquid', 'solid'.
2 Let the children mix a fruit syrup of their choice with enough water to fill

their film canister, put a lolly stick into the canister, then put the canister carefully into an empty ice cream container to go into the freezer. Talk to them as they are doing this and ask them what is going to happen when they put the lollies into the freezer. Encourage them to use the appropriate vocabulary to say what that means.

ASSESSMENT
Look at the children's work to give you an idea of the level of their understanding. During the Plenary session, note those children who are able to answer your questions and those who contribute sensibly to the discussion.

PLENARY
Bring the ice cubes out of the freezer and pass them around for the children to look at. (Put a tea towel under the trays or bags to prevent them sticking to the children's hands and to mop up any drips.) *How has the water changed? What would happen if we set these trays and bags aside in the warm classroom? What would happen if we put them into the freezer again once they have melted and changed from a solid to a liquid?* Tell them that this is what they are going to do. They will then see what happens in the next lesson.

Rehearse the appropriate vocabulary with the children, adding, or asking them to add, a definition every time. *What happened to the water as it froze?* (It got very cold and changed from a liquid into a solid.) *Did the same thing happen with the ice lollies?* Look at the jellies and ask: *What was different when the jellies set and changed from liquid to solid?* (They did not have to go into the freezer.) Look at some of the children's work and discuss it with them. Finish the lesson by enjoying the jelly and lollies!

OUTCOME
● Can describe how some materials change when they are cooled.

Differentiation
Group activity 1
In this activity, some children may need to draw pictures of the process and explain their pictures to you verbally. Other children will be able to use more of the appropriate vocabulary words in their writing and give a more detailed explanation of the process.
Group activity 2
All the children should be able to take part in this activity at their own level.

Lesson 10 ▸ Warm it up

Objective
● To know that some materials melt and change when they are heated.

Vocabulary
heat, heated, burn, melt, flame, wax, change, reversible, irreversible, solid, liquid.

RESOURCES
Main activity: Access to a freezer; a bowl or tank of ice cubes for each group of six, containing at least one ice cube per child; paper, writing and drawing materials.
Group activities: For both these Group activities you will need extra adult help to supervise the groups. **1** A candle and holder in a metal tray filled with sand for each group of four or six, matches (to be retained by the adult working with the group), paper and pencil (for the adult to note the children's comments and vocabulary – see Group activity 1), writing and drawing materials. **2** Flakes or a puffed rice cereal, chocolate, small cake cases, spoons, a double saucepan or a bowl that fits into a saucepan, access to a cooker.

PREPARATION
Freeze sufficient ice cubes for every child in the class to have at least one.

BACKGROUND
At this stage the children are learning that materials can be changed in a variety of ways. Water can be changed into ice and back again over and over again. Wax melts and then burns in the heat of a candle flame. Chocolate can be melted and hardened again to make chocolate cakes or shaped in to Easter eggs.

Some materials, such as dough or clay, change profoundly when heated or cooked. This leads eventually to an understanding that changes can be reversible or irreversible, and that changes are brought about in different ways such as heating, cooling, burning, using a force, and so on.

STARTER
Remind all the children about what they did in Lesson 9. Ask: *What happened when we put the water in the ice trays or bags and then into the freezer? Who can remember some of the scientific words that we used?* (Freeze, change, solid, liquid and so on.)

MAIN ACTIVITY
Tell the children that in this lesson they are going to find out what happens to ice when it is taken out of the freezer and kept in a warm room. Ask: *Can anyone predict what they think will happen?* Divide the children into groups of about six and sit them around a table with a bowl or tank of ice cubes. Ask them to look closely at the ice cubes to see what is happening to them. *Can you write down some words to describe what is happening?* (As they melt, the ice cubes are turning back to water. They are going from a solid to a liquid.) Perhaps they can draw some pictures of the process. Encourage the children to pick up an ice cube from time to time and hold it for a short while. *What does it feel like? What is happening as you hold it in your warm hand? Is your hand warmer than the room? Is the ice cube melting more quickly in your hand than it did in the bowl? Does it feel wet? What is it turning into? (Water, a liquid.)* As you work with the groups, ask: *What would happen if we put the ice that has melted back into the freezer? Would it turn back into solid ice? Would we be able to do the same activity over and over again? Is the change when water is frozen into ice a reversible or irreversible one?* Finish the activity by putting some of the water from the melted ice back into the freezer to look at with the children during the Plenary session (or the next day if it has not frozen in time).

GROUP ACTIVITIES
1 Organise the children into groups of four or six, each with an adult. (If you are working with the children yourself you may be happy to work with at least six children and manage the activity safely. If a classroom helper is in charge, he or she may feel more comfortable taking responsibility for only four children. Consult any other adults in advance.) Put the candle in the centre of the table and tell the children that they are going to watch it very carefully, and make as many observations as they can before, during and after it burns.

Ensure that the table is clear of papers and any other clutter, that long hair is tied back and that the children are seated at a safe distance from the candle. Give adult helpers a piece of paper with the initials of the group members written at intervals down the side so that they can note any appropriate vocabulary or comments that the children make during their observation. Remind helpers that the activity is about changes to the materials as they are heated and ask them to draw the children's attention to the change in the colour of the wick, the state of the wax near the flame, and so on.

2 Before starting this activity, make sure that the children have washed their hands and observe the rules of hygiene as they work. Children, again working in groups with an adult, should melt the chocolate and then add sufficient cereal, stirring gently until the chocolate has coated the cereal. Spoon the mixture into cake cases and leave to set. Encourage the adult working with the children to ask questions that will lead the children to observe the process closely and use the appropriate vocabulary. (See Group activity 1, above.)

ASSESSMENT
Look at the children's work from the Main activity to help you with your judgements. During the Plenary session, note those children who use the new vocabulary correctly and are able to answer your questions.

PLENARY
Talk to the children about what they have observed and learned during the three activities in this lesson. *What happened when the ice cubes were brought out of the freezer? Did they melt faster when you held them in your hand? What did the ice change into?* Bring some of the refrozen ice from the freezer to look at with the children and reinforce the idea that water can be melted and refrozen over and over again. This is a reversible change. *Is the same true of the wax that has melted and then burned as the candle was burning?* (Some of the wax that melted will have gone solid again and could be melted once more, but much of the wax will have vaporised and burned away.) *Could we get that back again? Is the wax gone forever? Is that an irreversible change? What about the chocolate? What happened when it was heated? What happened when it was cooled? Could we melt it again?* Look at, and read, some of the children's work with them and discuss what they have learned.

OUTCOMES
● Can describe how some materials change as they melt.
● Can describe how some materials change when they are heated.

LINKS
Technology: following safe procedures for food safety and hygiene.

Differentiation
Main activity
Some children will write detailed observations, showing a clear understanding of the process and using the appropriate vocabulary. Some children may need to tell you about their observations and rehearse the vocabulary verbally.
Group activities
All the children should be able to join in the Group activities at their own level.

Lesson 11 ◾ The uses of ice

RESOURCES ◉
Main activity: Four ice cubes in small foil dishes and a copy of photocopiable page 76 from Unit 2b (also, 'Fair test' (red), available the CD-ROM) per group of four; writing materials, timer or alarm.
Group activities: 1 Two flavoured ice cubes per child (see Preparation, below). **2** A copy of photocopiable page 121 (also 'The uses of ice' (red), available on the CD-ROM) for each pair of children, reference materials, drawing and writing materials.

PREPARATION
Make two flavoured ice cubes for each child by pouring a mixture of fruit syrup or fruit squash and water into ice cube bags (these can be bought at any supermarket) and freezing them so they are ready for the lesson. Allow the ice cubes to stand, at room temperature, for a few minutes before eating, to avoid it sticking to the children's fingers.

BACKGROUND
The ability to plan and carry out a fair test by understanding how to control and manipulate variables is not expected of children at KS1. However, even at this young age, children need to have experience of whole investigations in order to help develop this understanding. They need to practise at planning, managing and carrying out investigations, with your help.

Talking through the planning stage, with the whole class, is a good way to begin. It ensures that all the children understand what the investigation is about, what is expected of them and how to carry out their test fairly. If you go through this process in a questioning way, asking for ideas from the class, it gives those children who have the beginnings of an understanding a

Objective
● To know that ice will melt at different rates in different temperatures.
● To be able to plan and carry out a fair test with help.

Vocabulary
temperature, investigate, investigation, fair, melt, warm, cool, cold.

Differentiation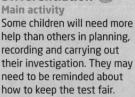
Main activity
Some children will need more help than others in planning, recording and carrying out their investigation. They may need to be reminded about how to keep the test fair.
Group activity 1
All the children should be able to participate in Group activity 1.
Group activity 2
For children who need support, use 'The uses of ice' (green), from the CD-ROM, which does not require them to provide reasons for the uses.

To extend children, use 'The uses of ice' (blue), which asks the children how people kept things cool before refrigerators were invented. They can use reference materials to help them.

chance to verbalise and reinforce their ideas. At this stage, give the children as much help as they need – investigating should be a fun, rather than a frustrating, experience!

STARTER
Remind the whole class about what they learned in Lesson 10 when they looked at ice cubes melting. *What happened when you held them in your hands? Did they melt faster? Why?* (Because their hands were warmer than the bowl.) Tell the children that they are going to do an investigation to see how quickly ice cubes melt in different places that are at different temperatures.

MAIN ACTIVITY
Put the children into groups of four and sit them around you. Show them four ice cubes in separate foil dishes. Tell them that each group is going to have four ice cubes and they will put them in different places to find out which is the best place for keeping ice frozen for as long as possible. Ask them to think about, and predict, which would be the best place and the worst place in the classroom or around the school. (In the fridge, in the shade, on the window sill, in the Sun and so on.) Discuss how often it would be sensible to check each ice cube. (Every ten minutes?) Ask: *How can we keep the test fair, so that each ice cube has the same chance?* (Make sure that the ice cubes are the same size, put them in place and check them at the same time.) *How can you check them all at the same time?* (Each member of the group could have responsibility for one of the ice cubes.)

Give each group a copy of photocopiable page 76 and ask them to plan their investigation. Ask: *Do you need to record anything as you go along?* (The check times, and whether each ice cube is still there or has melted completely.) Before they start, and as they are doing the activity, ask the children to complete the relevant sections of the record sheet. Check that the data they are recording is appropriate.

GROUP ACTIVITIES
1 Give each child two flavoured ice cubes on a plate. Ask them to predict which will melt first, if one is left on the plate and they put the other one in their mouth and suck it. Ask: *Where does ice melt more quickly- in a warm or cold place? Is your mouth warmer than the classroom?*
2 Put the children into pairs and give each pair a copy of photocopiable page 121. Ask them to think of as many uses as they can for ice and write these on their sheet in the correct section. Remind them that they can use the reference materials to help them.

ASSESSMENT
Use the children's work from the Main activity and from Group activity 2 to help you assess their level of understanding.

PLENARY
Look at the record sheets from the Main activity with the children and discuss what they found out. *Does ice take longer to melt in a cold or warm place? How did you keep your test fair? What did you record as you went along? Did your recording help you to remember what happened and which ice cube melted first?* Talk about some of the ways in which ice is used.

OUTCOMES
● Know that the warmer the environment, the quicker ice melts.
● Can plan and carry out a fair test with help.

LINKS
Unit 2b, Lesson 23, Fair test.

Lesson 12 ◗ Water and steam

Objective
● To know that water turns to steam when it is heated, but the steam turns back to water when it is cooled.

RESOURCES
An electric kettle; a large, cold plate or metal tray.

MAIN ACTIVITY
With the children around you, but at a safe distance, show them that the kettle is filled with water. Set it on the table and ask them to look closely: can they see any steam? Ask: *What is steam?* (It is what water turns into when it is heated.) Boil the water in the kettle. Ask the children to watch very carefully as the water boils. *What can you see?* (Steam.) When the water is boiling, hold the plate or tray over the steam, but be careful not to scald yourself. Say: *As the steam hits the plate, what can you see?* (Droplets of water forming.) Tell the children that as the water boils it turns into steam and that, when it cools again, it turns back into water. (Put the tray in a fridge for a short while before doing this activity to give a better, quicker, result.)

ASSESSMENT
During the Plenary session note those children who are able to answer your questions.

PLENARY
Ask the children to tell you what happens to water as it is heated and then as the steam is cooled.

Differentiation
All the children should be able to take part in this activity.

OUTCOMES
● Can describe what happens when water is heated.
● Can describe what happens when steam is cooled.

ENRICHMENT

Lesson 13 ◗ Things that use heat

Objective
● To know that heat is a form of energy and that it may be supplied by several sources.

Vocabulary
energy, heat, source, power, appliance

RESOURCES 💿
Group activities: 1 A copy of photocopiable page 122 (also 'Things that use heat - 1' (red), from the CD-ROM) for each child; writing and colouring materials. **2** A copy of photocopiable page 123 (also 'Things that use heat- 2' (red), from the CD-ROM) for each child; writing materials.
ICT link: 'Things that use heat' interactive activity, from the CD-ROM.

BACKGROUND
Energy is needed to make things work and we all need energy to make our bodies work. Energy comes in many forms and can be changed or transferred from one form to another, most of which are too complicated or abstract for children of this age. They should, however, be able to understand that energy is needed to make things work and give us heat.

Heat is just one form of energy. Others include light and sound. Some of our energy is provided by waves, water and wind or by nuclear power. These are all used to generate electricity. There is also increasing use of heat energy which is taken directly from the Sun: energy that is collected by solar panels. Houses can be heated and machinery run on electricity generated from solar energy so, in countries where a mains electricity supply is less certain and many daily hours of sunshine can be relied on, more appliances are solar-powered (water pumps, for example). Most of our heat energy comes from gas, electricity or solid fuel in various forms. This lesson concentrates on the everyday sources of heat energy and its uses.

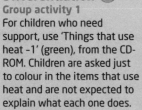

Differentiation

Group activity 1

For children who need support, use 'Things that use heat -1' (green), from the CD-ROM. Children are asked just to colour in the items that use heat and are not expected to explain what each one does.

To extend children, use 'Things that use heat – 1' (blue), which asks the children to think of two more household items that use heat and to explain what they do.

Group activity 2

The children who need support can use 'Things that use heat -2' (green), which lists the words that they will need to use. For extension, use 'Things that use heat – 2' (blue), You may need to talk to the children beforehand about places where we can obtain fuel – for example, power stations, the North Sea, trees and so on.

STARTER

The counting rhyme 'Six Fat Sausages Sizzling in the Pan' would be a good introduction to this lesson.

MAIN ACTIVITY

Ask the children when, where and why we use heat. (When we are cold, when we need hot water for a bath, when we want a cup of tea, for the hairdryer or the iron, to cook with or make the toast for breakfast and so on.) Ask them to close their eyes and try to imagine what it would be like if there were no heat. (Cold baths all the time, raw food, cold houses, crumpled clothes.) *It wouldn't be much fun would it?*

Tell the children that heat is a form of energy and that we get it from different sources. Ask: *Can anyone tell me what supplies the heat energy for* cooking? (Usually gas or electricity, although some children may have solid fuel or oil ranges in their houses.) *What about things like the iron, the hairdryer and perhaps the kettle?* (Electricity.) Ask the children if any of them have solar panels on their houses and get their heat energy directly from the Sun.

Help the children to understand that heat energy plays an important part in our lives. It helps to make our lives much more comfortable than they would otherwise be. Heat has been used in this way since very early people discovered fire. However, heat can also be very dangerous. Ask: *What would happen if you touched something that was very hot, like a hot iron, a kettle full of boiling water or an electric fire?* Tell the children that they need to be very careful with anything that uses heat energy and gets hot.

GROUP ACTIVITIES

1 Give each child a copy of photocopiable page 122. Look at the pictures with them and make sure that they can identify them all. Ask them to colour only those that use heat and to write under each one what it is used for.
2 Give each child a copy of photocopiable page 123. Ask them to identify and tell you what the pictures are. They should then write what fuel source or sources could provide the heat for each one. (For example, a barbecue might use charcoal or gas.) You may wish to put a list of fuel sources on the board or flip chart such as coal, gas, electricity, charcoal, wood, oil or rubbish.

ICT LINK

Children can use the 'Things that use heat' interactive, from the CD-ROM, to identify objects that work by heating up.

ASSESSMENT

Use the children's work to assess the level of their understanding. During the Plenary session note those children who know that heat is a form of energy.

PLENARY

Ask the children: *What is heat? What would we have to do without if we did not have sources of heat energy?* Look at the work that the children have done and discuss it with them. *How many sources of heat energy have we found out about? What appliances give us heat?*

OUTCOMES

● Know that heat is a form of energy.
● Know about different sources of heat energy.
● Can recognise different applications of heat in everyday life.

Lesson 14 ◻ Assessment

Objective
● To assess whether the children suggest everyday uses of some materials.
● To assess whether the children know that materials often change when they are heated.
● To assess whether children can describe how materials change when they are cooled.

RESOURCES ◉
Assessment activities: **1** Photocopiable page 124 (also 'Assessment – 1' (red), available from the CD-ROM), pencils. **2** Photocopiable page 125 (also 'Assessment – 2' (red), available from the CD-ROM), pencils.

STARTER
Ask the children to tell you about some of the things they have learned in this unit. You may want to revise some of the vocabulary that has been introduced to the children.

ASSESSMENT ACTIVITY 1
Give each child a copy of photocopiable page 124 and ask them to complete it by writing two uses for each of the materials pictured.

ANSWERS
Accept any reasonable answers for each material. You may wish to question children about any unusual use they have suggested.

LOOKING FOR LEVELS
Most children will be able to suggest two uses for each material. Some children may have difficulty suggesting uses for rock.

ASSESSMENT ACTIVITY 2
Give each child a copy of photocopiable page 125. Read it through with them and make sure that they understand each sentence. Ask them to complete the sheet by answering the questions.

ANSWERS
Accept any answer that indicates an understanding of the following:
1. It gets very cold and goes solid.
2. It melts and goes runny or changes to a liquid.
3. It melts and changes to a liquid.
4. It changes back to water.
5. It cooks and becomes solid.
6. The seeds pop. They get big and fluffy.

LOOKING FOR LEVELS
Most children will manage to write an answer to each question that indicates some understanding, although some children may need to explain their answers to you verbally. Some children will be able to indicate whether the change is temporary or permanent (reversible or irreversible).

PHOTOCOPIABLE

How is it used?

Material	Properties	Uses
wood		
metal		
glass		
plastic		

SCHOLASTIC

Where do materials come from?

Source	What do we get from the source?	What needs to be done before we use the material?
sheep	Wool	sheep sheared, wool spun, wool knitted or woven, clothes made.
tree		
sponges		
silk worms		
cotton field		
quarry		

Illustration © Ann Kronheimer

Make a cake

625g currants
225g sultanas
225g raisins
100g mixed peel (or use 1kg of mixed fruit)
175g glacé cherries (halved)
100g chopped nuts
grated rind of half a lemon
400g plain flour
level teaspoon mixed spice
level teaspoon cinnamon
350g butter or margarine
350g soft brown sugar
6 eggs (beaten)

Beat the butter or margarine and sugar together until light and fluffy. Gradually add the beaten eggs and beat again. Add the remaining ingredients and mix thoroughly. This mixture is sufficient for approximately 20–25 small cakes (depending on the size of your tins).

Bake at 150°C. The time needed will depend on the size of your tins and type of oven. Check after 45 minutes and test with a skewer: if the skewer is clean after pushing into a cake, the cakes are cooked.

The uses of ice

Ice is used in the home for:	because:
Ice is used in shops and supermarkets for:	because:
Ice is used when we are having fun for:	because:

Things that use heat –1

◾ Colour the things that work by heating up.
◾ Write underneath what each one does.

Illustration © Ann Kronheimer

◾SCHOLASTIC

Things that use heat – 2

■ Write which fuel or fuels each of these things uses for its heat energy.

Illustration © Ann Kronheimer

Assessment – 1

■ List two uses for these materials.

wood

1 _____

2 _____

glass

1 _____

2 _____

plastic

1 _____

2 _____

metal

1 _____

2 _____

paper

1 _____

2 _____

rock

1 _____

2 _____

Illustration © Ann Kronheimer

■ SCHOLASTIC

Assessment – 2

1. What happens to water when you freeze it? _____

_____

_____

2. What happens to chocolate when you heat it? _____

_____

_____

3. What happens to wax when you heat it? _____

_____

_____

4. What happens to steam when it is cooled? _____

_____

_____

5. What happens to a cake mix when you put it in a hot oven? _____

_____

_____

6. What happens to popping corn when you heat it? _____

_____

_____

CHAPTER 5 Forces and movement

Lesson	Objectives	Main activity	Group activities	Plenary	Outcomes
Lesson 1 Different forces	• To know that forces make things move.	Review Y1/P2 work on forces. Move objects and discuss the forces involved.	Identify forces. Play a game of 'Forces Snakes and Ladders'.	Talk about forces.	• Know that forces make things move.
Lesson 2 Stretch, squeeze, squash...	• To know that actions such as stretching, squeezing, squashing, twisting and turning can be explained as forces (pushes and pulls). • To plan and carry out a simple fair test with help.	Analyse stretching, twisting, squeezing and other actions into pushes and pulls.	Plan a test to find out which fabric sample will stretch most. Make a list of examples of twists at school and at home.	Discuss forces and report findings.	• Can describe a range of actions such as stretching, squeezing, squashing, twisting and turning in terms of forces (pushes and pulls). • Can plan and carry out a simple fair test with help.
Lesson 3 Investigating movement	• To know that forces can make moving objects go faster, change direction, or slow down .	Roll balls on the ground and hit them with a bat to examine forces.	Roll a painted ball on black paper, against a wall. Investigate pushing and pedalling toys	Talk about the effects of forces.	• Know that forces make objects speed up, slow down or change direction
Lesson 4 Vehicle investigation	• To develop further an understanding of how to make a test fair. • To know how to compare distances travelled by vehicles.	Push vehicles to compare how far they go. Make sure the test is fair.	Compare the distances vehicles travel down ramps. Write about how the test was made fair.	Discuss how the test was made fair. Interpret the graphs and compare results.	Gain a better understanding of how to make a test fair. • Can compare the distances travelled by vehicles.
Lesson 5 The effects of weight	• To investigate the effect of weight on distance travelled.	Organise a fair test to see the effect of increased weight on distance travelled.		Report findings.	• Can carry out a fair test with help. • Know that the weight of a vehicle affects the distance it travels.
Lesson 6 The effects of height	• To carry out a fair test with help. • To investigate the effect of ramp heights on distance travelled.	Organise a fair test to see the effect of ramp height on the distance a vehicle travels.		Discuss the findings.	• Can carry out a fair test with help. • Know that ramp height affects the distance a vehicle travels.
Enrichment Lesson 7 Introducing friction	• To know that there is a force of friction between two surfaces. • To know that friction is stronger between rough surfaces than smooth surfaces. • To plan and carry out a simple fair test with help.	Investigate friction, and how brakes work. Pull a brick over different surfaces.	Make a graph from the data collected. Play 'Shove 2p'	Rub hands together to experience friction. Look at and interpret the graphs.	• Know that there is a force called friction acting between two surfaces. • Know that the rougher the surface, the stronger the friction. • Can plan and carry out a simple fair test with help.
Enrichment Lesson 8 Rough or smooth?	• To know that friction is stronger between rough surfaces than smooth surfaces.	Race vehicles down ramps onto different surfaces.		Talk about the test.	• Know that the rougher the surface, the stronger the friction. • Can plan and carry out a fair test with help.
Enrichment Lesson 9 A rough ride	• To know that the rougher the surface, the stronger the friction.	Slide smooth and rough blocks down a slope. Write about what happened.		Discuss the children's writing about friction.	• Know that rougher surfaces slide less easily because the friction is stronger.
Enrichment Lesson 10 Will it float or sink?	• To know that some objects float because water pushes up on them.	Load margarine tub boats to see how much they will hold before they sink.	Predict, then investigate, what will float. Make plastic bottles sink and float.	Discuss the findings and compare these with the predictions.	• Can recognise that an object floats due to the upward push of the liquid being greater than the downward pull of gravity.

Assessment	Objectives			Activity 1	Activity 2
Lesson 11	• To assess whether the children know that forces can make moving objects go faster, change direction or slow down.. • To assess whether the children can explain actions such as stretching, squeezing, twisting and turning as pushes and pulls.			Complete sentences about friction.	Identify pictures of pushes and pulls.

SC1 SCIENTIFIC ENQUIRY

Rolling down ramps

LEARNING OBJECTIVES AND OUTCOMES
- To recognise when a test is unfair.
- To think about what might happen
- To make and record observations and measurements
- To make simple comparisons
- Review their work and explain what they did to others

ACTIVITY
Children are asked to predict which of two vehicles will go the furthest when pushed and they then test their predictions. Through discussion they decide if the test was fair and if both vehicles had the same chance. They are invited to suggest ways of making the test fairer. They then move on to carry out a fairer test by running the vehicles down a ramp and write about how they made their test fair, giving each vehicle a fair chance.

LESSON LINKS
This Sc1 activity forms an integral part of Lesson 4, Vehicle investigation.

Lesson 1 ▪ Different forces

Objective
- To know that forces make things move.

Vocabulary
force, push, pull, gravity

RESOURCES 💿
Main activity: A collection of wheeled objects such as toy cars, toy shopping trolleys, pull-along toys, toy wheelbarrows, bikes and tricycles; a range of balls; the hall or playground; a day when there is enough wind to move the bushes and trees.
Group activities: 1 A copy of photocopiable page 142 (also 'Different Forces – 1' (red), available on the CD-ROM) for each child; writing materials. **2** Sufficient game boards made from photocopiable page 143 (also 'Different Forces – 2' (red), available the CD-ROM; see Preparation, below), counters and dice for each group.
ICT link: 'Different forces' interactive activity, from the CD-ROM.

PREPARATION
Enlarge to A3 sufficient copies of photocopiable page 143 to give one to each group of four children. Colour and laminate these before use.

BACKGROUND
Forces are difficult for young children to understand because they are so abstract. At this stage children should understand that forces make things move and be able to identify them in simple terms. They should know that when someone is pushing a shopping trolley, or pulling a wheeled toy, that the forces they are using are making the objects move and that those forces are called a push or a pull.

Forces are often described in terms of the effect they have. When children jump, they move themselves by pushing against the floor and the force of gravity moves them back down again; they do not go on moving upwards. The concept of gravity is particularly difficult and abstract but is, perhaps, the force that has the most effect on our lives. Young children are not expected to understand gravity or to explain it, but they do need to experience the effect of gravity, understand that the force of gravity moves all objects downwards, not upwards, and that gravity is a pull force: it pulls things towards the centre of the Earth.

STARTER

Remind all the children about the work on forces moving things that they did in Year 1/Primary 2. Ask them to tell you what they remember and see if they can name any of the forces (pushes and pulls).

MAIN ACTIVITY

If you wish, you could do this activity in the hall or out on the playground so that the children have more room to move about. Show the children the collection of wheeled objects. Select a vehicle and ask: *Will this move on its own?* (No, we need to use a force to start it moving.) Push the vehicle along the ground. *What force am I using to make this move?* (A push.)

Put the children into pairs and give each pair a wheeled object. Ask them to take turns to move their object. *What force are you using to make your object move?* (A push or a pull.) When each child has had a turn they could swap their object with another pair and repeat the activity. Try to make sure that each pair has a chance to work with something that needs to be pushed and then with something that has to be pulled. Gather the children together to discuss what they did and the forces that they were using to move the things they were working with.

Now give each pair a ball, and ask them to take turns to throw the ball up in the air. *What force are you using to throw the ball up?* (A push.) Allow the children to do this several times, then gather them together again. Throw a ball up into the air yourself. Remind them that they were using a push force as they threw the ball. Now ask them to watch what happens to the ball. *Does it carry on going upwards?* Explain to the children that a force called 'gravity' pulls (moves) things downwards. Ask the children to jump as high as they can. *What are you doing?* (Using a push force to move up off the ground.) *What happens next?* (Gravity pulls you back to land on the ground again.) If you are outside, ask the children to look around at the bushes and trees. *What is happening to them?* (The wind is pushing them.)

GROUP ACTIVITIES

1 Give each child a copy of photocopiable page 142. Ask them to look carefully at the pictures and at the arrows showing which way the object in each picture is moving. Ask them to write under each picture the name of the force that is moving the object.
2 Put the children into groups of four with a 'Forces Snakes and Ladders' game board made from photocopiable page 143, counters and dice. Explain to the children how to play the game (like snakes and ladders). Ask them to notice the forces.

ICT LINKS

Children can use the 'Different forces' interactive, from the CD-ROM, to identify forces in action.

ASSESSMENT

During the Main activity discussion and the Plenary session, note those children who show an understanding that forces move things and who can name the forces involved (push, pull, gravity).

PLENARY

Talk about what the children did in the Main activity. *Would the objects or your bodies have moved by themselves?* (No, a force was needed to make them move.) *What were the forces involved?* (Pushes, pulls and gravity pulling things downwards.) Look at some of the work from Group activity 1 and discuss it with the children.

OUTCOME

● Know that forces make things move.

Lesson 2 ▪ Stretch, squeeze, squash...

RESOURCES
Main activity: A collection of objects and materials that can be stretched, squashed, squeezed and twisted such as: a range of strips of fabric and elastic, sponges, a jar or bottle with a screw top, play dough, a shoe with laces, a corkscrew (with cork to demonstrate), a cloth such as a tea cloth in a bowl of water that can be wrung out (twisted) before drying.
Group activities: 1 Writing and drawing materials, rulers; a range of strips of fabric of the same width and length (10cm ×1.5 cm) cut from fabrics of different 'stretchiness' such as nylon tights, wool, cotton, acrylic and so on. **2** Writing and drawing materials.

BACKGROUND
The concept of forces is very abstract and is therefore one of the most difficult areas of the science curriculum to teach, and for young children to grasp. We cannot see a force, only the effect of one - the resulting movement when something is pushed, pulled or twisted. Forces can start something moving (a push, pull or gravity), make it stop (a train hitting buffers), make it slow down (friction, travelling over a very rough surface or putting on a brake), make it go faster (an increased push or pull) or make it change direction (hitting a ball with a bat).

Eventually, in Key Stages 2 and 3, children will be expected to know that forces are acting all the time, even when there is no movement. They will also be expected to identify and name other forces and be able to say in which direction the main forces are acting. At Year 2/Primary 3 the children only need to be given experience of forces and to be able to identify them in simple terms.

STARTER
Remind the children that they learned something about forces in Year 1/ Primary 2, and again in Lesson 1 of this unit. Ask: *Who can remember what we learned? What do forces do?* (Make things move, slow down, speed up, change direction and stop.) *What are the names of some of the forces we learned about?* (Pushes and pulls.) *Can you remember that we talked about twists when we were investigating elastic during our work about materials?*

MAIN ACTIVITY
Show the children the collection of objects and materials and go through them one by one, asking the children to predict what force you are going to use and to identify the force each time. Help them if necessary. (Stretching the fabrics and elastics are pulls, squashing or squeezing the play dough, springs and sponges are pushes; opening and closing the jar or bottle, wringing out the cloth and using a corkscrew are twists - a push and a pull combined). Tying a shoelace into a bow is quite complicated, as it is a mixture of twists and pulls! When you have finished, go through the collection again, this time asking some children to come up and squeeze, squash, stretch or twist as appropriate, saying what they are doing and naming the force or forces involved.

GROUP ACTIVITIES
1 Put the children into groups of three. Give each group about three different strips of fabric (see Resources) that will stretch to different lengths. Ask them to look closely at and feel the fabric before they begin, and to predict which one they think will stretch the most and why. Allow them to plan a test to find out. As they are working ask questions such as: *How are you going to organise yourselves to find out which is the fabric that will stretch the furthest? Do you need to record anything as you go*

Differentiation
Group activity 1
Some children may need to be told how to organise their test and what to record, especially those that cannot read a ruler. You may wish to put the children into mixed-ability groups so that they can help each other. Other children will be able to use their experience of organising simple tests in previous units to manage this one on their own.
Group activity 2
You may need to revise some examples of twists and turns with some children.

along? (The length to which each fabric stretched.) Only intervene to tell the children how to organise the test if their method is clearly not going to give them a proper result. The children could hold one end of the fabric tightly against the edge of the table, measure its length, then stretch the fabric and measure again. Ask them what force they are using as they stretch their fabrics. (A pull.)

2 As individuals, ask the children to make a list, with pictures, of examples of twists at home and at school. (Door knobs, jam jars, corkscrews, taps, radio volume knobs, pepper and salt mills, wood screws, using a screwdriver, wind-up toys and so on.)

ASSESSMENT
Observe the children as they are stretching their fabrics and note their level of understanding. Do they know that a stretch is a pull force? Use their work from Group activity 2 to help you make your judgements. Also note those children who respond with understanding to your questions during the Plenary session.

PLENARY
Look together at the collection of objects and materials again, very briefly, and ask the children to tell you what squeezing, squashing, twisting and turning are examples of. (Forces, pushes and pulls.) Ask some children to report the findings from their test. *Which fabric stretched the most? Was it the one you expected?* Go through some of the work from Group activity 2 and look at the twists (pushes and pulls) that the children have listed. *Can anyone think of any more?*

OUTCOMES
● Can describe a range of actions such as stretching, squeezing, squashing, twisting and turning in terms of forces (pushes and pulls).
● Can plan and carry out a simple fair test with help.

Lesson 3 ▪ Investigating movement

Objective
● To know that forces can make moving objects go faster, change direction or slow down.

Vocabulary
force, speed up, slow down, change direction

RESOURCES
Main activity: A range of balls, bats and hockey sticks (enough for one between two); space on the playground or playing field.
Group activities: 1 Large sheets of black paper, small sponge or tennis balls, shallow trays of different coloured paint, newspaper, aprons or other covering for the children. **2** A collection of wheeled toys such as bicycles, tricycles and scooters. (If you do not have enough you could borrow from younger classes or ask the children to bring in their own for this lesson.)

BACKGROUND
Forces start something moving (a push, pull or gravity), make it stop (a train hitting buffers), make it slow down (friction, travelling over a rough surface or putting on a brake), make it go faster (an increased push or pull) or make it change direction (hitting a ball with a bat).

The children should be encouraged to develop the appropriate language of moving things and to realise that a throw is a type of push. Hitting a ball with a bat is a 'push' force that can change the direction of the object that is hit. They should begin to appreciate that the amount of force (push or pull) that they apply will affect the way in which the object moves: that a harder throw, hit or roll (push force) will make a ball go faster and further.

Differentiation
All the children should be able to take part in these activities.

STARTER
Singing the nursery rhyme 'Row, row, row your boat' would be a good introduction to this lesson. Ask the children to sit around you and mime the rowing action as they sing. *What happens to a boat when you row?* (It moves along.) *What are the oars doing?* (Pushing against the water and pulling the boat along.) *If you use a greater force on the oars what will happen?* (The boat will go faster.)

MAIN ACTIVITY
Talking to the whole class, tell the children that in this lesson they are going to find out more about push and pull forces and what they can do. Put the children into pairs, each with a ball and a bat or hockey stick, and take them out onto the field or playground. Ask the pairs to stand about two metres apart and to roll the ball very gently backwards and forwards. *What is happening?* (The ball is going slowly.) *What force are you using?* (A push.)

Now ask them to roll the ball harder and harder to each other. *What is happening?* (The ball has picked up speed and it is going faster.) *What is the difference between the push force that you are using now and the one you used at first?* (It is bigger.) *Can you use a force to stop the ball?* (Put your hand out so that the ball hits it and stops.)

Now put the children into groups of three with a bat or a hockey stick and a ball between them. Ask each group to stand in a triangle. The child with the ball should throw or roll it to the child with the bat or stick, who should hit the ball so that the third child in the group can catch it. Ask the children to notice what is happening. *When the ball has been hit is it travelling in the same direction?* (No, the push force of the bat hitting the ball has made it change direction.)

GROUP ACTIVITIES
1 Ask the children to roll a painted ball on black paper. This is a potentially messy exercise so make sure the children are well-covered! Place some large sheets of black paper on the floor against a wall or other solid obstacle (make sure this is covered with newspaper). Put the children into groups of three or four, each with a ball and a shallow tray of paint. Explain that the children should take turns to dip the ball into the paint and roll it across the black paper to hit the wall and roll back. *Can you see the track the ball has left? Has it changed direction? If so, when? What made it change direction?* Try rolling the ball gently, and then harder, to see what difference it makes to the track. You could use different colours for hard and soft rolls.
2 Put the children into groups of three or four and give each group a bike, tricycle or scooter. Ask them to take turns to push gently on the pedals or, for a scooter, push gently with their feet. *How fast do you go?* Push harder. *How does that change your speed? If you stop using your feet what happens?* (You slow down and eventually stop.) *How else could you stop?* (Put on the brakes or use their feet on the ground.) What is the force *slowing you down?* (Friction.)

ASSESSMENT
Throughout the lesson, note which children are able to answer your questions with understanding and can tell you that forces make things speed up, slow down, change direction or stop.

PLENARY
Ask the children to tell you how they made things speed up, slow down, change direction or stop. Look at some of the tracks made by the painted balls. Ask the children to explain what happened when the balls hit the wall.

OUTCOME
● Know that forces make objects speed up, slow down or change direction

Lesson 4 ◦ Vehicle investigation

Objective
● To develop further an understanding of how to make a test fair.
● To know how to compare distances travelled by vehicles.

Vocabulary
ramp, slope, measure, test, vehicle, fair, unfair

RESOURCES
Main activity: 'Mr Gumpy's Motor Car' by John Burningham (Picture Puffin); two different toy vehicles, a metre stick, a hall or corridor where there is sufficient room for the children to stand around you and watch what is happening; a slope and stand (see diagram below – a shelf or piece of stiff card and a pile of books will do if you have no slope and stand). A sheet of paper or card to record the distances travelled, pencils, a felt-tipped marker pen.
Group activities: 1 A ramp and stand and a selection of three or four vehicles for each group of four (vehicles could be made from construction kits or bought toy vehicles), metre sticks, coloured adhesive tape, scissors or chalk, writing materials, large squared graph paper, colouring materials.
2 Writing and drawing materials.

BACKGROUND
Children at this stage are not expected to be able to identify, control and manipulate variables in order to understand and devise a fair test on their own. This comes towards the end of Key Stage 2. Even so, Year 2/Primary 3 children need to be given help to organise and carry out fair tests as often as possible. Children, from a very young age, have a well-developed notion of social fairness and of things having the same chance, so developing their understanding of fair testing in this way can be very helpful.

Fair testing is important in scientific terms. Without fair testing any data collected is unreliable and cannot be used to draw valid conclusions. Children can be asked: *Have the vehicles had the same chance, have we treated them fairly?* Children need to be given the chance to interpret and compare results as often as possible – this is part of the expected Sc1 capability at the end of KS2 and is an area that is often neglected.

STARTER
Singing a song such as 'The wheels on the bus go round and round' or reading a story such as 'Mr Gumpy's Motor Car' would be a good introduction to this lesson.

MAIN ACTIVITY
Gather the children around you and show them the two different vehicles. Ask them which one they think will go the farthest if it is pushed along. Put a mark (with coloured adhesive tape or chalk) on the floor to indicate where the vehicles are going to start. Push one vehicle, then ask a child to come and use the metre stick to measure how far the vehicle has travelled. Use the felt-tipped marker to make a note on the sheet of paper: 'Vehicle 1 ...cm'.

Push the second vehicle from the same starting point and ask another child to come and measure the distance travelled. Make a note: 'Vehicle 2 ... cm'. *Which vehicle went further? Was it the one you predicted?* Ask the children whether they thought the test was fair. *Did both vehicles have the same chance? They started from the same place, so that was fair, but what about the push that they were given, was that fair? Can we be sure that I gave the same push to each vehicle? Is there any way of measuring that? If I gave one a harder push and one a more gentle push by mistake would that have been fair?*

Set up the slope and stand, marking on the slope where the starting point is. Repeat the test, this time running each vehicle down the slope from the same starting point. Be sure to place the vehicle and then let go without pushing it. Again, ask some children to measure the distances travelled and make a note on the sheet. *Did the same vehicle win?* Ask the children if they think that using the ramp made the test fairer. *How?* (They both ran

Differentiation

Group activity 1

Putting the children into mixed-ability groups so that they can help each other should enable all the children to take part in Group activity 1.

Group activity 2

Some children may need to tell you their ideas verbally. Some children, although they may write less, will show some understanding of making the test fair.

Other children will be able to offer a fairly detailed piece of writing showing a good level of understanding.

down the ramp, from the same starting point, with the ramp at the same height, and without pushing, so they both had the same 'chance'.)

GROUP ACTIVITIES

1 Put the children into groups of four or six and give each group a ramp and stand, a selection of three or four vehicles and a metre stick. Ask the children to test the distance each vehicle travels, making the test fair in the same way as was done in the Main activity. They should record the distance travelled by each vehicle, turn their recording into a block graph and compare the distances to find which vehicle travelled the furthest, which came next, and so on. Two or three groups could then join together to compare their graphs and find out which vehicle was the overall winner and which travelled the shortest distance. They could construct a master graph to show this.

2 As individuals, ask the children to write about how you made the test fair in the Main activity. They could draw the equipment used. *What did you need to do to give each vehicle a 'fair chance'?*

ICT LINK 💿

The children could use the graphing tool on the CD-ROM to convert their data into a block graph or pie chart.

ASSESSMENT

Use the children's work from both Group activities to help you make judgements about the level of their understanding. During the Plenary session, note those children who are able to answer your questions.

PLENARY

Discuss what was done in the Main activity and ask some of the children to read their piece of writing or tell you about the test and how they made it as fair as possible. Use the children's graphs from Group activity 1 to compare the distances travelled by all the vehicles. Ask some children to come to the front and interpret their graphs, comparing the distances their vehicles travelled.

OUTCOMES

- Gain a better understanding of how to make a test fair.
- Can compare the distances travelled by vehicles.

LINKS

Maths: graphs and measuring.

Lesson 5 ▪ The effects of weight

Objective

- To investigate the effect of weight on distance travelled.

RESOURCES 💿

For each group: a ramp and stand (shelves and a pile of books will do), a wheeled vehicle (one that can be loaded with play dough to increase the weight), metre sticks, play dough, writing materials, a copy of photocopiable page 76 (also 'Fair test' (red) from Unit 2b, available on the CD-ROM) for each group (if required).

MAIN ACTIVITY 💿

Divide the children into groups of four or six (four is better if you have enough ramps because each child in the group will then have a job to do - either rolling the vehicle, increasing the load, measuring or recording). Tell the children that they are going to find out if increasing the weight of a vehicle makes any difference to the distance it travels. Help them to organise their test to make it fair (same height of ramp each time, same car, same surface at the bottom of the ramp, release the vehicle from the same place each time, don't push the vehicle). Use photocopiable page 76, if you wish. The children should increase the weight by roughly the same amount each time. Remind them that they need to measure the distances and record them as they are working. They could go on to make a graph of their findings, using the graphing tool from the CD-ROM.

ASSESSMENT

As the children are working, note those who show some understanding of how to organise and carry out a fair test. Note those children who are, themselves, beginning to identify the things that should be kept the same (variables). Which children are able to read the metre stick and record accurately?

PLENARY

Ask some of the children to report what they did and what they found out to you and the class. *Did the weight of the vehicle make a difference to the distance it travelled? How did you keep your test fair?* They could refer to their recording sheet to help them.

OUTCOMES
- Can carry out a fair test with help.
- Know that the weight of a vehicle affects the distance it travels.

Lesson 6 ▸ The effects of height

Objective
● To carry out a fair test with help.
● To investigate the effect of ramp heights on distance travelled.

RESOURCES 💿

For each group: a wheeled vehicle, a slope and stand (if shelves and books are used, the books must all be of the same thickness to make the test fair), photocopiable page 76 (also 'Fair test' (red) from Unit 2b, on the CD-ROM), metre sticks, writing materials.

MAIN ACTIVITY

Divide the children into groups of four or six (four is better if you have enough ramps because each child in the group will then have a job to do – either rolling the vehicle, altering the height of the ramp, measuring or recording). Tell the children that they are going to find out if increasing the height of the ramp makes any difference to the distance their vehicle travels. Help them to organise their test to make it fair (increase the height of the ramp by the same amount each time, use the same car, same surface at the bottom of the ramp, release the vehicle from the same place each time, don't push the vehicle). Use photocopiable page 76 if you wish.

Remind the children that they need to measure the distances and record them as they are working. They could go on to make a graph of their findings, using the graphing tool available on the CD-ROM.

ASSESSMENT

Note those children who show an understanding of how to organise and carry out a fair test and those who are making accurate recordings of their results.

PLENARY

Talk to the children about their test. *What have you found out? How did you organise the test to keep it fair? Did the height of the ramp make a difference? Did the vehicle travel furthest when the ramp was as high as possible or was there a 'best height' somewhere in the middle?* Go through some of the recording sheets with the children and discuss how they have recorded their findings.

OUTCOMES
● Can carry out a fair test with help.
● Know that ramp height affects the distance a vehicle travels.

ENRICHMENT
Lesson 7 ◖ Introducing friction

Objective
● To know that there is a force of friction between two surfaces.
● To know that friction is stronger between rough surfaces than smooth surfaces.
● To plan and carry out a simple fair test with help.

Vocabulary
friction, force, surface, rough, smooth, rub, rubbing

RESOURCES 💿
Main activity: A large empty matchbox, a few matches, a bicycle. For each group of four; a force meter; a house brick with string tied around it and a loop at one end (see diagram, below); a range of surfaces of different degrees of roughness (tiled floor, rough carpet, plastic, linoleum and so on). Photocopiable page 76 (also 'Fair test' (red) from Unit 2b, from the CD-ROM) could be used if you wish.
Group activities: 1 The results obtained from pulling a brick across different surfaces in the Main activity, squared paper or graph paper for each child, writing and colouring materials. **2** 2p pieces; a range of surfaces of different roughness for each group, rulers.
ICT link: Graphing tool from the CD-ROM.

PREPARATION
Tie the string around each brick and put a loop in it so that a force meter can be hooked into the loop (see diagram, below).

BACKGROUND
Whenever two surfaces slide over each other there is a force called friction acting between them which tries to oppose one surface moving over the other. This slows them down and even stops them if the force of friction is big enough. The smoother the surfaces are, the less friction there is between them. Most people have experienced this when walking on ice! When working on friction and investigating surfaces using wheeled vehicles and slopes, always put the surface to be investigated on the floor at the bottom of the slope. This allows the slope to give each vehicle the same (fair) gravitational pull before it hits the surface.

   The vehicle slows and stops partly because of the friction between the wheels and the surface. There is also a certain amount of friction between the axle and the surface that it is rubbing on, and some air resistance (another form of friction). In some cases (rubbing a match across the rough surface of a matchbox) the force of friction is converted into heat energy. Children can easily observe this by rubbing their hands together.

STARTER
Gather the children around you and ask them to rub their hands together vigorously. What is happening? *What can you feel?* (Their hands get warmer and warmer.) Tell the children that this is the result of a force called friction that acts whenever two surfaces rub together.

MAIN ACTIVITY
Strike a match. Explain to the children that there is a force called friction between the surface of a match and the rough surface on the side of the matchbox. That friction can also produce heat, just as when they were rubbing their hands together. Pass the empty matchbox around so that the children can feel the rough surface. Remind them that matches are dangerous and that they should never play with them.

   Turn the bicycle upside down on a table. Point out the brakes to the

Differentiation
Group activity 1
In Group activity 1, some children may have difficulty transferring the information from the recorded results onto their graph. You may wish to put some children into pairs to help each other.
Group activity 2
All the children should be able to take part in Group activity 2.

children and tell them that brakes work by friction. When you put the brakes on, one surface rubs against the other and the friction between the two surfaces slows the bike down and stops it. Spin the wheel and operate the brakes so that they can see this happening. Do this several times, asking them to watch closely.

Divide the children into groups of four or six (four would be better if you have enough equipment) and give each group a brick, a force meter, a range of surfaces to investigate and a copy of photocopiable page 76 if required. Make sure the children know how to read a force meter. Ask them to look at, and feel, the surfaces. *Which one do you think it will be harder to pull the brick over? Do you think that the smoother or the rougher surfaces will cause more friction?* Tell them to hook their force meter into the loop of string at the end of the brick, then pull the brick over the various surfaces. They should measure the force needed with the force meter and record the results. Tell the children not to record anything until the brick is moving because the force of friction is not acting until one surface is rubbing against another. Discuss the results with the children. *Was it easier to pull the brick across the rougher or smoother surfaces? Which surface caused the most friction? Which caused least?*

GROUP ACTIVITIES

1 As individuals, ask the children to use the results from their brick-pulling activity to construct a pie or bar chart showing how much force was needed to pull the brick over different surfaces. They could use the graphing tool on the CD-ROM to create their charts.
2 Put the children into groups of four and give them a range of surfaces of different roughness. Tell them that they are going to play 'Shove 2p'. Place each surface, in turn, on the table so that the edge of the surface is at the edge of the table. Place the 2p piece on the surface so that half of it is sticking over the edge of the table. Now shove the 2p with the flat of the hand to send it across the surface. Ask the children to predict the surface on which they think the 2p will travel farthest. Over the rough surface or the smooth surface? They can use a ruler to measure the distance the 2p has travelled and record their findings. Remind them that, in order to make the investigation as fair as possible, they need to try to use the same force for each 'shove'!

ASSESSMENT
During the Main activity note the children who are predicting that the rough surface will produce more friction than the smooth. During the Plenary session note those children who show an understanding that the force that is acting between two surfaces is friction and that the rougher the surface, the greater the friction.

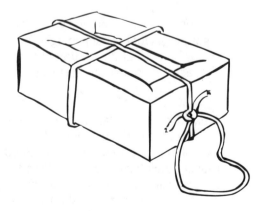

PLENARY
Ask the children to rub their hands together again. Can they tell you the name of the force that is acting when two surfaces are rubbing together? *When is the force of friction stronger?* (Between rougher surfaces.) Look at a few of the graphs with the children and ask some of them to come and interpret their graph, telling the class about their findings.

OUTCOMES
● Know that there is a force called friction acting between two surfaces.
● Know that the rougher the surface, the stronger the friction.
● Can plan and carry out a simple fair test with help.

LINKS
Maths: making graphs.

ENRICHMENT
Lesson 8 ▪ Rough or smooth?

Objective
● To know that friction is stronger between rough surfaces than smooth surfaces.

RESOURCES 💿
For each group: a wheeled vehicle, a ramp and stand (a shelf or plank on a pile of books will do), several surfaces (rough and smooth) to put on the floor at the bottom of the ramp, metre sticks, writing materials, a copy of photocopiable page 76 (also 'Fair test' (red) from Unit 2b, available on the CD-ROM).

MAIN ACTIVITY
Give each group their equipment (see Resources, above) and a copy of photocopiable page 76. Ask them to devise a test to find out which surface produces most friction. (The vehicle will travel the shortest distance on the surface with most friction.) Ask them to complete the first part of the sheet before doing the test, and then record their findings on it.

To keep their test fair they will need to use the same vehicle for each surface, keep the slope at the same height and start the vehicle in a fair way (without pushing), from the same place on the slope every time. Tell them that some groups will be asked to report to the whole class on how they organised their investigation and what they found out. Move around the groups as they are preparing to carry out their test, helping them where necessary.

ASSESSMENT
As you move around the groups note the level of the children's understanding and their ability to organise the test. Use the group recording sheets to inform your judgements. Note those children who are able to contribute sensibly during the Plenary session and who understand that the rougher the surface, the stronger the friction and its effect on the distance travelled by the vehicle.

PLENARY
Ask some of the groups to talk about how they managed their test and what they found out. Ask for the name of the force that is acting between the two surfaces. *When is friction stronger?*

Differentiation
Some groups may need more help with organising their test. You may wish to put the children into mixed-ability groups so that they can help each other.

OUTCOMES
● Know that the rougher the surface, the stronger the friction.
● Can plan and carry out a fair test with help.

ENRICHMENT
Lesson 9 ◦ A rough ride

Objective
● To know that the rougher the surface, the stronger the friction.

RESOURCES
A smooth slope and stand, a block of wood with coarse sandpaper stuck to one surface, a block of ice (freeze water in an empty tub or margarine pot roughly the same size as the block of wood), newspaper or paper towels for mopping up, writing and drawing materials.

MAIN ACTIVITY
Show the children the blocks of wood and ice. Ask them to point out which is rougher and which is smoother. *Which one do you think will slide down the slope more easily and quickly?* Try them out. *What happened? Did the smoother one slide more easily? Why?* (Because the rougher the surface, the stronger the friction, and that slows things down.) Ask the children to write about what happened, and why, and to draw pictures of the equipment.

Differentiation
More-confident learners will write what happened and why clearly and in detail. Some children may need help, and a list of words on a flipchart or board might be helpful.
Less confident learners may need to tell you their ideas. All the children should be able to draw the equipment. Some will be able to label it.

ASSESSMENT
Note the children's level of understanding from the way they answer your questions during the Main activity and the Plenary session. Use their writing to help you make judgements.

PLENARY
Ask some of the children to use their writing to tell everybody what was happening during the Main activity and explain why.

OUTCOME
● Know that rougher surfaces slide less easily because the friction is stronger.

ENRICHMENT
Lesson 10 ◦ Will it float or sink?

Objective
● To know that some objects float because water pushes up on them

Vocabulary
float, sink, push, pull, gravity, upthrust

RESOURCES
Main activity: One plastic tank or washing-up bowl per group (of four or six) filled with water; one small, empty margarine tub per group (or two per group of six); a selection of small heavy objects such as marbles, pebbles or washed gravel; paper towels for mopping-up!
Group activities: 1 A copy of photocopiable page 144 (also 'Will it float or sink?' (red), available on the CD-ROM) for each child; a flipchart or board, a tank or bowl for each group (as above) with a collection of objects, some of which will float and some of which will sink (stone, piece of wood, paper clip, cork, marble, lolly stick, coin and so on. Try to include some relatively light things that sink, like a paper clip, so that the misconception that light things always float is not reinforced). **2** A tank of water and two small empty plastic bottles with lids for each group.

PREPARATION
Write a list of the names of the objects to be used in Group activity 1 on the flipchart or board.

BACKGROUND
At this stage, children do not need to know about why things float or sink in any greater detail than in the outcome for this lesson. It is useful for you to have a bit more information in order to avoid reinforcing misconceptions and to help you answer the more difficult questions that able children

sometimes ask!

When an object is greater in density than water it sinks. It displaces the water molecules easily and sinks through the water because of the force of gravity. Water also exerts a force called 'upthrust'. When the upthrust of the water equals the weight of an object, that object floats. Plasticine is denser than water, so a ball of Plasticine occupying a volume of 50ml will displace 50ml of water, but will weigh more and therefore sink. If you then make the same piece of Plasticine into the shape of a boat it will have a greater volume and displace a larger amount of water than when it was rolled in to a ball. This amount of water weighs more than the boat itself does and so the boat will float.

STARTER
The story of Noah's Ark, or any story about boats and floating would be a good stimulus for this lesson. Some of the passages about Ratty and Mole going boating from *The Wind in the Willows* by Kenneth Grahame would also be suitable.

MAIN ACTIVITY
Remind the children about the work that they did in Year 1/Primary 2 when they pushed down on a ball that was floating and felt the water trying to push the ball up. They were feeling the upthrust of the water against the ball and when they let go of the ball it bobbed to the surface and floated again. Ask: *Do you remember that we talked about gravity in an earlier lesson? What does gravity do?* (Pull things down towards the centre of the Earth.)

Put the children into groups of four or six and give each group one or two empty margarine tubs (see Resources) plus a supply of small, heavy objects to load their tubs with until they sink. Groups of four would be preferable, but this may depend on how many tanks or bowls you can muster. Ask them to predict whether they think that their tub will float or sink when they put it on the water– then let them have a go.

Explain to them that their tubs float because the upward push of the water (upthrust) is greater than the force of gravity that is trying to pull them down and make them sink. Ask: *What do you think will happen if you load the margarine tub boats?* (They will sink.) Remind them that gravity is pulling down on everything, including the objects that they are going to load into their boats. Allow them to load their boats until they sink. Ask: *What do you think has happened? Why have the boats sunk?* (Because when the boats are loaded the force of gravity pulling down on the boat, plus the things in it, is greater than the force (upthrust) of the water pushing the boat up.)

GROUP ACTIVITIES
1 Give each group a tank of water and a collection of objects. Give each child a copy of photocopiable page 144. Ask the children to look carefully at the objects and predict whether they will float or sink, writing the name of the object (using the list on the flipchart to help them if necessary) and their prediction on the sheet. Set the sheets aside so that they don't get wet! The children should then place each object onto the water and make sets of things that float and things that sink. Mop up before checking the sets against the sheets! Ask: *Did you predict correctly?* Explain again that things float when the upthrust of the water is greater than the force of gravity pulling the object down and sink when the force of gravity pulling down is greater than the upthrust of the water.
2 Put the children into groups of four or six. Give each group a tank of water and one or two small, empty plastic bottles with lids. Ask the children to put the bottles in the water. *Do they float or sink?* Now ask them to fill each bottle, carefully replace the lid, and put them back in the water. *What*

Differentiation
Group activities 1 and 2
All the children should be able to take part in both these activities, but some may understand this difficult concept better than others.
To extend children in Group activity 2, use 'Will it float or sink?' (blue), from the CD-ROM, which asks the children to explain why some objects floated and others sank.

happens now? Ask the children if they can find a way to make the bottles float just below the surface of the water. (They need to partially fill the bottle and replace the top.) Remind them that when the bottles are floating the upthrust is greater than the pull of gravity. When they sink the reverse is true. When the bottles float just below the surface the increased weight of the bottle is not quite enough to overcome the upthrust of the water.

ASSESSMENT

During all the activities and the Plenary session note which children can answer your questions and show an understanding that an object floats due to the upward push of the liquid being greater than the downward pull of gravity.

PLENARY

Review what the children have done. *Why do things float? Why do they sink?* Look at some of the recording sheets from Group activity 1 and discuss them with the children. How accurate were their predictions?

OUTCOME

● Can recognise that an object floats due to the upward push of the liquid being greater than the downward pull of gravity.

Lesson 11 ▭ Assessment

Objective
● To know that forces can make moving objects go faster, change direction or slow down.
● To know that actions such as stretching, squeezing, twisting and turning can be explained as pushes and pulls.

RESOURCES ⊙

Assessment activities: 1 A copy of photocopiable page 145 (also 'Assessment – 1' (red), available on the CD-ROM) for each child; pencils. **2** A copy of photocopiable page 146 (also 'Assessment – 2' (red), available on the CD-ROM) for each child; pencils, a flipchart or board.
ICT link: 'Making things move' interactive activity, from the CD-ROM.

STARTER

Ask the children to remind you of some of the things they have learned in this unit. *What are forces? What do they do? How many different forces can you think of?*

ASSESSMENT ACTIVITY 1

Give each child a copy of photocopiable page 145. Go through it with them to make sure that they understand it and can read the words at the bottom of the page. Ask them to choose the correct words to complete the sentences.

ICT LINK ⊙

Children can complete this Assessment activity using the 'Making things move' interactive, from the CD-ROM.

ANSWERS

1 slow down
2 change direction
3 faster
4 higher
5 more slowly
6 ice is slippery; because ice is so smooth that there is little friction between it and shoes or skates.

LOOKING FOR LEVELS

All children should be able to answer at least three questions and most will answer at least five. As scientific understanding is being assessed rather than ability to write, accept a verbal explanation and annotate the child's sheet.

ASSESSMENT ACTIVITY 2

Give each child a copy of photocopiable page 146. Read the instructions at the top of the sheet with them, making sure that they understand what they have to do. Write 'push', 'pull' and 'push and pull' on the flipchart or board and remind the children that these are the forces they need to think about. Ask them to complete the sheet by writing the correct name of the force or forces being used underneath each of the pictures.

ANSWERS

1 pull
2 push and pull
3 push
4 push and pull
5 push and pull
6 push

LOOKING FOR LEVELS

All children should be able to complete at least four examples that appear on the sheet but some may write 'twist' rather than 'push and pull'. Some may have difficulty in thinking of any other examples of pushes and pulls.

Some children may need to explain their pictures to you. If the explanations show understanding, accept this and annotate the sheet. Most children should complete questions 1 to 6 correctly and be able to draw two examples of other pushes or pulls.

PHOTOCOPIABLE

Different forces – 1

◼ Write 'push' or 'pull' in the box under each picture.

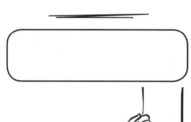

◼SCHOLASTIC

Illustration © Ann Kronheimer

Different forces – 2

33	40	39	38	**Finish**
32 Pull the light switch.	31	26	27 You fall out of a tree. Gravity pulls you down.	25
17	18	23	22	24 Push the ball down to make it bounce.
16	15	10	11	9
1 Push and pull yourself up a rope.	2	7	6	8

Gravity pulls you down the slide. (36 / 29 / 30)

Push and pull to climb the ladder. (21 / 28 / 37 / 20)

Pull your duck along to 14. (12 / 13 / 5 / 4)

Push yourself off the floor and jump up. (7 / 10)

Start

Illustration © Ann Kronheimer

PHOTOCOPIABLE

Will it float or sink?

Name of object	Prediction		Was your prediction correct? ✓ or ✗
	Will float ✓	Will sink ✓	

◣SCHOLASTIC

Assessment – 1

■ Complete these sentences with the correct words from the list below.

1. If I put the brakes on my bike will _____

2. When I hit the ball I am using a force to _____

3. If I push the car harder it will go _____

4. If I push the ball harder it will bounce _____

5. If I push the car less hard it will go _____

change direction	faster	more slowly	higher	slow down

■ Now write an answer to question 6.

6. Why do we slide about on ice? _____

_____

_____

_____

_____

Illustration © Ann Kronheimer

PHOTOCOPIABLE

Assessment – 2

■ Write the names of the forces being used in these pictures using the following choices: 'push', 'pull', 'push and pull'.

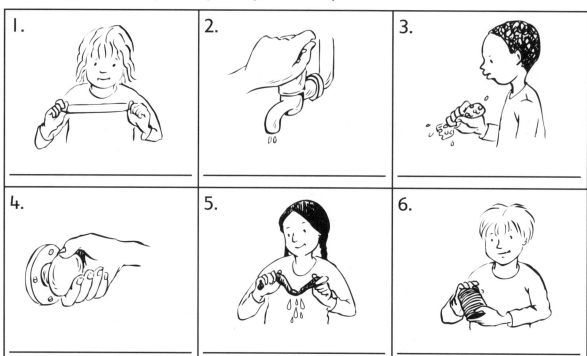

1.

2.

3.

4.

5.

6.

7. Draw two more pictures of a push force being used.

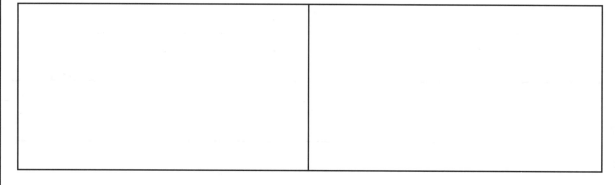

8. Draw two more pictures of a pull force being used.

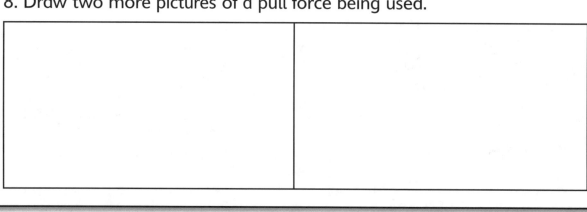

■SCHOLASTIC

CHAPTER 6 Using electricity

Lesson	Objectives	Main activity	Group activities	Plenary	Outcomes
Lesson 1 Using electricity	• To know that many appliances need electricity to make them work.	Look at a mains electrical appliance. Discuss how it is turned on and off. List other mains appliances.	Sort pictures of electrical appliances from other household objects. Identify the electrical appliances on a drawing of a house.	Work through both photocopiable group activities. Discuss the purposes of various household appliances.	• Can recognise a range of household electrical appliances. • Can identify the purposes of a range of household appliances.
Lesson 2 Matching game cards	• To know that electricity is obtained from the mains or from batteries (cells).	Sort electrical appliances into mains-operated and battery-operated.	Play card games to test knowledge of electrical appliances.	Discuss the usefulness of batteries and how some batteries can be recharged.	• Can distinguish between appliances that use batteries and ones that have to be plugged into the mains.
Lesson 3 Electricity snakes and ladders	• To know that electricity can be dangerous and must be treated with extreme care.	Write a list of rules for the safe use of electricity.	Make a poster to illustrate one of the rules. Play a board game to reinforce safety knowledge.	Discuss the usefulness of electricity, particularly for lighting.	• Understand that electricity can be dangerous. • Know some rules for keeping safe when using electricity.
Lesson 4 Torchlight test	• To plan and carry out a simple investigation with help.	Investigate a range of batteries to see which lasts the longest.	Use reference books to find out about situations where torches are used.	Review the investigation and the group work.	• Can plan and carry out a simple investigation in a group, with adult help.
Lesson 5 Mains and safety	• To know that electricity is used in many different ways. • To know that mains electricity can be very dangerous and must be treated with extreme care.	Revise safety rules. Look for devices, plugs and sockets around the school.	Make a plan of the classroom, marking on sockets and appliances. Suggest improvements. Write about the dangers of electricity and how to keep safe	Discuss electrical safety.	• Can identify electrical devices around the school. • Can explain why electricity should be treated with extreme care.
Lesson 6 Outdoor hazards	• To know that mains electricity can be very dangerous and must be treated with extreme care.	Consider safety outside – pylons, sub-stations, railway lines, lawnmowers – and the dangers of electricity and water.		Reinforce electrical safety.	• Can explain why electricity should be treated with extreme care.
Lesson 7 Match the battery	• To know that electricity can be supplied by batteries (cells).	Look at devices with and without batteries.	Complete a sheet matching batteries to devices. Practise putting batteries into devices to make them work.	Discuss how to insert batteries.	• Know that a range of devices use batteries for their electricity supply. • Can put a battery into a device and make it work.
Lesson 8 Circuits that will not work	• To know that a complete circuit is needed for a device to work. • To know the names of the components needed for a circuit to make a bulb light.	Make a circuit with a bulb.	Identify circuits that will not work and give reasons why. Make a circuit with two bulbs.	Talk about when a circuit works and name the components.	• Can make a simple circuit with one or more bulbs. • Can draw a circuit that works. • Can recognise why a simple circuit does not work. • Can name and label the components used to make a simple circuit.
Lesson 9 Buzzers and motors	• To make a circuit using buzzers and motors.	Make a circuit with a buzzer. Make a circuit with a motor.		Discuss and demonstrate the circuits that have been made.	• Can make a circuit including a buzzer or a motor.
Lesson 10 Switch it on	• To know that the flow of electricity in a circuit is controlled by a switch.	Use switches in a circuit.	Make a labelled drawing of a circuit with a switch. List electrical appliances that use a switch. Make a simple pressure switch.	Discuss the use of switches.	• Can make a switch and use it in a circuit. • Can make a drawing of a circuit with a switch.
Lesson 11 Circuit drawings	• To be able to record circuits as simple drawings.	Make and draw simple circuits.	Make a circuit from another child's drawing.	Decide which circuits will work and name components.	• Can record circuits as simple drawings.

Lesson	Objectives	Main activity	Group activities	Plenary	Outcomes
Lesson 12 Electrical models	• To know how to make a simple electrical device or model.	Discuss and plan how models could be made.	Apply knowledge to making models.	Demonstrate the finished models.	• Can make a simple electrical device or model.
Lesson 13 Using and misusing electricity	• To be able to identify appliances which need electricity to make them work. • To know the dangers of electricity.	Draw a flex and plug on things that need electricity to make them work.	Sort statements into sets of 'dangerous' and 'safe' actions.	Discuss answers to the worksheets.	• Can identify appliances which need electricity to make them work. • Can recognise the dangers of electricity.

Assessment	Objectives	Activity 1	Activity 2
Lesson 14	• To assess whether the children know that a complete circuit is needed for a device to work. • To assess whether the children know that mains electricity can be very dangerous and must be treated with extreme care.	Draw a complete circuit, labelling part appropriately using key words provided.	Write statements to describe how electricity is being used dangerously.

SC1
SCIENTIFIC
ENQUIRY

Make a circuit

LEARNING OBJECTIVES AND OUTCOMES
● To use first hand experience to answer questions.
● To think about what might happen and test their predictions.
● To review and explain their work to others.

ACTIVITY
Children are asked to predict what they will need to make a buzzer and a motor work (a complete circuit), and what would happen if they break the circuit. They make simple circuits to test their predictions.

LESSON LINKS
This Sc1 activity forms an integral part of Lesson 9, Make a circuit.

Lesson 1 ▫ Using electricity

Objective
● To know that many appliances need electricity to make them work.

Vocabulary
electricity, electric, appliance, mains, plug, flex, socket, dangerous, shock, generated

RESOURCES 💿
Main activity: A table lamp, computer or other mains electrical appliance.
Group activities: 1 Photocopiable page 166 (also 'Using electricity -1' (red), from the CD-ROM), A4 paper, scissors, adhesive. **2** An A3-sized copy of photocopiable page 167 (also 'Using electricity– 2' (red) , available on the CD-ROM); colouring materials.
Plenary: An A3 copy of photocopiable page 167, A3 paper.

BACKGROUND
Our mains electricity is mostly generated in power stations linked to the National Grid, and is brought into our homes via a system of cables that are either buried underground or carried overland by pylons. A small amount of electricity, in certain regions, is generated by water or wind power. At this stage, children need to know that electricity can be dangerous. Whenever you are working on the concept of electricity with children, always reinforce the potential hazards. Make it clear that the children should never play with mains appliances or touch the sockets. Very young children should not be allowed to plug anything into the mains themselves.

STARTER
Ask the class: *What do you know about electricity?* This gives the children a chance to voice their ideas, and gives you an opportunity to discover whether they have any misconceptions (such as the idea that electricity leaks, like water, out of the end of a wire that is attached to a battery).

MAIN ACTIVITY
Ask the children to look around the classroom. *Can you see anything that needs electricity to make it work?* Have a table lamp or computer switched off and unplugged. Show the children the plug and flex and ask whether they know the names of these parts of an appliance. *What has to be done to make something that uses electricity work?* (It has to be plugged in and switched on.) Explain and use the words 'appliance', 'plug', 'flex', 'electric', 'electricity', 'socket' and 'mains'. Reinforce the children's awareness that electricity can be dangerous, that young children should never plug things in for themselves and that mains electricity can give a very dangerous and painful electric shock. Explain that 'mains electricity' is generated (or made) in a power station and comes along wires to homes and schools.
Plug the appliance in and switch it on. Talk about the fact that it is using

Differentiation
Group activity 1
To support children in Group activity 1, use 'Using electricity 1' (green), from the CD-ROM, which contains a smaller selection of electrical and non-electrical items to sort. To extend children, use 'Using electricity 2' (blue), which includes a wider range.
Group activity 2
To extend Group activity 2, give children 'Using electricity 2' (blue), which asks children to name as well as colour in the electrical items.

electricity from the mains, and that it doesn't work when it is not plugged in. Switch the classroom lights on and off and explain that they, too, use mains electricity; but they do not have to be plugged in every time, like lamps and computers, because they have more permanent connections.

Can the children think of anything at home that uses mains electricity, has a flex and a plug, and has to be plugged into a socket to make it work? List their suggestions on the board. Can they think of anything that is used in the garden (such as a lawnmower)?

GROUP ACTIVITIES
1 Give each child a copy of page 166 and a sheet of A4 paper. Ask the children to divide the blank sheet into columns labelled 'Yes' and 'No' and then cut out the pictures, sorting them according to whether or not they use electricity. The children should then stick the pictures into the correct columns on the sheet. Ask the children to think, and talk to each other, about what the things in the 'Yes' column are used for.
2 Give each child, pair, or group of three an A3-sized copy of photocopiable page 167. Ask them to find all the things in the picture that use electricity and colour them in.

ASSESSMENT
Ask the children to name two or three appliances that use mains electricity. Ask them to describe what needs to be done to make these appliances work.

PLENARY
Pin up an A3 sheet with the heading 'Uses electricity' and divided into 'Yes' and 'No' columns. Go through the collection of pictures from photocopiable page 166 and ask the children to indicate whether each one should be put in the 'Yes' or the 'No' column. Stick the pictures in the correct columns. Ask all the children to check their own sheets. Look together at the picture on page 167. Ask the children to name the appliances and to say what each one is used for.

OUTCOMES
● Can recognise a range of household electrical appliances.
● Can identify the purposes of a range of household appliances.

Lesson 2 ▪ Matching game cards

Objective
● To know that electricity is obtained from the mains or from batteries (cells).

Vocabulary
batteries, mains, electricity, electric, appliance, mains, plug, flex, socket, dangerous, shock

RESOURCES
Main activity: A battery; a collection of appliances that use mains electricity only or batteries only (such as a torch, a table lamp, a kettle, a toaster, a personal stereo and a mobile phone); pictures of things that use mains electricity and of things that use batteries. Make sure that all the electrical appliances that use mains electricity have their flex with them, and that any appliance (such as a mobile phone) that uses rechargeable batteries have their charger flex and plug with them.
Group activities: 1 Sets of picture cards from photocopiable page 168 (also 'Matching game cards (red), available from the CD-ROM), mounted on stiff card and laminated. Base boards made from photocopiable page 168. **2** and **3** Sets of picture cards, as in Group activity 1.

PREPARATION
Make sets of cards from page 168. Cut out and colour the pictures, then mount them on card and laminate them (or cover them with sticky-backed plastic) for durability. Make base boards using the whole page, in a similar way. You will need a base board and set of cards for each child.

BACKGROUND
Some electrical appliances work on quite a low voltage, and can therefore be operated using batteries that provide a low-voltage supply. Other equipment may require a higher voltage in order to work, and thus may have to be connected to the mains supply.

Rechargeable batteries should not be used in situations where the children have direct access to them. In certain circumstances they can discharge all their energy at once, creating a great deal of heat. Children could receive a nasty burn if this happens. All batteries contain caustic substances, and should never be taken apart.

STARTER
Remind the class about the dangers of electricity and of putting anything into a mains socket. Talk to the children about what they did and what they learned in Lesson 1. Ask them if they can remember and name some of the appliances that they identified as using mains electricity.

MAIN ACTIVITY
Show the children a battery (cell). Discuss what it is. Warn the children of the danger of trying to take a battery apart: the contents are very harmful. Ask: *Can you think of anything that just uses batteries to make it work, and doesn't have to be plugged into the mains?* Show the collection of electrical appliances to the children and ask whether they can identify any of these.

Name the items and talk about what they are used for. Now ask the children to sort the collection into things that need to be plugged into the mains and things that use batteries. If some children say 'Both' for such items as a radio, put these between the sets and discuss this with the children. Ask them whether they can suggest any more things that use batteries or mains electricity.

GROUP ACTIVITIES
1 Play 'Electricity Lotto'. Each child will need a set of cards (from page 168) and a corresponding base board (also from page 168). Explain the rules of the game to the children, and sort them into groups of four or six. The cards are shuffled and placed face-down on the table. The children take turns to pick up a card. If they can name the appliance and say whether it uses the mains, batteries or either, they can put the card over the corresponding picture on their base board. If they cannot answer correctly, the card is returned to the bottom of the pack. The first child to cover every picture on his or her base board is the winner. Encourage them to talk about the pictures as they pick them up: can they explain what each appliance does?
2 Play 'Appliance Snap'. Sort the children into groups of four, with a set of cards per child. After saying 'Snap', a child has to say whether the appliance uses batteries or the mains before he or she can claim the pile of cards.
3 Use two sets of cards to play Pelmanism – each child takes it in turn to turn over two cards to find matching pairs.

ASSESSMENT
Ask the children to explain where they might find a supply of electricity. (Mains sockets or batteries.) Can they name some appliances that use the mains supply and some that use batteries?

PLENARY
Ask the children why they think batteries are useful. (They allow things to be used more flexibly; they make things more portable; some appliances can be used where there is no mains supply available.) *Where might there be no mains supply?* You could listen to the radio in the garden, use a cordless drill in the shed, or use a mobile phone in the street. *Why would it be inconvenient to have to connect these devices to the mains supply every*

time you used them? Explain the difference between an ordinary battery and a rechargeable one: an ordinary battery has to be thrown away when it no longer works, but a rechargeable one can be plugged in to a charging unit which in turn is plugged into the mains. It can then be re-used.

OUTCOME
● Can distinguish between appliances that use batteries and ones that have to be plugged into the mains.

Lesson 3 ▪ Electricity snakes and ladders

Objective
● To know that electricity can be dangerous and must be treated with extreme care.

Vocabulary
dangers, dangerous, care, shock, pylon, sub-station

RESOURCES ◉
Main activity: A large sheet of white paper, a large felt-tipped pen.
Group activities: 1 Drawing and painting materials, large sheets of art paper. **2** 'Electricity snakes and ladders' gameboards (see Preparation), dice, shakers, counters.

PREPARATION
Make one A3-sized copy of page 169 (also 'Electricity snakes and ladders' (red), available on the CD-ROM) per group. Colour it in, mount it on thick card and laminate it (or cover it with sticky-backed plastic) for durability.

BACKGROUND
Electricity can be fun and exciting, but can also be very dangerous. Working with batteries up to 6V is quite safe, and children can have a great deal of fun experimenting with these in circuits. Rechargeable batteries should not be used where the children have direct access to them, and batteries should never be taken apart. Some children may be curious about what the 'V' on a battery stands for – it is 'volts'. The voltage (or difference in electrical potential between the two terminals) determines the 'push' given to the electricity in the circuit. The higher the voltage, the greater the 'push'.

Electricity pylons may carry 30,000V, and are therefore extremely dangerous. Electricity sub-stations may carry even higher voltages, and should be avoided. Most batteries are between 1.5 and 9V.
Other electrical units that you may encounter (the children do not need to know these at this stage) are ohms and amps. Amps (A) measure the current or flow of electricity. An electrical current will flow very easily through some materials. Other materials are more resistant, and this resistance is measured in ohms (Ω).

STARTER
Talk to the children about the things they have learned from their work on electricity. Discuss some of their ideas about the dangers of electricity. *What dangerous things might some people do?*

MAIN ACTIVITY
Working with the whole class, devise a set of rules to keep people safe from the dangers of electricity. Ask the children for suggestions and make a list on the board, flipchart, or whiteboard. Help the children to think of any important aspects they may have missed. Discuss the list and decide on the order of priority. *Is everything on this list sensible? Do you want to make any changes?* Make a new list with the most important rules at the top.

GROUP ACTIVITIES
1 Ask the children to make a poster to illustrate one of the rules, working individually or in pairs. Help them to decide which rule they are going to illustrate, so that there is a variety of posters for a class display.

2 Let groups of four play 'Electricity snakes and ladders', using a gameboard copied from page 169 (see Preparation).

ASSESSMENT
During the Plenary session, ask the children to describe some of the dangers associated with electricity. *Can you tell me some of the rules for keeping safe?*

PLENARY
Talk to the children about the dangers of electricity, and remind them of the rules they drew up for its safe use. Now talk about how useful electricity is, and list some of the things it helps us to do. For example, we can use electricity to keep us warm, to make toast or to boil a kettle. Mention the fact that hospitals rely on electricity to run the machines that save lives and help people to get better. Discuss the importance of electric light, and how difficult we would find it to manage without electricity these days. If you are doing this activity in the winter, try to save it for late in the afternoon when it is getting dark. Then switch off all the classroom lights and say to the children: *Now carry on with your work! What would you miss the most if there was no electricity?*

OUTCOMES
● Understand that electricity can be dangerous.
● Know some rules for keeping safe when using electricity.

Differentiation
Group activity 1
This activity is accessible to all.
Group activity 2
Some children may need help in reading the instructions for the board game. This could be overcome by the children working in mixed-ability groups and helping each other with the reading. Some groups will need initial adult support while playing the game.

Lesson 4 ▪ Torchlight test

Objective
● To plan and carry out a simple investigation with help.

Vocabulary
investigate, test, plan, last longest, fair, unfair, torch

RESOURCES
Main activity: Pictures of miners or pot-holers with torches on their hats; several torches, a range of different torch batteries, a timer with an alarm, an A3-sized copy of photocopiable page 170 (also 'Torchlight test' (red), available on the CD-ROM).
Group activity: Reference books with information about other contexts in which electric torches are used.

PREPARATION
Obtain several torches that are of the same size and type and use batteries of the same voltage. Choose a selection of batteries of the same voltage for example, an ordinary cheap one and two different 'long-lasting' ones. Each battery and torch needs to be colour-coded, so that the children can record which battery is in which torch.

BACKGROUND
Children are not expected to have an understanding of fair testing until well into Key Stage 2 but they need to be given opportunities to discuss and participate in simple tests from an early stage, in order to develop their skills and begin to understand the concepts. Very often, children will be ready to understand when a test is not fair long before they can identify and manipulate variables in order to conduct a fair test. It is a good idea to talk to them about how to make a test fair, and to ask questions that highlight unfairness. *If we turn the torches on at different times, will that be fair? If the batteries are all in different kinds of torches, will all the batteries be getting the same chance?*

STARTER
Remind the children how useful electric light is, and how difficult they found it to work when it was getting dark and the lights were turned out. Talk

about how miners wear torches on the front of their hats when they go down a mine. Show the children some pictures of this and/or of other uses of electric torches.

MAIN ACTIVITY
Children at this age should be given opportunities to plan and carry out a simple investigation with help. Ask the class: *Can you think of a time when torches would be really useful? What about putting out the rubbish on a winter's night? Walking home with mum or dad when you have been round to a friend's house in the evening? Reading under the bedclothes?* Show the children the torches and the batteries. Tell them that they are going to do an investigation to find out which battery will last the longest.

Read the information on the battery packets with the children, pointing out that some packets say the batteries will last an especially long time. Ask them: *Which one do you think will last the longest? Why? What will you need to do to find out? Can you think of a good way to make the test fair?* Ask further questions such as: *Do you think, if we are using different batteries, then all the torches should be the same to make it fair? Would it be fair if we turned the torches on and off at different times? How often do you think we need to check the torches to see if the batteries are still working?* (A sensible answer would be: 'Every half hour or hour.') *Do you think you need to record anything while you are doing the investigation?* (They may suggest that each look at the torches should be recorded with its time.)

Help the children to set up the activity and leave the torches shining. A rota of children should look at the torches during the day and record whether they are still bright, recording on a class record sheet (an A3 copy of page 170). You might find it useful to set a timer to ring each hour to remind you that it is time to check. If any (or all) of the torches are still shining at the end of the day, ask the children: *What do we need to do now to keep the test fair and carry on tomorrow?* (Turn all of the torches off at the same time, then turn them all on again together the next day.)

GROUP ACTIVITY
Working as individuals, in pairs or in groups of three, ask the children to use reference books to find out what kind of people use torches in their work. (Miners, divers, firefighters, police and so on.) How many different examples can they find? Ask them to make a list. (If they are working individually, a lot of reference material will be needed.)

ASSESSMENT
Note which children show an understanding of when a test is not fair, and which children are aware of the importance of making regular observations and recording them.

PLENARY
Ask the children which of the batteries lasted the longest. *How do you know?* Discuss the record sheet and what it shows. *Did the one you thought would last the longest actually last the longest? Are the claims on the packet true?* Remind them of how they did the test and how they made it fair: that the different batteries all had to go into the same type of torch, and that the torches had to be switched on and off at the same times. Discuss the usefulness of torches, and when and where they are used.

OUTCOME
● Can plan and carry out a simple investigation in a group, with adult help.

LINKS
Maths: measuring time.

Lesson 5 ▪ Mains and safety

Objective
● To know that electricity is used in many different ways.
● To know that mains electricity can be very dangerous and must be treated with extreme care.

Vocabulary
danger, dangerous, safe, safety, appliance, plug, socket, pylon, sub-station, electrified

RESOURCES
Main activity: The inside environment of the school, a copy of the electricity safety rules generated in Lesson 3.
Group activities: 1 An outline plan of the classroom for each child, writing and drawing materials. **2** Writing and drawing materials.

PREPARATION
Prepare and photocopy an outline plan of the classroom for each child.

BACKGROUND
Children need to understand that electricity is very useful, even essential, but they also need to understand that it can be very dangerous. Make it clear that children should never play with mains appliances or touch electrical sockets.

STARTER
Ask the children what they can remember about electricity safety. This will tell you what they have retained and if they have any misconceptions.

MAIN ACTIVITY
Read out the safety rules devised in Lesson 3 to the whole class. Explain that in this lesson they will be learning more about electricity and then, at the end of the lesson, they will have a chance to improve or add to the safety rules, if they think they need to.

Tell the children that they are going to walk around the school looking for all the different ways in which the school uses electricity. Explain that they are also going to look for where and how the electricity is delivered. Tell them that wiring circuits are buried in the walls and can't be seen – all we can see of them are the switches to turn the lights on and off and the sockets into which electrical appliances can be plugged.

Walk around the school and look for computers, sound systems, tape recorders, radios, televisions, ceiling lights, vacuum cleaners, floor polishers, fridges, microwaves, electric kettles and so on. Find out if the school has any extension leads and why they are needed. (Multiple plugs in a single socket can cause a dangerous overload.) Perhaps they are needed to operate an appliance some distance from a socket (perhaps a sound system outside on sports day), or the sockets may be in the wrong place. Are the extension leads covered safely or tucked away under furniture so that no one can trip over them? If possible, take the children to look at the electricity meter that measures the electricity that the school uses.

GROUP ACTIVITIES
1 Give each child an outline plan of the classroom and explain that they are going to make an electrical plan of the classroom. Look at the plan with them to make sure that they understand, for example, where the doors and windows are. Ask them to look around and mark on the plan all the electrical sockets and appliances in the room. Then ask them to discuss, in groups of four or six, whether they think the sockets are in the best places. *Could you improve the positioning of the sockets? Are there any long flexes because an appliance, like a computer, is some distance from where it is plugged in? Are the light switches in the most convenient place?* Ask them to use a different colour to mark where they think the sockets would be better placed.
2 Allow the children, in groups, to discuss the dangers of electricity and what they need to do or think about to keep themselves safe. Ask them to writing about this. They could illustrate their writing if they wish.

ASSESSMENT

Use the children's work to help you make judgements about the level of their understanding. During the Plenary session, note which children have sensible ideas and a good understanding of the dangers of electricity and how to keep safe.

PLENARY

Ask the children to tell you what they saw as they walked around the school. *How many different appliances did you see? Were there any extension leads and what were they used for?* Look at some of the plans of the classroom. *Are there enough sockets? Are they in the best places? Has anyone thought of a better place for them? If they were changed would it make the classroom more convenient? Why?*

Read some of the children's writing about electrical safety and discuss their ideas. Make sure that they understand that too many plugs in one socket can be dangerous and could cause a fire. Remind them of the dangers of trailing flexes. Go through the rules again and ask the children if they would like to amend, add to or improve them.

OUTCOMES
- Can identify electrical devices around the school.
- Can explain why electricity should be treated with extreme care.

Lesson 6 ▪ Outdoor hazards

Objective
- To know that mains electricity can be very dangerous and must be treated with extreme care.

RESOURCES

'Understanding electricity' videos (these can sometimes be obtained from electricity suppliers); pictures of an electric lawnmower, pylons, sub-stations, railway lines.

MAIN ACTIVITY

Gather the children around you and ask them to tell you about some of the things they learned in the last lesson. Remind them that they looked for electricity inside, and tell them that now they are going to think about the dangers of electricity outside. Show them the pictures of the pylons and the sub-stations and tell them that both these things carry electricity. They are very dangerous and no one should ever go near them. If they ever see children playing near a sub-station or pylons they should tell a grown-up immediately. Show them the picture of the railway line and ask if anybody knows why this is a very dangerous place to be even when there are no trains coming. (One of the lines may be electrified and touching it could kill you.) Railway lines are very dangerous because of the trains, and because of the electrified rail. Show the picture of the electric lawnmower and explain its dangers. Tell them also that they should never use electrical appliances near water because water is a very good conductor of electricity; if the appliance falls into the water and anyone has contact with the water, the electricity could kill them.

ASSESSMENT

During the Main activity and the Plenary session, note those children who volunteer sensible ideas and show a good understanding of the dangers of electricity.

PLENARY

Show the video, if you have one, and discuss and reinforce all the aspects of electrical safety covered in the lesson.

OUTCOME
● Can explain why electricity should be treated with extreme care.

Lesson 7 ▪ Match the battery

RESOURCES 💿
Main activity: A collection of devices that run on batteries (radios, torches, cameras, toys, tape recorders, clocks) and their batteries. The items you choose should use a variety of battery types.
Group activities: 1 A copy of photocopiable page 171 (also 'Match the battery' (red), available on the CD-ROM) for each child, writing materials.
2 The collection of devices from the Main activity and their batteries.

PREPARATION
Check that everything works, then remove the batteries from all the devices you are going to use, but keep them to hand.

BACKGROUND
Many electrical appliances work using batteries. These appliances only require a low voltage and can therefore be operated by batteries that provide a low voltage supply. Some appliances, such as portable radios can work using either batteries or mains electricity. The Volt is a way of measuring electricity. A transformer converts mains electricity (which is usually 230-240V in Britain) to the lower voltage required by an appliance. Technically, the single battery should be called a 'cell' and it may be appropriate to introduce this term to the children.

Rechargeable batteries can sometimes discharge all their energy at once, creating a great deal of heat and children could receive a nasty burn if this happens. They should not be used in situations where the children have direct access. Batteries contain caustic substances and should never be taken apart.

STARTER
With the children around you, ask them to tell you some of the things that they have learned about electricity so far in this unit of work. Show the children one of the things from the collection of devices and tell them that this also works by electricity, but it does not have to be plugged into the mains supply.

MAIN ACTIVITY
With the children, look at the collection of devices without their batteries in. Try to switch one on: *Why won't it work?* Choose one or two devices and decide which battery goes in which device. Fit the batteries into them and switch them on. Tell the children that the battery supplies the electricity that the device needs to make it work. Look at the collection and the separate batteries again. How can they find out which battery is needed for each appliance? Look for information on the appliance and match it to the correct battery. (Look for voltage labels too.)

Invite the children to try fitting the batteries into the devices to make them work. *Which way do they go in?* Repeat this until all the children have had a go at putting a battery or batteries into one appliance and have successfully made it work.

GROUP ACTIVITIES
1 Give each child a copy of photocopiable page 171. Go through the sheet with them and make sure that they understand what they have to do. Tell them to choose devices from the collection and draw them, together with

the batteries they need to make them work.

2 Practise putting batteries into devices and making them work. Put the children into groups of four and give each group (if possible) two devices and their batteries. Allow the children to explore and practise putting the batteries into the devices and making them work. If you have a range of appliances, groups could swap when they have succeeded with their first two. Observe the groups as they are working, and ask questions about whether there is a right way and a wrong way to put the batteries in, how the children knew which battery to choose, and so on.

ASSESSMENT
Look at the work the children have done in Group activity 1. Note their answers to your questions in Group activity 2 and during the Plenary.

PLENARY
Ask the children to tell you what they have learned about how to put batteries into the devices in order to make them work. *How can you find out which battery a particular appliance needs?* (Read the label or instructions.) *Is there a right way and a wrong way to put them in?* (There is usually a guide on the appliance to say which way the battery or batteries should be fitted.) Look at some of the work from Group activity 1 and discuss it with the children.

OUTCOMES
● Know that a range of devices use batteries for their electricity supply.
● Can put a battery into a device and make it work.

LINKS
Technology: assembling components.

Lesson 8 ■ Circuits that will not work

Objective
● To know that a complete circuit is needed for a device to work.
● To know the names of the components needed for a circuit to make a bulb light.

RESOURCES 💿
Main activity: For each pair: writing and drawing materials; a battery (the 6V lantern batteries are best. Do not use rechargeable batteries – see Background to Lesson 7); two wires with crocodile clips; a bulb in a bulb holder mounted on a board (see diagram). Components mounted in this way are easier for the children to use since they can make a more positive connection with crocodile clips.
Group activities: 1 Copies of photocopiable page 172 (also 'Circuits that will not work' (red), available on the CD-ROM) for each child, writing materials. **2** As for the Main activity, but with the addition of a second bulb in a bulb holder and two more wires with crocodile clips.

BACKGROUND
At this stage, children are required to be able to make circuits and to understand that a complete circuit is needed to make an electrical device, such as a bulb, motor or buzzer, operate. Ensure that any batteries are the same voltage as the bulbs, buzzers and motors that you are using. For example, if you use a 6V battery with a 1.5V bulb, the bulb will blow as soon as the circuit is complete. Do not use rechargeable batteries for making circuits as in certain circumstances, such as a short circuit, the battery may discharge all its power in one surge and become dangerously hot.

MAIN ACTIVITY
Divide the children into pairs and give each pair the components to make a simple circuit. Go through the equipment they have been given, asking the

Vocabulary
battery, bulb, bulb holder, wires, crocodile clips, circuit, complete, break, simple, components

children to name each component, or naming it for them if they can't. Ask the children to use the equipment they have been given to make the bulb light.

Allow the children to investigate the equipment for themselves, intervening eventually, but only to help those who are struggling and becoming frustrated. *What did you need to do to make the bulb light?* (Connect the battery and bulb together using the wires to make a complete circuit.) Ask

the children to take their circuit apart. *Can you make it again?* Ask the children to detach one end of one of the wires and break the circuit. *Does the circuit work now?* Tell the children to reattach that wire and break the circuit somewhere else. *What happens? Will the circuit work if there is a break in it anywhere?* Finish the session by asking the children to draw a complete circuit and label the component parts. You may wish to put a word list on the board or flipchart to help them.

GROUP ACTIVITIES
1 Give each child a copy of photocopiable page 172 and ask them to explain why each of the circuits would not work.
2 In their pairs, ask the children to make a circuit, but this time lighting two bulbs. Allow them to explore initially, but check that they do not make both bulbs light by putting two wires on each battery terminal and making two separate circuits. Explain this and say that only one wire is allowed on each terminal (see diagram, below), then ask them to try again.

ASSESSMENT
Use the photocopiable sheet from Group activity 1 to help assess the children. Observe them as they are working to judge the level of their understanding.

PLENARY
If possible, project the photocopiable sheet onto a whiteboard and ask the children to tell you how to complete each circuit so that it will work. Invite the children to label the components shown in the diagrams. Make sure they understand that a complete circuit is needed for the bulb to light up.

Differentiation
Group activity 1
For children who need support use 'Circuits that will not work' (green), which asks them to complete the diagrams to make the circuits work, rather than explaining in writing why they would not work. To extend children use 'Circuits that will not work' (blue), which asks them to label the part of the circuits as well as explain why they will not work.
Group activity 2
All the children should be able to take part in Group activity 2, although you may need to intervene and help children if they are unable to make both bulbs light without putting two wires into each battery terminal. You may wish to organise the children into mixed-ability pairs so that they can help each other.

OUTCOMES
● Can make a simple circuit with one or more bulbs.
● Can draw a circuit that works.
● Can recognise why a simple circuit does not work.
● Can name and label the components used to make a simple circuit.

LINKS
Technology: assembling components.

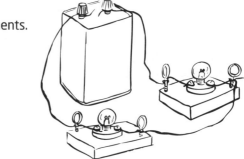

Lesson 9 ◗ Buzzers and motors

RESOURCES
As for Lesson 8, Group activity 1, with the addition of a buzzer mounted on a board and a motor mounted on a board; writing and drawing materials. If a buzzer fails to work try connecting it the other way round. A buzzer needs to be connected positive (+) to positive (+), and negative (–) to negative (–).

MAIN ACTIVITY
Working in pairs, ask the children to make circuits that include a buzzer, and then a motor. *What do you need to make a buzzer and a motor work?* (A complete circuit.) *What happens if you break the circuit?* Children could draw and label their buzzer and motor circuits.

ASSESSMENT
Observe the children as they are working and ask them to tell you what they need to do to make the buzzer and motor work. (Make complete circuits.)

PLENARY
Ask the children to tell you what they have done (you may wish some children to demonstrate their circuits) and what is needed to make a buzzer and a motor work.

OUTCOME
● Can make a circuit including a buzzer or a motor.

ENRICHMENT
Lesson 10 ◗ Switch it on

RESOURCES
Main activity: One or two electrical appliances (such as a table lamp or a kettle) that are turned on and off by the use of a switch; soft wood or fibreboard blocks, drawing pins, paper clips, circuit equipment as in Lesson 9.
Group activities: 1 Writing and drawing materials. **2** Folded cards (old Christmas or birthday cards will do), cooking foil, adhesive tape, scissors, circuit equipment as in Lesson 4.

BACKGROUND
A switch in a circuit is a convenient way of completing and breaking circuits in order to turn lights and other electrical appliances on and off. When the switch is open the circuit is broken and the flow of electricity interrupted; when the switch is closed the circuit is completed and the electricity is able to flow. Children in Year 2/Primary 3 need to experience the completing and breaking of a circuit with a simple switch and to understand that the switch is being used for this purpose. Learning about more sophisticated switches such as dimmer, and perhaps tilt, switches will come towards the end of Key Stage 2. Although commercial switches can be bought to put into circuits, they are enclosed and it is not possible to see how they operate. It is best if the children have the experience of making their own switch (see diagram) and putting it into a circuit.

In Group activity 2 the children will enjoy making and operating a simple pressure switch (see diagram, below). This will show them that there is more than one type of switch. The principle is the same as the switch that they will make in Group activity 1, or as in Lesson 8 when they completed and broke their circuits just by attaching or removing a wire.

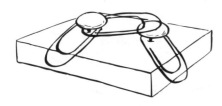

STARTER

Talking to the whole class, ask the children to remind you about what they learned in Lesson 8, when they were making circuits. Talk about how a complete circuit was needed to make their bulb light and that when the circuit was broken the bulb did not work. Tell them that they are now going to make switches to turn their bulb on and off.

MAIN ACTIVITY

Turn the electrical appliances that you have on and off so that the children can see that when switched on the appliance works and when switched off it does not. Explain that opening the switch interrupts the flow of electricity around the circuit and the circuit is broken. When the switch is closed the circuit is complete, the electricity can flow, and the appliances work. Relate this to the work the children did in Lesson 8.

Turn the classroom lights on and off and explain to the children that wherever there is a switch it works to complete or break a circuit. Put the children into pairs and give each pair a set of components. Demonstrate how to make a switch using paper clips and drawing pins (see diagram below). Ask the children to make a switch using paper clips and drawing pins (see diagram on page 160) and put it into a circuit so that they can turn their bulb on and off by completing or breaking the circuit.

GROUP ACTIVITIES

1 As individuals, ask the children to draw the circuit with the switch in it that they have made and then to label their drawing. (You may want to put a list of words on the flipchart or board to help them.) Underneath their drawing they can make a list of some electrical appliances that use a switch to turn them on and off.
2 Again in pairs, use the materials provided to make a simple pressure switch and include it in a circuit (see diagram, above). A fun extension of this activity is for one pair's pressure switch to be included in a circuit containing a buzzer. Place the pressure switch under a thin mat just inside the door so that anyone entering the classroom closes the switch and makes the buzzer buzz.

ASSESSMENT

Observe and question the children during the Main activity and note their level of understanding. Use their drawing of a circuit to help you make judgements.

PLENARY

Ask the children to tell you what a switch in a circuit is used for. *How does it work?* Look at some of the pressure switches that the children have made and ask them to demonstrate them. Ask: *Do these pressure switches work in the same way as the other switches? What is happening to the circuit as the switch is opened and closed?*

OUTCOMES

● Can make a switch and use it in a circuit.
● Can make a drawing of a circuit with a switch.

LINKS

Technology: making a switch.

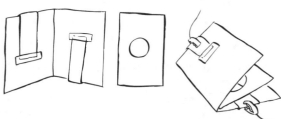

Lesson 11 ▪ Circuit drawings

Objective
● To be able to record circuits as simple drawings.

RESOURCES
Main activity: Components to make simple circuits – wires, batteries, bulbs, buzzers and so on.
Group activity: writing and drawing materials.

BACKGROUND
Children need to be able to record the simple circuits they have made and the easiest way for them to do this is by drawings. At this stage they will draw a representation of the actual component. Later they will learn to represent components by symbols.

STARTER
Remind the children of the work they have in other lessons in this unit. Can they tell you what is needed to make a complete circuit? Can they name the simple components?

MAIN ACTIVITY
Ask the children to use the components to make simple circuits and to draw each one as they make it. They should make, draw and label circuits that will or will not work. Ask them to make as many circuits as they can from the equipment they have. Can they remember how to make a switch to turn their bulb on and off?

GROUP ACTIVITY
Ask the children to exchange their drawings with another child. Can they make the circuits from their friend's drawings?

ASSESSMENT
During the Main activity note those children who can readily make several circuits and say why they will or will not work. Also note those children that can name and label components correctly.

Differentiation
The children will make models according to their abilities. Some children may get on better if they adapt a pressure switch that they have already had experience of.

PLENARY
Look at some of the circuit drawings that the children have made. Can they tell you which of them will work and name some of the components? Remind the children that making circuits using batteries is safe and fun but that they should never play with mains electricity.

OUTCOME
● Can record simple circuits as drawings.

Lesson 12 ▪ Electrical models

Objective
● To know how to make a simple electrical device or model.

Vocabulary
model, circuit, battery, wire, bulb, switch, wire cutters, buzzers, component, device

RESOURCES
Main activity: Battery, wire, bulb, switch.
Group activity: Batteries, wire, wire cutters, screwdrivers, card, paper, boxes, insulating tape, scissors, a flashing light bulb circuit (optional), bulbs, buzzers, adhesive, found materials as required, paint for decorating.

PREPARATION
Prepare a selection of bulb holders, buzzers, switches or motors (according to the models being made) ready-wired with about 15cm of wire from each terminal. Some children may be able to do this for themselves but it is quite a tricky job. The majority of children of this age will find it easier to attach an

extra length of wire to a prepared component by twisting the bare wires together and covering the join with insulating tape. The objective of this lesson is to make a simple model including an electrical circuit, not to spend the lesson chasing missing screws around the classroom!

BACKGROUND
Keep the models simple and with simple circuits. Leads with crocodile clips attached can be used but are rather cumbersome and it may be better to attach wires directly to the component being used (see Preparation). Circuits within models may be difficult for children to manage if the routing of the wires becomes complex. A very simple model of a room can be made by using a shoebox, pushing a bulb through a hole in the top to make a ceiling light. The wires can be taped to the outside of the box leading to a battery and switch at the back.

A soft drinks bottle can be used as the basis for a lighthouse. Make a hole in bottle near the base and thread the wires through and up to the top where the bulb holder will rest on the neck of the bottle. A flashing bulb will give a more realistic effect. Put a clear plastic cup over the bulb and finish off with decorations in order to make it look like a lighthouse.

Some children may have made a pressure switch in Lesson 10. This idea could be adapted to make an alarm which alerts the class of the end of a marble's run for example. Children may want more than one light, for the eyes on a robot and may unwittingly slip into making parallel circuits which could become too complicated. It may be better to make two separate circuits - one for each eye.

STARTER
Remind all the children that a complete circuit is needed if a device is to work. Ask a child to come out and make a simple circuit to make a bulb light.

MAIN ACTIVITY
Talk about how a simple circuit can be incorporated into a model to make it more interesting. Ask the children for ideas about what they could make and discuss the feasibility of their suggestions. You may wish to give more or less guidance on the models the children make according to your resources. Do not take too long over these discussions as the children will need lots of time to get on with their models.

GROUP ACTIVITY
Divide the children into pairs or threes. Friendship groups work well in this type of activity and more than one pair of hands may help when trying to stick things together. Encourage the children to talk about what they are going to make and to think carefully about what they need before raiding the materials box! You may need more than one lesson to complete the models.

ASSESSMENT
Observe the children while they are making their models and note those who have particular difficulties. During the Plenary session ask the children to explain how their model works.

PLENARY
Look at the finished models. Ask the children to demonstrate how they work.

OUTCOME
● Can make a simple electrical device or model.

LINKS
Technology: making models.

Lesson 13 ▸ Using and misusing electricity

Objective
● To be able to identify appliances which need electricity to make them work.
● To know the dangers of electricity.

RESOURCES ◉
Photocopiable page 173 (also 'Using and misusing electricity –1' (red), available on the CD-ROM), pencils, scissors, adhesive and photocopiable page 174 (also 'Using and misusing electricity – 2' (red) available on the CD-ROM.

STARTER
Ask the children to tell you something they have learned about electricity in this unit. Can they remember some of the special words that go with electricity? (Appliance, mains, plug, socket, flex and so on.)

MAIN ACTIVITY ◉
Give each child a copy of photocopiable page 173. Go through the pictures with the children to make sure they recognise each one. Ask them to draw a lead (or flex) and plug on all the things that need mains electricity to make them work.

Check that the children have drawn a lead and plug on the table lamp, washing machine, TV, computer, toaster, iron and vacuum cleaner. This could be completed as a class activity by showing 'Using and misusing electricity – 1' on an interactive whiteboard and using the drawing tools to annotate the worksheet on screen.

GROUP ACTIVITY
Give each child a copy of photocopiable page 174, scissors and adhesive. Ask the children to put their finger under each instruction as you read through them together.

Working in small groups, ask the children to cut out the instructions and stick each one into the correct box: 'dangerous' or 'safe'.

Differentiation
Main and group activities
Most children will manage these activities quite easily but others may need help with reading as they complete the worksheet on page 174.

PLENARY ◉
Discuss the answers to the worksheets; display 'Using and misusing electricity –1' and 'Using and misusing electricity – 2' on the interactive whiteboard and complete them as a class using the drawing tools.

OUTCOMES
● Can identify appliances which need electricity to make them work.
● Recognise the dangers of electricity.

Lesson 14 ▸ Assessment

Objective
● To assess whether the children know that a complete circuit is needed for a device to work.
● To assess whether the children know that mains electricity can be very dangerous and must be treated with extreme care.

RESOURCES ◉
Assessment activities: 1 A copy of photocopiable page 175 (also 'Assessment – 1' (red), available on the CD-ROM) for each child, pencils. **2** A copy of photocopiable page 176 (also 'Assessment- 2' (red), available on the CD-ROM) for each child, pencils.

STARTER
Ask the children to remind you of some of the things that they have learned about electricity and the benefits and dangers associated with it.

ASSESSMENT ACTIVITY 1
Give each child a copy of photocopiable page 175. Go through it with them

and make sure that they understand what is required. Ask them to complete the sheet by writing what is needed to make a device work and then drawing a complete circuit, labelling its parts using the words provided.

ANSWERS
1 Make a complete circuit with a bulb, a battery and two wires. **2** A drawing of a circuit which includes a battery, two wires and a bulb, all connected together correctly to form a complete circuit.

LOOKING FOR LEVELS
Most children should understand that a complete circuit is needed to make a bulb light. Some children may also list the equipment needed for the circuit. Most children should be able to draw a complete circuit and some will label the components of the circuit without help.

ASSESSMENT ACTIVITY 2
Give each child a copy of photocopiable page 176. Ask them to look carefully at the pictures and write why each one is dangerous.

ANSWERS
Accept any answer that conveys an understanding of the following:
1 The flex is trailing and could cause someone to trip.
2 The socket is overloaded and could cause a fire.
3 Pylons carry a high voltage of electricity so you should never play near them.
4 Electrical appliances should never be used near water; if the hairdryer fell into the bath the electricity could kill you.

LOOKING FOR LEVELS
Most children should be able to answer these questions correctly though some will only manage to answer questions 1 and 3. Some children will answer all the questions correctly and in detail. Accept correct verbal answers and note them on the children's sheets. Remember that you are assessing their scientific understanding, not their ability to write.

Using electricity – 1

Illustration © Ann Kronheimer

◼ SCHOLASTIC

Using electricity – 2

■ Colour in the things that use electricity.

Illustration © Ann Kronheimer

Matching game cards

◀ Play a game of 'electricity lotto' and say which of these objects use mains electricity and which use batteries.

Illustration © Ann Kronheimer

▲SCHOLASTIC

Electricity snakes and ladders

33	34	35	36	37	38	39	40
		Play on the pylons			Play near sub-station		**Finish**
32	31	30	29	28	27	26	25
Make sure friends stay away from sub-station							
17	18	19	20	21	22	23	24
			Switch light on with wet hands				
16	15	14	13	12	11	10	9
					Take radio into bathroom	Switch light off when leaving the room	
1	2	3	4	5	6	7	8
Start	Remember safety rules	Never poke things in sockets					

Illustration © Ann Kronheimer

PHOTOCOPIABLE

Torchlight test

■ Use this sheet to record the results of your investigation.

Battery	Time (hours)									
	1	2	3	4	5	6	7	8	9	10
1										
2										
3										
4										

■ Colour in a square for each hour that the battery lasts.

Illustration © Ann Kronheimer

■SCHOLASTIC

Match the battery

◼ Draw a picture of each device that you choose and the type of battery it needs to make it work.

◼ Write the voltage (V) of each battery on your picture.

PHOTOCOPIABLE

Circuits that will not work

◢ Look at each of these circuits and write why they will not work.

This circuit does not work because

_____

_____

_____

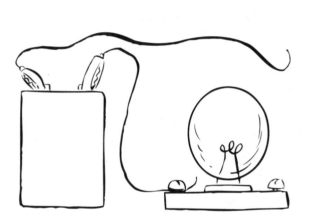

This circuit does not work because

_____

_____

_____

This circuit does not work because

_____

_____

_____

Illustration © Ann Kronheimer

◣SCHOLASTIC

Using and misusing electricity – 1

◀ Draw a lead and plug on all the things that need mains electricity to make them work.

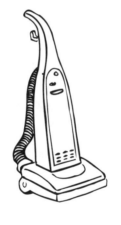

Illustration © Ann Kronheimer

PHOTOCOPIABLE

Using and misusing electricity – 2

dangerous

safe

◼ Cut out these instructions and stick each one into the correct box.

1. Poke something into a socket.	2. Allow grown-ups to plug things in for you.	3. Play near a sub-station.	4. Never play with electrical things near water.
5. Never go near a railway line.	6. Climb on pylons.	7. Never play near sub-stations.	8. Take a battery to pieces.

◖SCHOLASTIC

Assessment – 1

1. To make a bulb light up I need to _____

_____

_____

2. Draw a circuit that will make a bulb light up in the space below. Label the equipment you have used using the words below.

battery	wires	bulb

Assessment – 2

What is happening in the pictures below? Why is it dangerous?

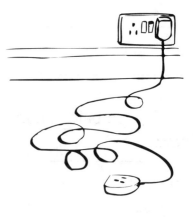

1. This is dangerous because _____

_____

_____

_____

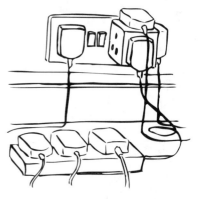

2. This is dangerous because _____

_____

_____

_____

3. This is dangerous because _____

_____

_____

_____

4. This is dangerous because _____

_____

_____

_____

Illustration © Ann Kronheimer

SCHOLASTIC

CHAPTER 7   The sky

Lesson	Objectives	Main activity	Group activities	Plenary	Outcomes
Lesson 1 What do you do in the sunshine?	• To know that the Sun is a sphere and that we see it in the daytime. • To understand the dangers of looking directly at the Sun.	Look at pictures of the Sun; discuss its shape and nature. Watch a tealight burn.	Write about sunshine activities. Make a large collage of the Sun, using the colours seen in the tealight flame.	Discuss the importance and dangers of sunlight.	• Know that we see the Sun during the day. • Know about the dangers of looking directly at the Sun.
Lesson 2 The Moon changes shape	• To know that the Moon is a sphere and we see it at night-time. • To know that the Moon appears to change its shape.	Discuss why the Moon's shape appears to change. Demonstrate using a ball and OHP. Observe the Moon in the sky.	Identify different shapes that represent phases of the Moon. Make a large collage of the Moon.	Review ideas about the phases of the Moon, and when we can see the Sun and the Moon.	• Know that the Moon is a sphere. • Know that we see it best when the sky is dark. • Know that the Moon appears to change its shape.
Lesson 3 The Sun, Moon and stars	• To distinguish the Sun and the Moon from the stars.	Watch a tealight burn. Discuss the nature and location of the Sun and the stars. Make a stars mobile.		Compare the Sun, Moon and stars; discuss when each can be seen.	• Can distinguish the Sun and Moon from the stars.
Lesson 4 Nocturnal	• To know that the pattern of day and night affects animals.	Discuss which animals are active at night and why. Talk about how humans cope with working night shifts.	Make a zigzag picture diary of their own day and night. Identify nocturnal animals from a selection of pictures.	Discuss the various reasons why animals (including people) may need to be active at night.	• Know the difference between day and night. • Know that some animals prefer to come out at night.
Lesson 5 Winter or summer?	• To know that the pattern of day and night changes with the seasons.	Discuss the seasonal changes in daylight hours. Use a display to represent the changes.	Draw summer and winter pictures. Draw or paint pictures of daytime or night-time activities.	Ask questions to help the children interpret the graph display.	• Know that the pattern of day and night changes according to the season.
Lesson 6 The Sun in the sky	• To know that the Sun appears to move across the sky in a regular way.	Make a class display of the apparent movement of the Sun.	Create and position collage shapes of a cat and a mouse. Order pictures of the Sun	Discuss the class display and the progress of the Sun.	• Can describe how the Sun appears to move across the sky.
Lesson 7 Seasonal change	• To know that the Sun is higher in the sky at midday in summer than in winter.	Compare pictures of the Sun and shadows in different seasons. Examine shadow lengths.	Interpret the results of the investigation. Draw a picture showing midday in either summer or winter.	Report findings.	• Know that the Sun is higher in the sky at midday in summer than in winter.
Lesson 8 The summer Sun	• To know that the Sun appears to have a longer path through the sky in summer than in winter.	Create a picture and measure the Sun's track.		Discuss the difference in hours of daylight in summer and winter.	• Know that the Sun appears to stay longer in the sky in summer than in winter.
Lesson 9 How much light?	• To know that we only see the Moon because it reflects light from the Sun.	Use a ball and an OHP to show reflected light.	Complete a sheet to show how much light we see. Comment on differences between the Sun and the Moon.	Review that we see different amounts of light reflected from the Moon each night.	• Know that the Sun is a light source but that the Moon is not. • Know that the Moon reflects sunlight. • Know that we see a different amount of the reflected light each night as the Moon moves around the Earth.
Lesson 10 Weather data	• To use weather records to see the pattern of the seasons. • To collect, present and interpret data.	Discuss weather patterns and examine weather recordings.	Use weather data to create a block graph of sunshine, rain, snow, wind and so on. Write about 'birthday weather'.	Interpret the block graphs.	• Can use records to describe how the weather changes from season to season. • Can transfer data to a graph. • Can interpret data from a block graph.

Lesson	Objectives	Main activity	Group activities	Plenary	Outcomes
Lesson 11 Stargazing	• To be able to distinguish the Sun from the Moon. • To know that the pattern of day and night changes with the seasons. • To know that the pattern of day and night affects living things, including humans.	Complete sentences and draw pictures on a worksheet to show the sky in the daytime and at night.	Complete sentences on a worksheet to describe the seasonal pattern of daylight hours. Know and draw some nocturnal animals.	Discuss the answers to the worksheets.	• Can distinguish the Sun from the Moon. • Recognise that the pattern of day and night changes with the seasons. • Recognise that the pattern of day and night affects living things, including humans.

Assessment	Objectives	Activity 1	Activity 2
Lesson 12	• To assess whether the children know that the Sun appears to move across the sky in a regular way. • To assess whether the children know that we see the Moon by the light it reflects from the Sun.	Draw the apparent path of the Sun across the sky.	Complete a sheet to show how a person on Earth sees moonlight.

SC1 SCIENTIFIC ENQUIRY

Handling and Interpreting data

LEARNING OBJECTIVES AND OUTCOMES
- To use weather records to see pattern of the seasons
- To collect, present and interpret data

ACTIVITY
Using simple weather records the children look for simple seasonal patterns in the weather. The children then use the weather data to create block graphs showing amounts of snow, rain and other types of weather. The children then answer questions by interpreting data from their graphs.

LESSON LINKS
This Sc1 activity forms an integral part of Lesson 10, Weather data.

Lesson 1 ▶ What do you do in the sunshine?

Objective
- To know that the Sun is a sphere and that we see it in the daytime.
- To understand the dangers of looking directly at the Sun.

Vocabulary
Sun, Moon, stars, gas, burning, shining, sphere, danger, orbit

RESOURCES 💿
Main activity: Pictures of the Sun (both photographs and cartoons), a large ball (yellow if possible), a globe, a tealight, matches, a metal baking tray with sand, a small table, paper and drawing materials.
Group activities: 1 Photocopiable page 196 (also 'What do you do in the sunshine?' (green), available on the CD-ROM), writing materials. **2** A large circle of light-coloured paper (the size will depend on the size of the display area); tissue paper in shades of red, orange and yellow; gold foil, adhesive, spreaders.

BACKGROUND
Throughout this lesson, emphasise to the children that they should never look directly at the Sun, even through sunglasses: it can damage their eyes. The Sun is necessary for life on Earth to exist. It gives us warmth and light. Plants need light in order to make food by photosynthesis, and we depend on plants for food. We also need sunlight to remain healthy: our skin is able to manufacture vitamin D (which helps us to develop strong bones) in the presence of sunlight.

The Sun is really just another star in the Universe, but it is very important to us. There may be other solar systems like ours, with planets that have life on them, but no one really knows. There is still a great deal of research going on to find out, and science fiction stories often speculate about what life might be like in other planetary systems. For your information (the children don't need to know this), the Sun is 93 million miles away from the Earth. Other stars are so far away that the distances are measured in light years. A light year is the distance travelled by a beam of light in one year (about six million million miles). After the Sun, the next nearest star is Proxima Centauri; this is 4.2 light years away, an unimaginable distance.

PREPARATION
Fill the tray with sand and place it on a small table.

Differentiation
Group activity 1
For children who need support in Group activity 1, give them 'What do you do in the sunshine?' (green), which asks them just to draw, rather than write about, what they like to do in the sunshine.
To extend children, use 'What do you like to do in the sunshine?' (blue), which contains some additional questions about the Sun.
Group activity 2
Group activity 2 is accessible to all children.

STARTER

Working with the whole class, ask the children to draw and colour a picture of the Sun. Almost certainly, they will draw a stereotypical yellow disc with spikes or lines coming from it.

MAIN ACTIVITY

Gather the children together on the carpet and talk about why they think the Sun is the shape they have drawn. Ask them to explain why they have drawn 'spikes' around it. We usually do this to indicate the rays coming from it. Look at some of the pictures you have and compare cartoon versions with actual photographs. *Which one is really the Sun?* Use a large ball to explain that the Sun is really a huge ball that is very, very hot, and is made of gases that are burning all the time. Emphasise that it is also very bright and can damage their eyes if they look at it, even through sunglasses. Introduce the word 'sphere' if the children have not met it before. Using a globe map, explain that the Earth is also (roughly) a sphere, but a much smaller one than the Sun. The Earth orbits around the Sun, and also spins – like a football that has been kicked at a slant so that its path will curve. At night, we cannot see the Sun because it is on the other side of the Earth. The Sun only seems small to us because it is so far away. Some children may find it difficult to accept that the Sun is a sphere. Talk about how we draw a ball as a circle, even though we know it is a sphere.

Discuss all the colours that you might see in the Sun if you could look directly at it. Put the tealight in the middle of the sand tray on the small table, and make sure that the children are sitting well back. Light the tealight, watch it burning and discuss the colours you can see in the flame. Some children may never have encountered a 'living' flame, so take this opportunity to talk about the dangers of playing with fire and matches.

GROUP ACTIVITIES

1 Give the children a copy of photocopiable page 196 to record a sentence about what they like doing in the sunshine.
2 A group of four to six children can make a large collage of the Sun, using tissue paper in all the colours they have seen in the candle flame (plus gold foil).

ASSESSMENT

Ask the children when they see the Sun. Ask them to describe its shape, and to explain why the Sun is important to us.

PLENARY

Talk about the crucial role that the Sun plays in our lives: it gives us light and warmth. Discuss how most of us enjoy being out in the sunshine.

Remind the children about the dangers of looking directly at the Sun, and talk about the need to wear a sunscreen to stop our skin from burning. *What other things can we do to protect ourselves from the Sun's harmful rays?* (Keep in the shade, wear a hat.) Ask the children to think about what it might be like if there were no Sun. Discuss the fact that it is colder at night, when we can't see the Sun in the sky.

OUTCOMES

● Know that we see the Sun during the day.
● Know about the dangers of looking directly at the Sun.

LINKS

Maths: solid shapes.

Lesson 2 ■ The Moon changes shape

Objective
● To know that the Moon is a sphere and we see it at night-time.
● To know that the Moon appears to change its shape.

RESOURCES 💿
Main activity: Pictures or posters of the Moon (particularly a full Moon), a large ball, a strong torch or OHP, paper, pencils.
Group activities: 1 Photocopiable page 197 (also 'The Moon changes shape' (red), from the CD-ROM), scissors, adhesive. **2** A large paper circle (smaller than that for the Sun in Lesson 1), collage materials in shades of grey and black, silver foil, paper, adhesive, spreaders.

BACKGROUND
The Moon is a satellite of the Earth. It moves in orbit around the Earth about once every 28 days. It has no light of its own, and shines only because it reflects the light of the Sun. The Moon appears to change shape because of the way we see the sunlight reflected from it. Young children can observe the changes in its shape, but understanding why these changes happen is too difficult for this age group. Until they have a firm grasp of how shadows are formed and can grasp the complexity of multiple movements, they cannot begin to understand why the Moon appears to change shape in such a regular pattern. Many adults find this difficult.

Choose the time when you do this lesson carefully. It is possible to see the waxing (growing) Moon in the late afternoon or early evening, and the waning (diminishing) Moon in the early morning. The full Moon is only visible in the middle hours of the night, and the new Moon is in the sky in the middle of the day (when we can't see it, because the light from the Sun is too strong). What we call the 'new Moon' is really the first thin crescent that we see in a darker sky. What we call a 'half moon' is really a quarter Moon, since what we can see is a quarter of the whole sphere illuminated. The shape in between the 'half' and 'full' shapes is called a 'gibbous Moon'. It is not necessary for the children to know these names at this stage, but someone might ask! Some daily newspapers publish the phase of the moon along with the weather forecast and lighting-up times; if you choose to do the lesson during a waxing or waning period, you may be able to see the Moon while the children are in school.

While Moon-gazing, you may also be lucky enough to see a few stars. This may be difficult if you are in the middle of a town, where light pollution from street lamps and buildings may prevent you from getting a clear view. Many children do not appreciate that the stars are still in the sky during the daytime; it is just that the light from the Sun is so intense that we are unable to see the fainter light from the stars. The first bright 'star' to appear each evening, often called the Evening Star, is really the planet Venus and not a star at all. Planets, like the Moon, shine with the reflected light of the Sun; they shine steadily, whereas stars appear to flicker (because they are masses of burning gases).

STARTER
Ask the children to draw a picture of the Moon. The majority will probably draw a crescent Moon, possibly with a face.

MAIN ACTIVITY
Talk with the children about when we see the Moon in the sky. *Do you see the Moon every night?* Sometimes we cannot see the Moon because of clouds, but sometimes it is because of the phase of the Moon. Ask them whether the Moon is always the shape they have drawn. Look at some pictures or posters showing the full Moon. Show the children the large ball and say that the Moon is really a sphere or ball shape. Discuss the fact that we see the phases of the moon because of the way light is reflected.

If possible, work in a dark place so that light and shadow are more pronounced. Sit the children with their backs to a bright light source, such as a strong torch or overhead projector. Move a large ball slowly from one side of the light beam to the other, in front of them. Can they always see the whole of the ball lit up - or do they sometimes, as the ball crosses the edge of the light beam, see a crescent shape? Project a copy of the photocopiable on a whiteboard and discuss the shapes. Which are the shapes they may see the Moon take? Drag and drop the shapes into the circles to test the predictions.

If possible, go out each day and look for the Moon. The children should draw the shape they see. On some days you will not see the Moon at all, because it is only visible later in the night sky - or it is in the daytime sky, but cannot be seen because of the intensity of the Sun's light. If the Moon is coming towards full, the children may be able to make some observations at home before they go to bed and bring the results to school the next day.

GROUP ACTIVITIES
1 Give each child a copy of the appropriate photocopiable page 197. They have to identify, cut out and stick down the different shapes that represent phases (shapes) of the Moon.
2 Ask groups of four to six children to make a collage Moon to go with the Sun from the previous lesson. The Moon should be smaller than the Sun. They should collage most of the circle in black and grey, with a crescent of silver on one edge. This will help them to understand that the Moon is always complete, even though they can sometimes only see a small part.

ASSESSMENT
Ask the children to draw a picture of the Moon or describe some of the Moon shapes they might see. Some children may find this a difficult concept: even though you have talked about it being a sphere, they may still draw the stereotypical crescent shape. Other children may understand that the Moon reflects the light from the Sun. Ask whether anyone can explain why we sometimes see a half Moon or crescent shape.

PLENARY
Look at the large ball and talk again about the Sun and the Moon really being spheres, even though we see and draw them as circles. Talk about why we sometimes see only part of the Moon. Look at the shapes again using the whiteboard. Ask the children to describe some of the shapes that we see. Discuss when is the best time to see the Sun or the Moon in the sky.

OUTCOMES
● Know that the Moon is a sphere.
● Know that we see it best when the sky is dark.
● Know that the Moon appears to change its shape.

LINKS
Maths: solid shapes.

Lesson 3 ▪ Sun, Moon and stars

RESOURCES
Pictures of the Sun, Moon and night sky (with stars), a tealight, a metal tray filled with sand, matches, silver foil, card, scissors, star templates.

MAIN ACTIVITY
Observe a tealight burning (in the dark if possible). Remind the children of the Sun burning and glowing. The stars are like this, but so far away that they appear to be very, very small. Talk about when we can see stars, the

Moon and the Sun. Go out and look for stars in the evening sky if possible. The children cut out silver stars to hang as mobiles in front of the collaged Sun and Moon display.

ASSESSMENT
Take note of those children who contribute sensibly to the Plenary session.

PLENARY
Talk about the things that are seen in the sky. Can the children identify the Sun, Moon and stars in pictures, and say when they are most likely to see each? Can they describe the differences between them?

OUTCOME
● Can distinguish the Sun and Moon from the stars.

Differentiation
Most of the children will be able to draw round a template to make their own stars, but some may need to have the shapes drawn for them. Some children might be able to find out that some stars have names, or are grouped together in constellations that have names.

Lesson 4 ◖ Nocturnal

Objective
● To know that the pattern of day and night affects animals.

Vocabulary
day, night, dark, light, dawn, dusk, active, hunt, nocturnal

RESOURCES ◉
Main activity: Pictures of nocturnal animals (hedgehogs, foxes, bats, owls and so on); picture books about nocturnal animals.
Group activities: 1 Thick paper or thin card, drawing materials. **2** Photocopiable page 198 (also 'Nocturnal' (red), available on the CD-ROM), colouring materials.

PREPARATION
Make a zigzag book for each child from thick paper or thin card.

BACKGROUND
Sunlight is essential to life, and we might therefore expect living things to 'close down' at night, to sleep and await the dawn. Some creatures, however, started coming out at night to feed so that they had a better chance of avoiding their predators. But the predators responded by adapting their own feeding patterns so that they, too, came out at night. Many insects are most active at dusk, and some plants have adapted to attract the insects they need to pollinate them by producing their strongest scent at this time of day. Bats feeding on these insects are adapted to hunting in the dark, navigating by sound rather than sight. Owls have developed exceptional night vision, so that they can locate small creatures such as mice and voles in the dark. Some cold-blooded creatures, such as lizards, need the warmth from the Sun in order to get their systems working. They may be seen soaking up the early morning Sun before setting off on their hunt for food.

Humans are naturally diurnal, but many have needed to become nocturnal because of the work they do. Some people can adapt quite well to a nocturnal lifestyle, but others find it very difficult and may become ill.

Plants, too, are affected by the pattern of day and night. They are unable to photosynthesise in the dark. Since many of the insects they depend on for pollination are not abroad during the night hours, many plants close their flowers as night falls.

STARTER
Read a story such as *The Owl Who Was Afraid of the Dark* by Jill Tomlinson (Mammoth) or *Hoot* by Jane Hissey (Red Fox) to the class.

MAIN ACTIVITY
Ask the children if they know of any other animals that come out at night. Look at some pictures of nocturnal animals. *Why do you think they prefer to*

Differentiation

Group activity 1
All the children should be able to take part in this activity 1.

Group activity 2
To support children in Group activity 2, use 'Nocturnal' (green), from the CD-ROM, which does not include 'nocturnal' humans.

To extend children, use 'Nocturnal' (blue), which asks the children to write the names of the animals underneath the pictures.

'work' at night and sleep during the day? Why do they need to sleep? Discuss the fact that many animals (including humans) need to sleep if they are to remain healthy and alert. Discuss with the children the kinds of animals they might see during the day. *What things are they doing? Are they feeding, playing or sleeping? What do they feed on? Does anything feed on them?* For example, talk about snails eating plants and birds eating snails.

Some of the children may have a family member who works at night. *How does working at night affect them? When do they sleep? When do they eat? Do they have their dinner in the middle of the night? What happens at the weekend or on their day off? Do you have to change your own behaviour if a parent is sleeping during the day? Do you have to be very quiet?*

GROUP ACTIVITIES

1 Give each child a zigzag book and ask them to make a picture diary of their own day and night. They should draw daytime activities on one side and night-time activities on the other.

2 Give each child a copy of photocopiable page 198. Ask the children to colour in the animals (including humans) that come out at night and complete the sentence appropriately.

ASSESSMENT

Ask the children to describe some differences between day and night. Can they name some animals that come out at night? Use the photocopiable sheet to assess their understanding.

PLENARY

Discuss with the children what animals (including humans) do during their waking hours. All have to find food. Some animals may hunt directly; humans often work to earn money to buy food. Pets rely on us to provide their food.

Talk about why and how some animals have adapted to become more active at night. *Why do some humans work at night?* For example, nurses and doctors are needed to look after people who are ill. Some people work at night to provide electricity and gas, which are needed at all times. Other people clean and repair public places ready for the next day.

OUTCOMES

● Know the difference between day and night.
● Know that some animals prefer to come out at night.

Lesson 5 ▸ Winter or summer?

Objective
● To know that the pattern of day and night changes with the seasons.

Vocabulary
month, season, day-length, daylight, longer, shorter, evening, morning, spring, summer, autumn, winter

RESOURCES

Main activity: A prepared display board; 'Bed in Summer' by Robert Louis Stevenson (in A Child's Garden of Verses, Puffin), labels for each month.
Group activities: 1 Photocopiable page 199 (also 'Winter or summer?' (red), available on the CD-ROM), pencils. **2** Drawing or painting materials, art paper.

PREPARATION

Use yellow and dark blue (or black) paper to cover a display board as shown in the diagram (see bottom of page 185). If you choose to do this activity during the autumn term, you will need to cover the board as shown in the second diagram; otherwise, you should follow the first diagram.

Make name labels for the months of the year from January to July. For the Plenary session, make a large arrow out of card, to pin to the display board, in order to show the present month of the year.

BACKGROUND

The number of daylight hours varies considerably according to the season and the latitude (distance from the Equator) at which you live. At this stage, the children will just be observing or remembering that there is a change, and will not be expected to understand or explain the reasons for the change.

The variation is less in the tropics, but becomes more noticeable the nearer you get to the Poles. This is because the Earth is tilted on its axis. The angle and direction of this tilt does not change. This means that for part of the Earth's orbit the southern hemisphere is tilted toward the Sun, and for the other part the northern hemisphere is receiving more direct sunlight (see illustration below). In summer in the northern hemisphere, that part of the Earth is tilted towards the Sun. The northern regions are thus exposed to sunlight for longer during each daily rotation than in the winter, when they are tilted away from the Sun.

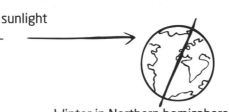

sunlight

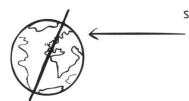

Summer in Northern hemisphere
Sun appears high in sky

Winter in Northern hemisphere
Sun appears lower on horizon

STARTER

Read Robert Louis Stevenson's poem 'Bed in Summer' to the class.

MAIN ACTIVITY

Ask all the children if it was dark this morning when they got up. *Do you think it will be dark when you go to bed tonight, or will you have to go to bed while it is still light? Is it always like this, or does it change? Can you remember [the opposite season], when things were different? Do you know what season it is when it is dark in the morning and at bedtime?* Talk about the daylight time being shorter in the winter. Briefly discuss other changes: it is warmer in summer, leaves fall in autumn, and so on.

Look at the display board. Explain that the yellow strip is daytime and the dark parts are night-time. Some of the shortest 'days' are in January, so where do they think the January label should go? Put the label at the top of the cone shape. Continue in this way until the June label is at the bottom of the cone, indicating the longest 'days'. Talk about how the days seem to get longer in the summer: it is lighter for longer, and it is light enough in the evening for the children to play outside until bedtime. *As the yellow part of the board becomes wider, what happens to the darker parts?*

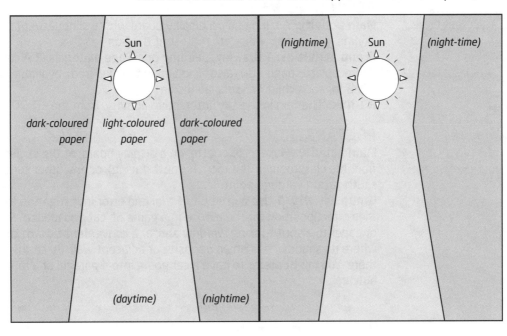

Group activity 1
To support children in Group activity 1, use 'Winter or summer?' (green), from the CD-ROM, which asks the children to draw just morning and bedtime pictures for winter and summer.

To extend children, use 'Winter or summer?' (blue), which asks the children to write a sentence to accompany their drawings.

Group activity 2
All the children can take part in Group activity 2.

GROUP ACTIVITIES

1 Give each child a copy of photocopiable page 199 to complete. Remind the children about the differences between summer and winter days, and ask them for some ideas about what they might draw on the sheet before they begin.

2 Ask each child to draw or paint a small picture of one of their daytime or night-time activities. Discuss some possibilities before they start, so that there are a variety of pictures. Add these to the display.

ASSESSMENT

Ask the children to describe the difference between getting up (or going to bed) in winter and in summer. Can they explain the display board?

PLENARY

Look at the display board and ask the children to explain it. Can they say why the yellow strip is narrower in January and wider in June? Pin the arrow to the board to indicate which month of the year you are in now. *What is going to happen to the day-length in the next few weeks? What shape would the display be if it went from June to December? What season is it when it is light for longest? Which season has the least daylight?*

OUTCOME

● Know that the pattern of day and night changes according to the season and that some animals come out at night, either to avoid their predators, or to hunt for their food (because that is when their food is available). The children's pictures should show nocturnal animals such as the badger, mouse, owl, hedgehog and so on. Pictures of foxes, rabbits, slugs and snails are acceptable, though these are mainly active at dusk and dawn.

LOOKING FOR LEVELS

Most children should be able to answer questions 1 to 7 and give at least one reason to answer question 8. They should be able to draw three or four nocturnal animals. Some children may answer around five of the questions and know two or three nocturnal animals.

Lesson 6 ▪ The Sun in the sky

Objective
● To know that the Sun appears to move across the sky in a regular way.

Vocabulary
Sun, orbit, Earth, rotate, axis, sunrise, sunset, east, west, apparent

RESOURCES 💿

Main activity: A sunny day, a display board with a silhouette of the local skyline, yellow paper discs to represent the Sun.
Group activities: 1 Drawing, painting or collage materials. **2** A copy of photocopiable page 200 (also 'The Sun in the sky' (red), available on the CD-ROM) for each child, scissors, adhesive.
ICT link: 'The Sun in the sky' interactive activity, from the CD-ROM.

PREPARATION

Main activity: Make a silhouette, on a display board, of the skyline you see from the classroom (if the room is south-facing), or any other convenient south-facing vantage point.
Group activity: 1 Use a little bit of trial and error investigation to work out the correct position for the mouse in a game of 'cat and mouse'. Stick a piece of paper to a south-facing window and, at a convenient time of the day, note where its shadow falls on an opposite or adjacent wall. Place the mouse there. You might prefer to have a car going into a garage, or a rabbit into a hutch.

BACKGROUND

The fact that the Sun is stationary and the Earth is moving seems to contradict the evidence we see with our eyes. It is important, therefore, to make sure that you always talk about the 'apparent' movement of the Sun, or the Sun 'appearing' to move. Emphasise the fact that it is the Earth moving, not the Sun. The Earth is spinning at almost 2000 miles an hour, and takes a day to complete one full rotation. The Sun appears to rise in the east because of the direction of rotation of the Earth. (Anti-clockwise, looking down on the North Pole.)

MAIN ACTIVITY

Ask the children: *Is the Sun in the same part of the sky all day?* (Many children will know that the Sun is in the sky, but may never have noticed that it appears to move.) If no one volunteers this information ask: *Where was the Sun as you came to school this morning? Was it shining in your eyes or was it on your back? Can anyone remember?*

Remind the children that they should never look directly at the Sun as it can damage their eyes, even if they are wearing sunglasses. Draw the children's attention to the silhouette on the display board and point out any particular landmarks. You may have a church tower, a block of flats or a particular tree. Go outside and decide where the Sun is now, in relation to your silhouette. Note what the time is and write it on one of the yellow discs. Go back into the classroom and stick the disc, in the appropriate place, on the display.

Go out each hour through the day, if possible, and repeat the exercise. Encourage the children to note the height of the Sun, as well as its apparent movement across the sky. You will obviously get a better idea of the apparent movement if you can start this activity as early in the day as possible. The positions may be approximate, as you will not be able to look directly at the Sun but, by the end of the day, you should have several 'Suns' progressing across the display.

Remind the children that it is the Earth that is moving (rotating) and not the Sun. If you have a south-facing window in your classroom, you could stick the 'Suns' directly onto the window using the actual skyline. Watch how shadows move around the classroom and help the children to relate this to the direction the sunlight is coming from (see diagram, below).

GROUP ACTIVITIES

1 Working in groups of three or four, ask the children to create collage shapes of a pouncing cat and a mouse. Cut out the cat and stick this on a south-facing window. Then cut out the mouse and stick this on an opposite or adjacent wall, where the Sun casts shadows (see Preparation). *What time is it when the cat catches the mouse?* Other groups could work on variations of this theme.

2 Give each child a copy of photocopiable page 200. Ask them to cut out the pictures and stick them in the right order in their books or on a separate piece of paper. Remind the children that the Sun rises in the east.

ICT LINK

Children can use 'The Sun in the sky' interactive to sequence the apparent movement of the Sun across the sky.

ASSESSMENT

Use the children's work from Group activity 2 to assess their understanding.

Differentiation
Group activity 1
Most children will be able to take part in Group activity 1. Some children may go on to explain why the cat moves to catch the mouse. (As the Sun appears to move across the sky the direction of the shadows changes.)
Group activity 2
To support children in the Group activity 2, use 'The Sun in the sky' (green), from the CD-ROM, which does not require any written work. Some children may find this activity easier once the class display has been completed in the Main activity and they have watched the Sun's apparent progress throughout the day.
To extend children, use 'The Sun in the sky' (blue), which asks children to explain why the Sun appears to move across the sky during the day.

PLENARY

After completing the class display, discuss how it shows the Sun appears to move across the sky. Ask the children to notice where the Sun is, in the morning, when they come to school. Tell them to also observe the Sun's position on the following morning, just to check that it does the same thing every day. You could finish by telling the story of Ra (Re), the Ancient Egyptian Sun God. Ra travelled across the sky each day, in his boat. He was swallowed up each evening by the sky-goddess Nut and spent the night battling the monster Apep who, every day, failed to prevent Ra re-emerging.

OUTCOME

● Can describe how the Sun appears to move across the sky.

Lesson 7 ▪ Seasonal change

Objective
● To know that the Sun is higher in the sky at midday in summer than in winter.

Vocabulary
Sun, apparent, rotate, rotation, shadow, length, seasons, spring, summer, autumn, winter

RESOURCES

Main activity: Pictures of winter and summer daytime scenes showing clear shadows, a lump of play dough, a metre rule, a torch (one with a narrow beam will give a clearer shadow), a large sheet of white paper, a model tree, coloured pencils or crayons; a darkish working area where shadows will show up.
Group activities: 1 Paper and writing materials. **2** Drawing and painting materials.

BACKGROUND

The Sun appears higher in the sky at midday in summer than in winter because the Earth is tilted on its axis. Throughout the Earth's orbit of the Sun, the angle and direction of the tilt remain more or less the same (apart from a slight wobble). Because of this, in the summer, we see the Sun from a more direct angle and this makes it appear higher in the sky. In the winter the angle is more acute and so the Sun appears lower on the horizon.

STARTER

Ask the children to name the four seasons. *What is the main difference between summer and winter?* (Summer is usually warmer than winter.)

MAIN ACTIVITY

With the class gathered around you, look at pictures of a winter scene and a summer scene which show clear shadows and (if possible) the Sun. Ask: *Which picture do you think is of summer and which one is of winter? How can you tell the difference?* (People are dressed differently, trees have leaves, there may be snow or flowers on the ground, the summer picture may be brighter and so on.) If nobody mentions the shadows say: *Look at the shadows. Can you see that those in the winter are longer than those in the summer?* Explain that this is because the Sun seems to climb higher in the sky in the summer than it does in the winter.

In your darkish working area stand a metre rule in a large lump of play dough (or sandwich it between books) to hold it upright. Similarly, stand a model tree in play dough and place it on the white paper, about a metre away from the rule. Shine the torch onto the model tree, from the metre rule, to make a clear shadow. (You may have to move the tree and paper to find the best place.) Explain to the children that the torch represents the Sun and the model tree something down on Earth.

Now shine the torch down from near the top of the metre rule and ask the children to look at the shadow. Mark the length of it with a coloured crayon. Move the torch about half-way down the metre rule and look at the shadow of the tree again. *Has it changed?* Mark the end of this shadow with a crayon of a different colour. Now move the torch near to the bottom of the metre stick. *What has happened to the shadow now?* Mark its length with another colour. Allow time to repeat the investigation and ask: *Where was the torch when the shadows were shortest? Where was it when the shadows were longest?*

GROUP ACTIVITIES

1 Divide the children into groups of four or five to talk about what they have observed. Pin the winter and summer pictures up so that the children can see them. Tell them that the torch represented the Sun. Ask them to think about where the torch was on the metre rule when the shadows were longest and shortest. Was it high up or low down? Ask them, individually, to write, explaining in which season the Sun is highest in the sky and in which the lowest.

2 Working individually, ask the children to draw or paint a picture showing the Sun in the sky in the middle of the day in either the summer or the winter. Ask them to show how long the shadows would be from any houses, trees or figures that they include. Make sure that there are a mixture of summer and winter pictures. Mount the pictures to make a display and label these: 'In winter the shadows are long because the Sun is low in the sky at midday.' and 'In summer the shadows are short because the Sun is high in the sky at midday.'

ASSESSMENT

Use the children's writing or pictures to assess their understanding. Some children may struggle to grasp this concept and may have trouble understanding that the torch represents the Sun.

PLENARY

Ask one or two children from each group to read out their sentences or give a verbal report. Look at some of the pictures they have drawn or painted and ask the artists to explain which seasons they represent, and why the shadows are the length they have drawn them. Help them to understand that when the Sun is higher in the sky the shadows are shorter, when it is low the shadows are longer, and that shadows are shortest in the summer and longest in the winter.

OUTCOME
● Know that the Sun is higher in the sky at midday in summer than in winter.

Lesson 8 ◗ The summer Sun

Objective
● To know that the Sun appears to have a longer path through the sky in summer than in winter.

RESOURCES
The display of the Sun's track made in Lesson 6, yellow and orange discs to represent the Sun, string, tape measures, sticky labels, sheets of paper stuck together to make a very large sheet (about the size of the window you used previously).

MAIN ACTIVITY
Remind the children about there being more daylight hours in summer than in winter. Look at the display of the Sun's track that you made in Lesson 6 and use extra yellow discs to transfer the shape of this track to the large sheet of paper. Remind the children about the Sun being higher in the sky in summer than in winter. If you are doing this lesson in winter, ask the children what shape they think the track would be in summer (or vice versa). *Will it be higher or lower than the one in Lesson 6?* Place the orange discs on the paper to form this track, either higher or lower than the original.

Ask several children to hold a piece of string around the shape of the first track. Cut it off and attach a sticky label so that you know which is which. Repeat for the second track. Measure the length of each string and decide which is longer. *Was it the summer one or the winter one?*

ASSESSMENT
Discuss the fact that the piece of string representing the track of the Sun through the sky in the summer was longer than that for winter. Explain that this means that the Sun is in the sky longer in the summer than in the winter and that therefore there are more hours of daylight.

PLENARY
Note during the Main activity and in the Plenary session which children understand that the length of the string relates to the length of time the Sun is in the sky.

OUTCOME
● Know that the Sun appears to stay longer in the sky in summer than in winter.

Lesson 9 ▪ How much light?

Objective
● To know that we only see the Moon because it reflects light from the Sun.

Vocabulary
Moon, Sun, rock, reflect, light, shine, illuminate, phases, light source, crescent Moon, half Moon, full Moon

RESOURCES
Main activity: OHP, a 'Moon on a stick' (see Preparation, below), a room that can be blacked out, extra adult help (optional).
Group activities: 1 A copy of photocopiable page 201 (also 'How much light?' (red), available on the CD-ROM) for each child, writing and drawing materials. **2** Writing and colouring materials.
Plenary: Flipchart or board.

PREPARATION
Make a 'Moon on a stick' by pushing a thin piece of dowel into a polystyrene ball. The size of the ball is not very important, but the bigger the better. If you have no curtains with which to black out a room, stick sheets of black paper over the windows. Choose a dull day if possible.

BACKGROUND
The Moon is a natural satellite of the Earth. It is made of rock covered in a thick layer of dust and orbits the Earth about once every 28 days. A full Moon can appear to be very bright, but the Moon has no light of its own. Moonlight is merely a reflection of the light from the Sun. Because the Earth and the Moon are moving in orbit around the Sun, the light is reflected at different angles during the orbit, and this makes the Moon appear to change shape. Although the Moon orbits the Earth in approximately 28 days the movement of the Earth and Moon around the Sun means that we see a new Moon approximately every 30 days.

Children in Year 2/Primary 3 are not expected to understand this concept. They will need a firm understanding of how shadows are formed and a grasp of the complex movements involved before they can do so. (Many adults still struggle with the concept!) Even so, try to avoid reinforcing the misconception that the Earth's shadow causes the phases of the Moon. The Earth's shadow only crosses the Moon during a lunar eclipse and the different phases are seen purely because of the way light is reflected from a sphere (the Moon). Eclipses occur because the Moon's orbit is not in the same plane as the Earth's and, just occasionally, the Earth comes between the Sun and the Moon, causing a shadow to pass across the Moon.

STARTER

Working with the whole class, remind the children what they learned about light in Year 1/Primary 2. We can only see things when there is light, and we see things because light is reflected from them.

MAIN ACTIVITY

For this lesson you will need a room that can be blacked out (see Preparation), but with room for the children to sit in a circle. It is also helpful, but not essential, to have the assistance of a second adult.

Sit the children in a tight circle facing outwards. You may need to sit them in two circles, one inside the other, to keep the circle as small as possible. Explain that they are sitting in a band right around the Earth and they are going to look up into the sky to look at the 'Moon'. Hold up the 'Moon' (the ball on a stick) and ask if the children can see it. They may be able to see it, but not very well, depending on the level of light in the room.

Turn on the OHP and place a piece of paper over part of the glass so that the light shines upwards, but not into, the children's eyes. Stand outside the circle, on the opposite side to the OHP, and hold the 'Moon on a stick' in the beam of the light. *Can you see it now? What shape can you see?* They may describe it as round, or as a circle. Explain that this is the shape we see when we have a full Moon.

Telling the children that they must only look straight in front of them, walk slowly around the circle (anti-clockwise), keeping the 'Moon' in the beam of light and above the children's heads so that there are no shadows on it. (This is where a second pair of eyes and hands can help to adjust the 'Sun' to keep the 'Moon' in full light). Tell the children to look at the illuminated (bright) part of the ball. *Does it change shape as it goes past you?* Stop at regular intervals and ask the children how much of the 'Moon' they can see. (All, not quite all, half, just a bit, and so on.) Point out to the children that the light is travelling from the Sun to the Moon and then is reflected (travels) to the Earth. (See Assessment activity 2, photocopiable page 207.) Explain to the children that it takes a whole month (or 28 days) for the Moon to go around the Earth and that each night we see a slightly different amount of the reflected light. Rearrange the children and repeat the activity so that they get a different view of the 'Moon'. If you have access to the internet NASA has a very good site with pictures of the Earth and the Moon which could be projected on a whiteboard.

GROUP ACTIVITIES

1 Give each child a copy of photocopiable page 201 and ask them to complete it. Remind the children that sometimes we only see a small amount of the light that is reflected from the Moon so the Moon appears as a crescent shape, and sometimes we see all the reflected light: we call that a 'full Moon'.
2 Ask the children to draw pictures of the Sun and the Moon and to write a few sentences to explain how they are different. They should comment that the Sun is a light source and the Moon is not, and that we only see the Moon because it reflects light from the Sun.

ASSESSMENT

During the Plenary session ask the children: *What is it that shines in the day and gives us light?* (The Sun.) *Why do we get light and heat from the Sun?* (Because the Sun is a big ball of burning gas.) *Why do we get light from the Moon?* (Because it reflects the light from the Sun.) Check their understanding from their answers.

Use the children's completed photocopiable sheets, from Group activity 1, to assess their understanding that we sometimes see different amounts of sunlight reflected from the Moon.

PLENARY

Ask the children what it is that gives us light during the day. (The Sun.) *What do we see at night?* (The Moon.) *Why do we see the Moon?* (Because it reflects the light from the Sun.) Draw a diagram on the flipchart, board or whiteboard to show how the light travels from the Sun to the Moon and then to the Earth. Remind the children of when they were sitting in a circle and looking at the 'Moon on a stick'. *Did you see the same amount of light reflected all the time?* Explain that the Earth and the Moon are moving around the Sun, so we see different amounts of light reflected each night.

OUTCOMES

- Know that the Sun is a light source but that the Moon is not.
- Know that the Moon reflects sunlight.
- Know that we see a different amount of the reflected light each night as the Moon moves around the Earth.

Lesson 10 ▪ Weather data

Objective
- To use weather records to see the pattern of the seasons.
- To collect, present and interpret data.

Vocabulary
weather, season, record, data, pattern

RESOURCES

Main activity: Weather data. If you have no school records from previous years, you can obtain information and data from the Meteorological Office over the internet (www.met-office.gov.uk). Simple information is supplied free of charge to schools, but more complex data carries a charge. You can ask for fairly specific information over a given period of time for your area, for example the rainfall over the last six months. This can be useful if you have no school records, but apply in plenty of time.

If these alternatives are not available a fictitious set of recordings is supplied on photocopiable page 202 (also 'Weather data –1' (red), available on the CD-ROM). This data is purely fictional but could be used to give children practice in reading a chart and gaining information. The chart represents an aggregate of weather information for the three months of each season in order to simplify the data sufficiently for Year 2/Primary 3 children. These records should help the children to see that there is a pattern in the weather (even though it is rather stereotypical). Use local records if they are available, or adapt this record to suit the conditions in your area.

Group activities: 1 A copy of photocopiable pages 202 and 203 (also 'Weather data – 1' (red) and 'Weather data – 2' (red), available on the CD-ROM) for each child; pencils. **2** Writing materials.

ICT link: Graphing tool from the CD-ROM.

PREPARATION

You may have weather data from previous years, or choose to use data obtained from the internet (see Resources). Alternatively you could start a system of weather recording with the class early in the year so that you have sufficient data to use by the time you do this lesson. Weather recording need only take a few minutes each day but can build into a very useful school resource if carried out regularly throughout the year. One year's records may then be compared with another year, but they will be records of your own area. Young children may keep a fairly simple 'tick if we have it' record while older children could keep more detailed records on a spreadsheet.

BACKGROUND

Even though weather patterns in the British Isles seem to be getting more confused it is still basically warmer in the summer than in the winter. Northern areas often get a significant snowfall in the winter but many southern areas have seen very little snow over the last few years. (If you want to do a lesson on snow take the opportunity as it arises and sort out the planning later!)

This lesson is really about handling and interpreting data, which is just as important in science as it is in maths. It is meant to help the children to see that there is a pattern to the weather, and that we are more likely to get certain types of weather in particular seasons. (It is more likely to be frosty in the winter than the summer; in spring and autumn the weather may be fairly similar but in spring we are moving from colder to warmer weather and in autumn from warmer to colder.) It does not matter too much if you were unable to collect data yourself, but interpreting your own data is always more interesting.

STARTER
Ask the children if they can name the four seasons. *Can you say how we tell the difference between them?* (Warm in summer, cold in winter, flowers come out in spring, we collect conkers in the autumn, and so on.)

MAIN ACTIVITY
Ask the children: *Why is it useful to know the pattern of the weather? Who might need to know?* Point out that weather patterns are very important for some people. A farmer relies on the pattern of the weather to know the best time to sow crops and harvest them. He sows seed in the autumn or spring so that the crop has time to grow and ripen in the warmer summer weather.

Holiday-makers also choose the best time for their holiday, depending on whether they want to sunbathe or ski. Fishermen and sailors need to make special preparations for bad weather, as do the people who look after our roads. They need to make sure that they have supplies of salt and grit to put on the icy roads that they expect in the winter.

Some people say that our weather patterns are changing but how do they know? It is because people have kept records of the weather for years and years. It is therefore possible to look back at records to see how the weather changes from season to season and to check if, and how, the pattern is changing.

Divide the children into groups of three and give each group a copy of the weather data you have. If you have no local records, you could use those on photocopiable page 202, which have been kept very simple. If you do have local records you may need to edit them to make them accessible for the children.

Help the children to find which season had the most rain, sunshine, or fog. Ask: *Is there a pattern? Is it always the same season that has more rain, frost, and so on?*

GROUP ACTIVITIES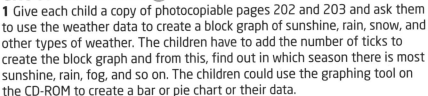
1 Give each child a copy of photocopiable pages 202 and 203 and ask them to use the weather data to create a block graph of sunshine, rain, snow, and other types of weather. The children have to add the number of ticks to create the block graph and from this, find out in which season there is most sunshine, rain, fog, and so on. The children could use the graphing tool on the CD-ROM to create a bar or pie chart or their data.
2 Make a list of whose birthdays fall in spring, summer, autumn and winter respectively. Ask the children, to use the weather data to write about the sort of weather that they might expect to have on their birthdays.

ASSESSMENT
During the Plenary session note which children can explain that there is a pattern in the weather.

PLENARY

Look at the block graphs the children have prepared. Ask them to tell you what kinds of weather you are most likely to experience in each season.

OUTCOMES

● Can use records to describe how the weather changes from season to season.
● Can transfer data to a graph.
● Can interpret data from a block graph.

LINKS

Maths: handling data.

Lesson 11 ▸ Stargazing

Objective
● To be able to distinguish the Sun from the Moon.
● To know that the pattern of day and night changes with the seasons.
● To know that the pattern of day and night affects living things, including humans.

RESOURCES ◉

Group activities: 1 Photocopiable page 204 (also 'Stargazing – 1' (red) available on the CD-ROM); writing and drawing materials. **2** Photocopiable page 205 (also 'Stargazing – 2' (red), available on the CD-ROM); writing and drawing materials.

STARTER

Review the class display about day-length (from Lesson 5) Ask: *What does it show? What have you learned in the last few lessons?*

MAIN ACTIVITY ◉

Give each child a copy of page 204 and ask them to complete it individually. Make sure that they understand what is required. Alternatively, 'Stargazing – 1' from the CD-ROM, could be displayed on the interactive whiteboard and the activity could be completed as a whole class.

GROUP ACTIVITY

Give small groups or pairs of children, a copy of page 205. Read through the sentences with them and make sure they understand that they have to complete each one.

Differentiation
Main and Group activities
Most children should be able to complete the sheets successfully. More able children should be encouraged to draw both the Sun and the Moon as circles (indicating spheres), and may colour one yellow and the other white or silver. Point out that the Moon may also be seen in the daytime. You may wish to provide a bank of key words for Group activity 1.

PLENARY

Discuss the answers to the worksheets; display 'Stargazing – 1' and 'Stargazing – 2' from the CD-ROM, on an interactive whiteboard and complete, as a class, using the drawing tools.

OUTCOMES

● Can distinguish the Sun from the Moon.
● Can recognise that the pattern of day and night changes with the seasons.
● Know that the pattern of day and night affects living things.

Lesson 12 ▸ Assessment

Objective
● To know that the Sun appears to move across the sky in a regular way.
● To know that we see the Moon by the light it reflects.

RESOURCES ◉

Assessment activities: 1 Copies of photocopiable page 206 (also 'Assessment - 1' (red), available on the CD-ROM), drawing materials. **2** Copies of photocopiable page 207 (also 'Assessment - 2 '(red), available on the CD-ROM).

STARTER
Remind the children about what they have learned in this unit. They have been thinking about how we get light from the Sun and how the Moon reflects this light, how the Sun appears to move across the sky, and how the Moon seems to change its shape.

ASSESSMENT ACTIVITY 1
Give each child a copy of photocopiable page 206. Explain that they are to draw circles to represent the path of the Sun across the sky.

ANSWERS
The Suns should describe a shallow arc across the picture. (See diagram in Lesson 6, page 187.) The Sun is higher in the sky during the summer.

LOOKING FOR LEVELS
Most children will draw the Suns in a line across the sky showing a slight curve. Some may draw the Suns in a straight line across the page.

ASSESSMENT ACTIVITY 2
Give each child a copy of photocopiable page 207 and ask them to draw lines to show how the person on the Earth sees the moonlight. They must show the direction in which the light is travelling.

ANSWERS
There should be a line from the Sun to the Moon and from the Moon to the person on the Earth. For the extension questions, accept answers showing that the child understands that we see the Moon because it reflects light from the Sun.

LOOKING FOR LEVELS
Most children will be able to draw the lines required. Some children may get the lines in the wrong place or be unable to show the direction in which the light is travelling. Other children may be able to provide an explanation of what is happening.

What do you do in the sunshine?

When the sun is shining, I feel _____

_____

_____

I like to _____

_____

_____

◼ Draw what you like to do.

◣ SCHOLASTIC

Illustration © Ann Kronheimer

The Moon changes shape

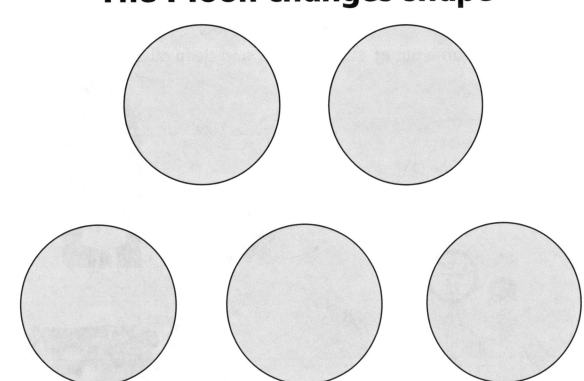

___

◀ Choose the Moon shapes and colour them in.

◀ Cut them out and stick them in the grey circles to make Moon shapes.

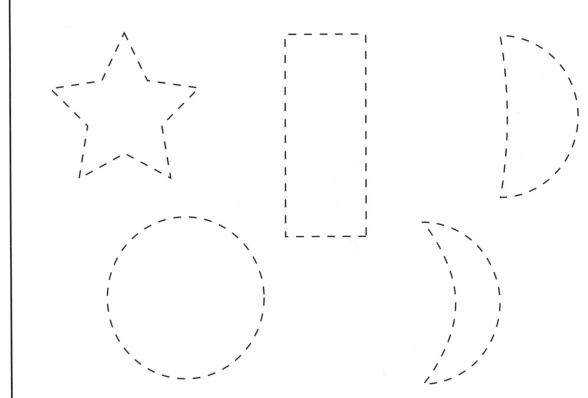

PHOTOCOPIABLE

Nocturnal

These animals come out at ＿＿＿＿＿＿ and sleep all ＿＿＿＿＿＿ .

◼ SCHOLASTIC

Illustration © Ann Kronheimer

Winter or summer?

■ Draw a picture in each box.

When I get up, it looks like this:

winter	summer

When I get home, I play like this:

winter	summer

When I go to bed, it looks like this:

winter	summer

PHOTOCOPIABLE

The Sun in the sky

◼ Cut out the pictures and put them in the correct order.

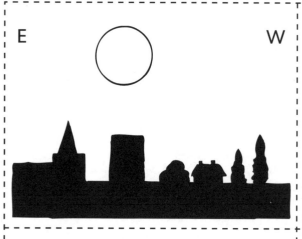 

◼ Complete the following sentences:

1. The Sun rises in the _____

2. The Sun sets in the _____

Illustration © Ann Kronheiner

◼SCHOLASTIC

How much light?

■ Draw the shape of the Moon to match each sentence.

When the Moon looks like this it is only reflecting a little light back to Earth.	When it looks like this it is reflecting all the light back to Earth.	When it looks like this it is only reflecting half the light back to Earth.

PHOTOCOPIABLE

Weather data – 1

season	sunshine			cloud			rain			hail			snow			frost			fog		
	Yr 1	Yr 2	Yr 3	Yr 1	Yr 2	Yr 3	Yr 1	Yr 2	Yr 3	Yr 1	Yr 2	Yr 3	Yr 1	Yr 2	Yr 3	Yr 1	Yr 2	Yr 3	Yr 1	Yr 2	Yr 3
spring	✓	✓✓	✓✓	✓	✓✓	✓✓	✓✓	✓✓	✓✓			✓			✓	✓	✓	✓✓	✓	✓	✓
summer	✓✓	✓✓✓✓✓	✓✓✓✓	✓	✓	✓	✓	✓✓	✓		✓	✓									
autumn	✓✓	✓✓	✓✓	✓	✓	✓✓	✓✓	✓	✓✓			✓					✓		✓✓	✓✓✓	✓✓
winter	✓	✓	✓	✓	✓✓✓✓✓	✓✓✓✓✓	✓✓✓✓✓	✓✓	✓✓✓✓✓				✓✓	✓	✓✓	✓✓✓✓✓	✓ ✓✓✓✓	✓✓✓✓✓	✓	✓	✓

FOG

Which is the wettest season?

Which season has most sunshine?

When are we most likely to have frost?

When is it most likely to snow?

Illustration © Ann Kronheimer

■SCHOLASTIC

Weather data – 2

sunshine				cloud				rain				hail			
spring	summer	autumn	winter	spring	summer	autumn	winter	spring	summer	autumn	winter	spring	summer	autumn	winter

snow				frost				wind				fog			
spring	summer	autumn	winter	spring	summer	autumn	winter	spring	summer	autumn	winter	spring	summer	autumn	winter

Stargazing – 1

■ Fill in the missing word in each sentence, then draw a picture to show what you might see.

We see the _____ in the sky in the daytime.

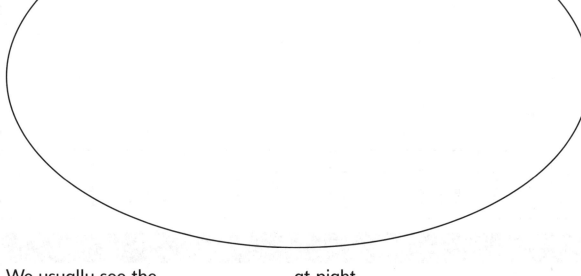

We usually see the _____ at night.

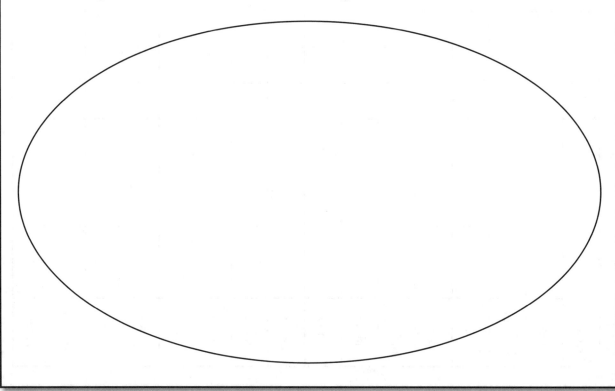

■ SCHOLASTIC

Stargazing – 2

1. It is light enough to play outside until bedtime in the _____

_____

2. It grows dark early in the _____

_____

3. In the winter it is still quite _____ when I come to school.

4. When I wake up early in the summer, it is already _____

5. It is light for longer in the _____ .

6. It is dark for longer in the _____ .

7. Most humans work in the _____ and sleep at _____

8. Some animals sleep all day because _____

Draw a picture of four animals that come out at night.

PHOTOCOPIABLE

Assessment – 1

▪ Draw five circles to show how the Sun appears to move across the sky during the day.

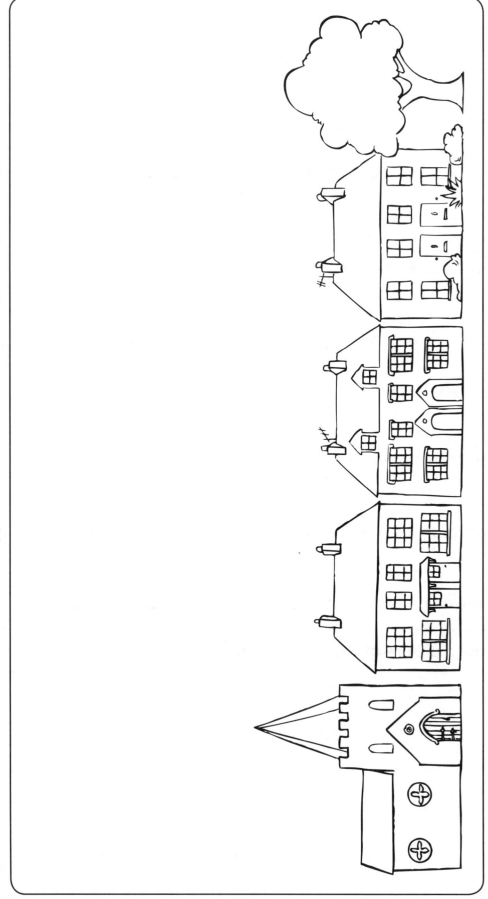

In the summer the Sun is _____ in the sky than in the winter.

Illustration © Ann Kronheimer

Assessment – 2

■ Draw two arrows to show why we see light from the Moon.

Moon

Earth

Sun